Other Books by the Author

The Ochre Robe
The Tantric Tradition
A Functional Analysis of Indian Thought
    and Its Social Margins

THE LIGHT AT THE CENTER:
Context and Pretext of Modern Mysticism

Agehananda Bharati

ROSS-ERIKSON / *SANTA BARBARA*

THE LIGHT AT THE CENTER: CONTEXT AND PRETEXT OF MODERN MYSTICISM. Copyright © 1976 by Agehananda Bharati. All rights reserved. Printed in the United States of America. No part of this book may be used or reproduced in any manner whatsoever without written permission except in the case of brief quotations for purposes of review.

ISBN 0-915520-04-4

Second Printing

ROSS-ERIKSON, Publishers, Inc.
223 Via Sevilla
Santa Barbara CA 93109

FOR
JANE
CAROL
GLENDINNING

TABLE OF CONTENTS

"... das zeigt sich.
Das ist das Mystische"
L. Wittgenstein, *Tractatus*

PREFACE

All sorts of people volunteered to write a preface to this work, foremost among them Alan Watts from among mystics and saints, and R.C. Zaehner from among scholars and gentlemen. Both of them died recently, and checking the other volunteers I have decided to write the preface myself.

I think this opus is timely. The incipient, abortive cultural rebellion of the sixties is gone, and forgotten by the young who were then children; their elder siblings who participated, on the campuses and in Washington, on many more communes than are extant into the mid-seventies, have realigned their social priorities and are doing other things. The devout and persistent from a decade ago are now the teachers of those who want to follow in the way of the gurus. Transcendental meditation has waxed very strong indeed, and it has become establishmentarian—its teachers are and look like golfers and business executives and there is no stylistic link between the first generation of transcendentalists and ecstasy seekers of the sixties and the new guru generation, except in its Indian founder figures who survived the demise of the ecstasy of the sixties. The century's greatest event as heralded for the Houston Astrodome faded into history somewhat meekly. The Guru Maharaj and his *premis* have been performing in a low key ever since. Hare Krishna and the International Society for Krishna Consciousness is going strong, their books and their incense sell well at airports and on busy streets. The post-Christians of the theologians of the sixties have become Christians, and God has resurrected once more from being dead.

As this opusculum goes into print, I just received a beautifully printed brochure by Dr. Robert Keith Wallace, Professor of Physiology and President of the Maharishi International University, *Neurophysiology of Enlightenment*, developed from his keynote address to the twenty-sixth International Congress of Physiological Science held in New Delhi, India, in October 1974. The brochure contains sixty-four charts, it presents the World Plan generated by the teachers of the science of creative consciousness. The Maharishi university bought up the defunct Parsons College in Iowa. For people who do not realize the cosmic humor involved in this extended milking of the scientific paradigm, these efforts seem commandingly respectable, both scientifically and spiritually. The Maharishi set is at pains to keep out the *term* "religious," denying its applicability, pains matched perhaps only by modern Hindu's zest for proclaiming Hinduism scientific.

To the outsider to the anthropology of religious behavior faced with these movements, there seems to be a wide chasm between the trimmings of transcendental meditation, the Hare Krishna gymnastics, the dilated smiles of Jesus Freaks, and the now defunct hippydom of the sixties. This book, however, aims to show up their common base through their common errors, and as such it aims to be a perennial critique of mystical movements and of utopia in general.

One thing is sure: the India-originated religious movements—whatever their actual or fictitious link with the Asian base—have come to stay. To wit the Yellow Pages in the telephone directories of the largest American and Canadian cities: only a decade ago, the entries were listed under such odds and ends sections as *Churches, non-denominational.* Increasingly, we find full sections on *Yoga Schools* and such entries as Vedanta, Hindu, Zen Buddhist, Tibetan Dharma, etc. under *Churches*, on a par with *Methodist, Episcopalian, Latter-Day Saints*, etc. Until recently, these Asian imports were marginal, interesting at best; now they are competitors—some of them will probably eclipse smaller Judaeo-Christian establishments in the not too distant future in this part of the world. Semi-facetiously, the late Alan Watts once suggested that in the next century, people in India will wear ties and jackets and drive in limousines, and people in America will sit crosslegged in Colorado and Oregon caves, meditating. Even as he said it, both these suggestions were true in part; urban Indian males do wear coats and ties and pants, and thousands of Americans do things converging on the cave and meditation scene. But I think that matters will be somewhat different in the next five decades or so: Hindu and Buddhist teachings, progressively ensconced in the West will be much like Christian and Jewish places of assembly now. Transcendental meditation has made a beginning, its orderliness and organizational expertise is very much like any well run church organization.

A word to my fellow anthropologists: we have been taught, have tried to do, and have taught our succeeding generation the mysteries and the magic of 'participant observation.' This book, however, is the result of *participation* rather than 'participant observation.' It belongs more to the genre of reinvented, radical anthropology, its texts and meetings which have been panelling from the mid-sixties. And because participation means more concern than the old-time participant observation, the participant anthropologist has the right and the duty to criticize his subjects where criticism is due in the light of intellectual integrity. At Sam Goody's in New York, I once saw an LP record titled ALOHA AMIGO. I felt physically sick when I saw it. The all-American mental retardation as I see it is pathological eclecticism—and I don't think the new anthropology can leave it at that with a shrug and a note—it has to be chastised. Aloha and Amigo don't go together except in the realm of the phoney. Neither do yoga, Sikhism, kundalini, T'ai Chih', and macrobiotic diet. The silliness of *dal* and curry powder being sold in health-food stores all over America is blatant: Indian food is nutritionally among the poorest in the world; *dal* is a staple for lack of other protein sources; and spices are part of the Indian cuisine because they have to fry away at least part of the germs, hopefully, where there is no refrigeration. The syllogism in the minds of the health-food store owners and their customers "India is spiritual—*dal* and curry are Indian—hence *dal* and curry are spiritual" is just one instance of the aloha-amigo syndrome; any two or more items that are different from the immediately surrounding ecosystem are desirable, hence can be grooved upon jointly. But these *mèlanges* preclude genuine quest, and this has to be pointed out. It has to be pointed out not by an outsider who is only a critic—for this is being done all the time in the *New York Times Sunday Magazine Section* and similar subversive publications; nor can it be done by an insider-believer—this, of course, is also done in tons of pious pamphlets emerging from gurus and followers. It must now be done by one who is an insider, an initiate, a professional in the field of mysticism, but who is also a professional social scientist and hence a social critic. Voilà, here we are.

Agehananda Bharati

11

THE LIGHT AT THE CENTER:

Context and Pretext
of
Modern Mysticism

Chapter One

Definitions and Descriptions

People who read have a number of ideas about what mysticism is and what sort of persons mystics might be. But a book on mysticism and mystics needs something as close to a definition as the subject permits.

Let me first get rid of several dysfunctional uses of "mystic." Some modern anthropologists use the term for the putatively supernatural or superhuman, and the belief systems involved. This is far too wide, for it includes such categories as shamans in primitive societies and many sorts of priests and magicians, as well as people who call themselves mystics or who are called mystics by others. These latter may be priests, religiously engaged specialists; laymen, literary people who need a term of contrast to the worldly; and a heterogeneous crowd of seekers after ultimate truth. The common anthropological use of "mystic" would be unacceptable to them because it is too inclusive and hence probably derogatory. But there are certain attitudes and acts which would be recognized by *all* mystics, among whom are people of very different theological and ideological traditions. These attitudes include the turning away from worldly things, or viewing them quite differently from the majority of people; also, certain types of committed reliance such as faith, devotion, sacrifice—but *not* adherence to any one type of moral or social behavior.

I once thought that the cognate Greek and Indic etymology of "mystic" might provide a basic meaning, not because etymologies provide operational clues (which they don't) but because mystics in the east and in the west share an element of silence and secrecy—the meaning of the Greek *my-* and the Indic *maun-mun*. The Indian *muni* or sage, a person of canonical status in ancient and modern days, is one who keeps silent, temporarily at least. But there are many mystics whose practice and spiritual career have never included silence, such as the followers of Sri Chaitanya and other singing and dancing practitioners of religion.

Modern philosophy has taught its practitioners to declare

their axioms. There is much reason to believe that the distinction between the moral and the aesthetic is at best a weak one, and I suspect that radical analysis will disintegrate it. A. R. Louch[1] has shown that all decisions about the choice of a science or of a discipline, and the choice of one method over another within a discipline, are eventually moral choices; they are not enjoined by the chosen science itself, nor by the ratiocinations at the disposal of any or all of the sciences. Thus, whether I choose to be an anthropologist or a philosopher, am "exact," "hard," scientist or humanist, my selection is prompted by moralistic motivations, not by the greater validity of one discipline; similarly with the method or style within the discipline, whether a quantifying method or a discursive, quality-based style when either is permitted by the content.

When we talk about definitions—some philosophers believe that this is their chief or even their only job—we can list all possible definitions and then proceed to give our own, not claiming that it is exclusively better than the others. But in offering our definition we have made our moral and aesthetic choice (and at this point the distinction between "moral" and "aesthetic" becomes academic). My choice of a non-quantitative, humanistic, yet behavioral approach, using the tools of linguistics and analytical "ordinary language," over a statistically informed approach is a moral-aesthetic choice. My combination of methods is rare at this moment, and has few friends.

In defining a type of human action we usually presuppose a common denominator among the events—in this case, those constituting the mystical way. But the question "who is a mystic" does not lend itself to a neat definition, just as the rules of old-time philology had to provide a sub-section for exceptions. As an anthropologist I find the analogy between social structure and linguistical structure (of which the speaker is unaware, but which is definable through analysis) rich and rewarding. Throughout this book I shall deduce linguistic parallels as heuristic devices to aid the understanding of the *social* components of the mystical experience. Yet when it comes to studying the mystic as an individual, the linguistic analogy does not work well. I cannot define "mysticism" or "the mystic" except by *pointing him out*, listing the things he does, says, and feels—but with a *caveat* on what he feels: he can report only himself, and likely not too well. Inasmuch as this writer is a mystic—of this I am sure—I can and will attempt to state discursively what I feel.

If we grant that ostensive definition, i.e. pointing out a

16

person or a case, is a definition of sorts, the task becomes easier. I can define a circle as $\pi 2r$, or use some verbal device which implies these formulae; and I can point to a circle. I can call both procedures definitions. *Definire* means precisely "setting limits;" what limits can be more narrowly set than those of a thing which I point out to set it off from its environment?

If there is a common denominator to all mystical events and persons, it is not to be found in the descriptions of most religious leaders today. It is not of a speculative or prescriptive character proposed by my Indian colleagues, monastic and lay; nor theologically stipulated, as most Christian teachers suggest. Christian and Hindu-Buddhist doctrinarians want it this way: a mystic is a person who does something special with the teachings, something beyond the call of duty, "supererogatory" in scholastic jargon, perhaps incomprehensible to his Christian, Hindu, or Buddhist contemporaries. And then the doctrinarians would append quotations and commentaries relating those persons' lives, deeds, and words to the doctrine in question. Such procedure is outdated and misleading because doctrine-based categories are both too wide and too narrow for our purpose. They include people and actions under the rubric "mystical" that are not; and they keep out people and actions that are. Two examples: Christians would call St. Thomas a mystic, Jews call Martin Buber a mystic, Hindus today call Swami Vivekananda a mystic; I doubt that any of these men was a mystic. But doctrinarily informed Christians, Jews and Hindus would not call Arthur Koestler a mystic, yet he is.

The Hindu theologian is closest to a viable definition of the mystic. I say this not because he is shrewder or more "tolerant" than the Christian spokesman, nor because I am a Hindu. But because of some complex historical developments, Hinduism happens to espouse a theology in which the mystical experience is *doctrinally* crucial and orthodox. As we thumb through modern Hindu apologetic literature in English, we find "mystic" and "mystical" much more frequently than in comparable Christian literature; in Buddhist pamphleteering from Srilanka and Thailand, the word hardly ever occurs, for reasons to be explained later. Among proclaimed Hindu mystics, there are some we should investigate as genuine mystics; yet in the same breath the Hindu Renaissance booklets and pamphlets include persons and actions that are not mystical by an operational definition: many saintly persons and altruistic actions are called "mystical" for lack of knowledge of a better word in English.

17

Official exegeses and homiletics of the world religions give us little help and no directions toward building a viable definition of the mystical. It would be advantageous for us to create definitions through critical consideration and analysis of eccentric religious behavior, or behavior which deviates from the standstill perceptions of most spokesmen for religious doctrine.

Ego-involvement in a discipline does not cancel the duty to analyze and criticize that discipline, nor does it jeopardize the skill of analysis during periods of discursive detachment. There is no reason why a composer should not also be a musicologist, and a connoisseur of wines a social scientist who describes and criticizes the social or antisocial use of alcohol. From the fact that very few mystics have been anthropologists studying mysticism critically, it does not follow that they cannot or should not be—and vice versa.

The catch-all use of "mysticism," "mystical" etc. by social scientists, especially by cultural anthropologists, is more annoying than the misuse of these terms by theologians; for however negatively the latter may be disposed toward the mystical—orthodox Christians and 'ulema-oriented Muslims must need frown upon it—theologians at least take it seriously. Anthropologists, however, despite their ambition to talk "hard science" and to eschew the romantic, the poetic, and the involving, use the term "mystical" sloppily to cover everything related to the supernatural. I suspect that their sloppiness is studied; they apparently fear that the profession will regard their study of potentially so involving a thing as mysticism as non-professional, that their colleagues will regard them as converts. Else why should not their terminological meticulousness extend to mysticism? An example: Talking about the Fipa of southwestern Tanzania, Roy G. Willis[2] has a whole section on "mystical agencies": "Sociological understanding of notions of 'mystical' [Willis' quotation marks] causation properly began with Evan-Pritchard's explication of his Zande material, an achievement which itself owed much to the pioneer work of Lévy-Bruhl . . . Zande ideas of witchcraft . . . had a dual aspect . . . . In traditional Fipa belief, mystical agencies were ranked in an immutable hierarchy . . . ; the lowest ranked mystical agency was that associated with evilly disposed human beings. . . ." If we thus misuse the term "mystical" for superhuman, supernatural, witchcraft, and sorcery, we destroy the term's focus.

Another discipline, professionally in opposition to the aspirations of mystics, is closer to an exact and critical use of the term. I refer to the theologians of the world's great faiths, the ecclesiastics who fear mysticism as an endemic poison.

Even while formal religion retains its age-old reservations about mystics, who by their very nature must be antinomian in attitude and practice, a new appreciation of mystical attitudes is growing in an unexpected ground, the playing fields of the Western intellectual. Radicalized by their traditional exercises of verbal analysis and objective criticism (radicals of the right seldom call themselves "intellectuals" any more because of the term's leftist associations), academics find themselves alienated from the institutionalized former centers of leftist allegiance, the Soviet complex. The new radical ideology finds the Russian leaders, for example, indistinguishable from the western politicians: hypocritical bores, puritans, incredibly square. Influenced by the counter-culture of alienation and drugs, the academics have opened up for themselves new fields of radical thought, in personal as well as in political relations.

Not too long ago, at a panel discussion among anthropologists, psychologists and other passionate people, under the auspices of a Society for the Study of Alienation, Professor Stanley Diamond, disciple of the late Paul Radin, and an admitted latter-day Rousseauian, spoke admiringly of the primitive mind: that it was moral, not moralistic, that it was holistic; that it was existential, not essential; that there was no hoarding and no competition for rank; he recommended that modern man take his cue from the primitive mind in order to survive, spiritually at least. Diamond, however, is all wrong, and so were Radin and Rousseau. There is no primitive mind, and the categories which Diamond imputed to the primitive were the armchair categories of nineteenth century Weltschmerz romanticists. But a significant fact emerged from that lively discussion: the western radical intellectual, whether his inspirations are those of Herbert Marcuse or of Norman Brown, demonstrates a kind of mystical engagement: he thinks in terms of merging with some larger entity. He rejects the Russian and Chinese leaders' intention to merge the individual in the people, as he decried the Nazis' perverse rituals to merging with the *Volk*; and he damns both poles as anti-intellectual. But the modern intellectual has abandoned isolation and detachment. He seeks communication on a level that includes but is higher than the political—as a lover, an aesthetician, a utopian. I am not restricting this observation to those who have taken LSD or similar potions, for whom mystical practice has become a hope both disturbing and salutary. The great majority of intellectuals have not taken psychedelic drugs, but still they are responding to a new contagion, arising from the growing interest in Eastern religions, and western research into brain wave activity and parapsychology. Mysticism is moving closer to sober investigation and therefore perhaps, even to exact definition.

I have elicited definitional responses from several dozen people who must be called intellectuals in the refined sense suggested by Hofstadter.[3] The intellectuals are likely to circumscribe the mystic and mysticism, and if pressed to attempt a formal definition, feel uncomfortable. They seem to be aware that the mystical is antithetical to both the religious and the secular, probably as a result of the pervasive confrontation between establishment and counter-culture. But they do not quite know its parameters and, with the exception of the stauncher Jungians, tend to include too many phenomena under the rubric—like the anthropologist with his loose attributions. Indian intellectuals,[4] who are more likely to be highly motivated by religious matters than their Western counterparts, bracket all sorts of full-time or part-time religious practitioners as "mystics" when using English: astrologers, magicians, curers of all sorts, and of course, the wide category of sadhus or holy men, many of whom are indeed mystics by my definition.

R.E. Stanfield exemplifies the occidental intellectual's contemporary view about the mystical when he writes: "Science and technology have in the modern world assumed the role of theology—a rational system making sense of the nature of things. The reassurance of ritual that all is well is provided in this nation today by its mass culture, particularly in the weekly cycle of television programs, fixed in format and varying slightly in content. Against this order of rationality, mysticism manifests itself, *favoring experience over reason, ecstasy over control* [italics added]. Dionysian cults, pentecostal revivals, and rock festivals are not merely analogues; they are manifestations of the same basic response to life. In the absence of spiritual forces to take possession of the communicant's body, physical drugs become sacraments. The record of our history is that technology and ritual have prevailed over mysticism. Mystics are an embarrassment to the established order. If they cannot be suppressed, they will be neutralized. They may be permitted to withdraw to cloistered retreats, there to remain hidden from the eyes of the world (as some do now in communes and colleges). The more reputed of their number may be sainted—saints to be revered but not imitated (a state that Allen Ginsberg may well have achieved). Some of the excesses of their experiences may be transformed into

20

acceptable ritual . . . ."[5]

I do not know the author of this letter, but as an anthropologist I like to let the natives talk, then interpret what they have said. The modern intellectual seems highly sympathetic to the mystical scene even though he rarely participates in it. He stands in contrast to his parental generation, which did not recognize that mysticism was more than potentially inimical to religion—ecclesiastic, establishmentarian, moralistic. Until the late fifties the intellectuals of the western world included mysticism, commonly seen as a religious expression, in their cherished antagonism against established religion. Theologians know better.

Some intellectuals view the mystic and his works the way natural scientists view moon rock or DNA—extremely important for their work, but nothing to upset their way of life, even in theory. Others view the mystic as some sociologists and anthropologists view the natives they describe: as people who can teach them something and help them toward greater realization. The dispute between those who are sympathetic to the mystic and those who regard him as simply a subject of study has a simple etiology: social scientists have not heeded ordinary philosophy of language: the distinction between descriptive and persuasive uses of language. Some few social scientists believe that the only valid way of being sympathetic to the mystic or to the native is to adopt his ways, or at least to admire them; the more tough-minded say "Not so"—getting involved is not their job.

A fairly typical example of the inexact use of our term appears in a statement by John J. Honigman, an American researcher who has published extensively on psychological anthropology. He has not, to my knowledge, tried to define the mystic, and we must take his casual reference as typical. Speaking about the Devils of Loudon incident, he says of Sister Jeanne: "classics of spiritual life . . . gave her a taste for mysticism"; and he defines witchcraft as "an automatic mystical propensity in someone to promote evil."[6] Like most of my colleagues in the social sciences who are sympathetic to mysticism, Honigman probably thinks he has implied a definition of the mystic; but if we accept the implication, then we might as well declare all supernatural events as examples of the mystical. If a spirit, a religious curer, a witch, a shaman, a witch-doctor are all referred to as "mystics," then what term do we use for a person whose main concern is mystical practice strictly defined?

Following an ancient Indian scholarly tradition in which a

21

commentator reserves the best argument—his own—for the end, after having exposed the inadequacy of other possibilities, I now proceed toward my own definition of a mystic, the one I want my readers to keep in mind throughout the book.

The model for my definition is provided in part by the most recent and, to me, the most exciting branch of social anthropology, called *ethnoscience* and *ethnosemantics*. The principle of ethnoscience is quite simple. Formerly researchers in ethnography and in philology brought along with them ready-made, preconceived categories of a philosophical and grammatical sort. They then saw the natives, studied their language, and fitted both into categories held in store: metaphysical notions like "Dionysian" or "Apollonian" and linguistic notions like subject-predicate-verb-case, taken straight from Latin or Greek. Ethnoscience states that you cannot understand the native or his idiom if you insist on torturing him into your own Procrustean categories. You must take the cultural and linguistic categories supplied by the native, and then find the things that fit into *them*. You can no longer do what that old ethnographer did: he reportedly took a native interpreter and asked him to ask the chieftain if the latter had an Oedipus complex; the chieftain said no, and the researcher wrote a learned piece showing why the natives of X do not have an Oedipus complex. To the new anthropologist, the ethnoscientist, the words and the categories supplied by his subject or his "informant" are the one and only *corpus*. In other words, we now try to understand the native as he is, not what we think he ought to be. In line with ethnoscience, anthropology is now developing other modes of research where the terminology and the information on the sundry types of human reaction are supplied by the subject, *not* by the researcher and his home-library. Thus, ethnohistory studies the history of a tribe or any other ethnic group as given by that tribe or group, then arranged, and analyzed for the sake of an orderly, often highly formalized understanding of what the native really said; ethnozoology analyzes the zoological terms which the native uses, not in standard terms of zoology and biology textbooks; ethnobotany investigates the botanical taxonomies which the *subjects* use. Of course, once these indigenous categories are assembled, research and interpretive sophistication must begin at home; but the *corpus* must not be tampered with.

The lexical aspect of this all-important innovation will make the matter even clearer. Whereas the old-time lexicographers, philologists, orientalists, Indologists, Sinologists etc. tried to translate native terms into English, French, or German, trying to find lexical equivalents, the modern anthropological linguist tries to find what things, events, and persons fit the words and phrases the native informants use as they speak with each other.

One specific ethnosemantic tool is crucial in this book, and as it is not likely to make its way into non-technical literature for some time, it will be helpful if I explain it here. Ethnosemanticists speak of -etic and -emic statements; the terms are derived from structural linguistics, where the phoneme is studied as the minimal significant sound unit. Within any specific language, there is a limited number of phonemes, and any native speaker handles these perfectly without reflection. If he were taught phonology, and understood the meaning of a phoneme, he would then be able to write down all sounds of his own language, geared to its phonological conditions. Theoretically, if we succeeded in writing the sounds of a language by using a transliteration which *takes no account of the specific phonemic structure* of the language, we would get a *phonetic* alphabet. An example of a phonetic alphabet for the English language: to the alert non-English speaker, there are two different *k* sounds in English, the *k* of "king" and the *k* of "sky"; the former is aspirated, the latter is not. In Hindi and Sanskrit and all other Indian languages, these two *k*'s are different phonemes and different letters and can not be confused by any native speaker, any more than the English listener and speaker would confuse *g* and *k*. But to the native speaker of English, the aspirate *k* of "king" and the non-aspirate *k* of "sky" are not different *phonemes* (they bear no difference in meaning), so mentally he counts them by one symbol, viz. *k*. For his use, one sign *k* is quite sufficient—his transliteration, which has one *k* only, would be a *phonemic* transliteration; a phonetic transliteration would have to spell "khing" for king and "skai" for sky. Now the ethnoscientific terms -emic and -etic were artificially created so as to incorporate the distinction into a much wider, nonlinguistic set.

Marvin Harris, in his *Rise of Anthropological Theory*, 1968, gave what I regard as the best succinct definition of *emic* and *etic*.

> . . . *Emic* statements refer to the logico-empirical systems whose phenomenal distinctions or "things" are built up out of contrasts and discriminations significant, meaningful, real, accurate, or in some other fashion regarded as appropriate by the *actors themselves* (italics supplied; the "actors" are the members of the society

23

investigated by the anthropologist). An *emic* statement can be falsified if it can be shown that it contradicts the cognitive calculus by which relevant actors judge that entities are similar or different, real, meaningful, significant, or in some other sense "appropriate" or "acceptable" (p. 571).

. . . *Etic* statements depend upon phenomenal distinctions judged appropriate by the community of scientific observers. *Etic* statements cannot be falsified if they do not conform to the actors' notion of what is significant, real, meaningful, or appropriate. *Etic* statements are verified when independent observers using similar operations agree that a given event has occurred. An ethnography carried out according to *etic* principles is thus a corpus of predictions about the behaviour of classes of people (p. 575).

An *etic* statement, then, is one made in a universal context under the assumption that all adult sane people in the world would understand the meaning of the statement; an *emic* utterance, on the other hand, is one which is understood (or thought to be understood) only in a specific social or cultural segment. To simplify this seemingly abstruse notion, let me give you an example: when a person says "I am a Jew" and says so consistently, and means it, then he IS a Jew, notwithstanding some people's notions that the Jews are a race (which, of course, they are not), or that you have to be born of Jewish parents etc. When Sammy Davis, Jr. says "I am a Jew" he is a Jew, or when Elizabeth Taylor says "I am Jewish," then she is.

Now take another case. In Britain, there is an officially recognized Church of Witches; in fact, the head-witch is respected here in the States and the church has some following. When a churchgoing Englishman asks a person to what church she belongs, and she says "I am a witch," then she will be understood in that context, as simply being a member of the witches' church. Here in America, there is a fashion among some women who espouse the mysterious and think and say they are witches. But the trouble is that these "witches" are spurious. They are *not* witches either in the anthropological sense, where a witch is a person—male or female—who causes physical harm, consciously or unconsciously, by supernatural means; nor are they "witches" like those on the membership lists of the Church of Witches. Hence when a witch-church-member says "I am a witch," she is making an *etic* statement, one that could be understood by all people who happen to

24

understand English. But when the American woman says "I am a witch," she *thinks* she is making an *etic* statement, whereas in reality she is making an *emic* utterance—which is to say that she identifies her status within a circle which shares her linguistic habits of talking about "witches." The confusion between *emic* and *etic* statements, in speech and intent, accounts for the difference between genuine and spurious self-identifications.

Now to "mystic." Without this distinction, the ethno-scientific definition of a mystic would be incomplete, shallow, and in many cases just wrong. But with it in mind, here is what I regard as a thoroughly operational definition of a mystic: *A mystic is a person who says "I am a mystic,"* or words to that effect, *consistently,* when questioned about his most important pursuit. Further, his statement must be an *etic* statement—that is to say, it has to have a general widely applicable meaning, and must not be a term used only by a group of people in a manner peculiar to them, *emically* that is. Consider the American woman interested in the spiritual, yet too lazy to read the abundant anthropological material on witches—male and female—all over the world; when she says "I am a witch," she makes a spurious statement, one that makes sense only among people who share her situation; as she uses it, it is an *emic* term, not a term to be found in the ideal dictionary. Now, no English dictionary so far has defined a mystic as I do—but then no dictionary has so far been written or compiled by ethnoscientists. Whatever the traditional dictionaries' definitions of a "mystic" or "mysticism," they are quite irrelevant. We are concerned here with people, not with words; but we have to gauge people by words properly chosen, from observing certain complex experiences in ourselves and in others. Ethnosemantics provided the first part of my definition: a mystic is he who says he is, with certain exceptions and limitations which I indicated. The second, material part of my definition is one specific experience out of the vast number of religious experiences: it is the person's *intuition of numerical oneness with the cosmic absolute, with the universal matrix, or with any essence stipulated by the various theological and speculative systems of the world.* This alone is the mystical effort; a person who pursues it, and pursues it as his overwhelmingly central avocation—doing everything else marginally, so to speak—and who at the same time *states* that he has embarked on this quest, is a mystic. The shorthand expression for doing these things, seeking these intuitions etc., is "I am a mystic"; but since most mystics don't know the word "mystic," we should seek the statement in any language which, directly or obliquely, relates this intuition of numerical oneness as central, and use it as another way of saying "I am a mystic." The statement must be intelligible to anyone who understands his language; it must not be a secret code for some people, some illuminati who think their special thoughts but don't tell anyone about it, and who decide to call themselves "mystics." Their use is *emic*; only the *etic* use of "mystic" as a self-identificatory term suffices to identify a person as a genuine mystic.

The aid given to us by ethnoscience can hardly be overrated: we have finally *acquired* an instrument to obtain irrefutable criteria. No longer can we impose our own categories on other people's ideas; they themselves have to supply them. Whatever order we confer upon them is a posterior, heuristic undertaking for us, which does not make their experiences richer or poorer. The mystic is native: he tells us propositions which state "I am a mystic," and the circumlocutions he uses have to be broken down and decoded—not for his benefit, but for ours. Just like the statement "I am a Jew," when consistently made in relevant dialogue, the statement "I am a mystic" really provides the only exterior criterion of a mystic. The Śaivites of South India gleaned something of this sort many hundred years ago: "If a man who wears the monk's robe says he is a holy man, we must not doubt it. Only Śiva himself knows whether he is or whether he isn't." Let us hold fast to this: when a person says "I am a Jew" he says this in a setting where the term Jew *is understood*; when a person makes the statement "I am a mystic"—or statements which could be abridged into "I am a mystic" *on the speaker's terms*—he assumes that it is understood. There is a simple test: the American women who call themselves witches (because they think it makes them mysterious and sexy) will drop the claim the moment they are told that a witch is a person who causes physical harm through supernatural means, for that's not at all what these women meant. Suppose a woman or man is told that a witch is one that does harm (or thinks so) by supernatural spells etc., and *assents* to it by word or nod. In that case, by our ethnoscientific criterion, he or she is indeed a witch. When the person who says "I am a mystic," or words to that effect, is told by an expert what a mystic is, a seeker of the experience of numerical oneness with the cosmic ground, through meditation or some kindred procedures, and that person then exclaims "Yes, that's what I am after"—then he is a mystic, if he says the truth. As we shall see later in the book, rather few people do these things. They meditate, they strain to achieve ecstasy, euphoria, a contemplative state of mind directed toward some divine target, yet they do not see it this way. They believe that they can never merge with the target, that the target, God, or some god, must remain separate from them, that they want to get near but neither want to nor can become one with it numerically. What about these? Do they qualify as mystics by the ethnoscientific criterion? They do, but their case is a bit more complicated. I would call them mystics by courtesy. Again, there are seekers after transcendental intuition who do not look for euphoria, and some among them would shun it. I claim that ecstasy, or better *enstasy* to use M. Eliade's term,[7] is part of the objective description of what the mystic does. Rejection of euphoria does not disqualify a person from the mystic title: but he falls into a somewhat marginal category.

Now the readers who do not feel persuaded by the ethnoscientific argument, as well as those who have never heard of it, will be tempted to say that the definition was "purely subjective." This is not so, and the phrase "purely subjective" refers correctly to a much smaller number of phenomena than popular parlance would presume. We might say that dreams are purely subjective; genuine hallucinations are, but that's about all. Articles of faith, when held by a single person, are not "purely subjective," and it would be quite naive to claim they are, for components of a system of faith, however idiosyncratic and bizarre they may seem, share large chunks of the surrounding belief system. We might call the definition which the ethnoscientist elicits "inter-subjective"—a term that has been used off and on in contemporary analytical philosophy and in the sort of psychology *MIND* incorporated in its title as a journal of "philosophy and psychology." "Inter-subjective" simply means "subjective, but potentially shared by people within the same accidental, historical, or cultural radius."[8] In other words, an inter-subjective experience is one that is potentially shared by a group each of whose members understands the phenomena concerned. Our definition of a mystic is inter-subjective, since it is understood by other mystics, who then constitute the group which shares the same type of experience. However, this really begs the question, for obviously we don't say much about any cook by saying he is recognized as a cook by other cooks. The ethnosemantic approach takes note of the persons, things, and states which fit the term; it is more fertile and certainly more elegant, and accommodates many marginal cases which would either have to be excluded or which would necessitate a new terminology to account for them.

This does not prevent me from attempting a final definition which is "purely objective"—a term I do not like too much in my more technical work. Let me adduce an analogy from mythology, one that carries an important ethical message. When King Yudhiṣṭhira, the eldest of the five Pāṇḍava princes in the Mahābhārata epic, was asked by a minor vassal prince, "Tell me o king, what is the universal moral law," the king gave a sound anthropological, relativistic answer at first: "Different lands have different laws at different times, which one must see; and different castes have different laws, which one must see." But the vassal persisted, he was trying to get at some sort of objective, absolute moral law. So Yudhiṣṭhira said "The one universal law is ahimsa (non-violence)." The implication seems to be that this one law, comparable perhaps to the sixth commandment, was singled out as radically more important by the Hindu king, not just as one important injunction, but as universal, valid presumably at all times, in all societies, and in all situations. Obviously, such a declaration would be *etic* just as "tuberculosis" is in medicine.

If we now transfer this analogy into mystical speech we shall have to choose a set of phenomena which could be ascribed to all mystics at all times, regardless of what people in their society call them, regardless even of what they call themselves. I believe there is such an additional objective criterion: *a seeker of intuitive union with the cosmic ground, who chooses experiments which would lead to such intuition*, preferring the available enstatic or euphoric experiments to available less ecstatic and less euphoric ones. Such merging with the cosmic ground is proposed by some theological doctrines, discouraged by others. Now non-mystics—ecclesiastical doctors, for instance, or simply consistently pious and self-abnegating saints and people—may also be striving to attain union with the cosmic matrix (which, of course, is never called by such a term except by philosophers and anthropologists; but which is variously called "God," "the light" and scores of other names which were generated by sundry religious traditions and by conventional religious parlance). Now as I tried to show a bit earlier, orthodox Jews, Christians, and Muslims really cannot seek this union and be pious at the same time, because losing one's identity and becoming the cosmic ground is a deadly heresy in these teachings. But we certainly have in South Asia today hundreds of people who are pious Hindus, self-effacing ascetics, gentle or eager souls, who regard spiritual merger with the absolute ground (Brahman) as their life's aim. Yet, by my definition, that does not make them mystics right

28

away: for they must make a choice in favor of the euphoric, the more ecstatic procedure, accepted or forbidden by their surrounding religious tradition. In other words: all things being equal, if a man strives for the intuition of (numerical) identity with the absolute, however conceived, but does so without courting euphoria and ecstasy as his method, and if another man in the same community strives for the same identification, but uses ecstatic means of approaching the target, then the latter is a mystic, the former is not (although few mystics in any tradition would dispute the *possibility* that a man of the former, non-ecstatic, non-euphoric type could still achieve oneness).

People who are familiar with the Indian scene today will object that some modern mystics didn't act ecstatically at all, that they did seek union with the Absolute, that they did use highly poetic language, but that they did not choose euphoria and ecstasy when euphoric and ecstatic means were available to them. Such critics might juxtapose Ramakrishna Parama-hamsa [9] and Ramana Maharshi [10] of Tiruvannamalai, pointing to the fact that whereas the former seemed constantly "high," the latter hardly ever left his couch and if he did, he walked gently about and around the cow and the people in his *āśram*. Not so—Ramana Maharshi was a mystic of the first order, for he did indeed use ecstatic language, though being a Smārta [11] brahmin of a very conservative and orthodox tradition, he used the medium of Sanskritized instruction to convey the ecstatic; and anyone who knows the monistic scriptures and commentaries also knows that there are oft-repeated, highly coded terms which connote ecstasy, delight, euphoria, very directly—*ānanda* "bliss" being the big catch-all. The frequent occurrence of these terms tends to blunt the edge: western observers might feel that talking about *ānanda* "bliss" all the time is akin to the pastor's Sunday clichés about "grace," "peace that surpasseth . . . ," even "bliss" and other literally pleasant things. The analogy is plausible, but it isn't correct; for the basic content of the Hindu doctrine *is* hedonistic, the canonical scriptures talk overtly about delight and pleasure, and even the last five centuries of puritanical subversion have not quite succeeded in suppressing them.

In the *Taittirīya Upaniṣad* [12] there is a famous long passage called the "hierarchy of *ānanda* (pleasure)." Now official Hindu exegesis today, informed by that puritanism which I view as verging on the pathological, declares that *ānanda* does not mean pleasure, it has no hedonistic underpinnings; rather, it means controlled spiritual well-being, etc. But the passage resists these dampening attempts, and if you really want to get a rise out of a modern Hindu pandit who speaks English, you quote the *ānanda-mimāṃsa*, the "hierarchy of pleasure." There it says that one unit of *ānanda* is what a young, mature man, in full control of his senses, enjoys when he does his thing—which is being like other active, loving men and women according to the natural rule, being wealthy, having cattle and kin, etc. This basic delight-unit multiplied by a hundred is what a "human satyr" (*manuṣyagandharva*—a mythical being, much lower than the gods, but more powerful than men, cognate perhaps with fauns and nymphs of western Indo-european traditions) enjoys; then multiply this satyr's delight by a hundred, and we get a "divine satyr" (*devagandharva*); multiplied by a hundred, it is the pleasure experienced by a "long-lived heavenly ancestor" (*pitṛ-ciraloka*); times one hundred, we get the delight felt by the Vedic high-gods; then the text keeps multiplying by a hundred at a time, going through various kinds of divinities, and then in the end, beyond the pleasure of Indra, arch-hedonist and lecher of the Veda, comes the pleasure experienced by the person who has reached intuitive identity with the supreme self (*ātma-brahma*): the mystic, in our terms.

Another canonical passage says *raso vai saḥ* "verily, He (the universal absolute) is *rasa*," lit. "sauce," but the term is highly diversified lexicographically, and connotes essential pleasure, highly sophisticated aesthetic sentiments, etc. "Wrong," Prof. V. Raghavan, one of India's greatest Sanskritists and a very orthodox brahmin, said to me when I suggested this. "*Rasa* is not what you think it is—it is spiritual purity. It has nothing to do with the senses." Professor Raghavan is a very senior spokesman for the Hindu Renaissance, and even if he wanted to, he could not admit any literal reading of the text, for it is sensuous in the very real sense that it measures spiritual growth by the pleasure principle. There are many ways in which any text in the Indian tradition can be defused. I am not impressed by the Renaissance jargon. When Raghavan says that *rasa* does not connote sensuous pleasure, and that the "hierarchy of delights" in the *Taittirīya Upaniṣad* does not really talk about hedonistic things, his dissimulation is part of the modern apologetic of India.[13] What he rejects, and what the religiously most highly committed in India reject is precisely that the hedonistic element is quite crucial to the canonical texts, and that it is a co-defining factor for mysticism, in India as elsewhere. That the mystic's mind zeroes in on the orgasmic situation, anywhere in the world, is as distasteful to the committed Hindu ecclesiastic as it is to the fundamentalist Christian. Nevertheless, my thesis stands for an "objective" definition of a mystic as one who seeks numerical unity with the cosmic ground, the absolute, says he does, and does so by espousing the psycho-experimental which contains the pleasure-principle, rather than other, non-hedonistic means to achieve union, within the tradition which he knows.

The ethnosemantic, I think, remains the formally more important component of the definition. As we listen to all people who say "I am a mystic" or, in hundreds of other languages, when a person makes an equivalent statement, repeats it, modifies it, always coming up with a token which *means* "expansive numerical oneness," we can then observe, talk to, analyze, perhaps even love or hate that person; and we shall learn a lot about mysticism. The hedonistic clause, however, has but ancillary status: insisting on it dogmatically might effect unwarranted exclusions. For obviously there may be a practitioner of the art whose use of the pleasure principle is so rarefied or so highly submerged in exegetical or homiletic language, that the hedonic ground remains all but invisible. He may feel the pleasure principle work in him in many strange ways, and he may so modify the orgasmic syndrome that neither he nor anyone else could trace it in his thoughts, actions, and words. And yet, if he consistently identifies himself as a mystic making utterances which are reducible to the proposition "I am a mystic," we shall have to observe him as a mystic, even without the "objective" justification.

Let me adduce two very different men living at different times: Jesus Christ and Allen Ginsberg. Quite clearly, the latter is a mystic, on the ethnosemantic, as well as on the objective criterion: he says and sings that he is a mystic, and he certainly uses the pleasure principle without embarrassment. Jesus Christ said "I and the Father are One"—a statement of numerical identity quoted more than any other of his sayings in modern English-speaking Hindu India; but did he espouse the pleasure principle? I do not know; I somehow doubt it—but he made an authentic identificatory statement, and that is enough for the ethnoscientist.

31

Chapter Two

The Mystical Experience

"The flowing together and dissolution of all things in the ultimate identity of non-duality can be attained in different ways: through the affective identity of universal suffering, through sympathy, and through the theoretical identity or the non-differentiation of subject and object."[1] There are, of course, less pompous ways of stating an important number of affects which make up a mystical experience. The author of this declaration has obviously read many things—neo-Vedānta in English translation, some stuff written by modern Hindu college teachers of philosophy, and the inevitable Jungian texts. There are two important complaints about this way of talking about the mystical experience, its sources and its agents: first, the idioms involved are too woolly and too wide *to be refuted*; and it is the problem of refutation rather than verification that bothers me, for anything that claims to refer to real persons and events must be in theory falsifiable. But how does one set about to suffer "universal suffering?" What kind of sympathy must one engender to have the sympathy that makes a mystic? I am pretty sure I know what the author means when he says that mystical experience can also be reached by "theoretical identity of the non-differentiation of subject and object": he has the somewhat clumsy, somewhat Victorian English-language treatises of the modern Hindu Renaissance in mind, where such effusions abound. Suppose I translate this last clause into permissible English, into an idiom which does not presuppose the reading of Vivekananda, Radhakrishnan, and the scores of assorted swamis that roam the earth. The phrase would then have to be edited to run somewhat like this: one of the ways in which to achieve a genuine mystical experience is to grasp the speculative theory, or theories, which claim that there is really no numerical difference between the subject and the object, or that such difference is somehow erroneous, a delusion. Unfortunately, such cognitive understanding does not yield the mystical experience at all. Now of course, the author would say, this was not what he meant to say; the theoretical

32

understanding of the postulated unity of subject and object presupposes an intuitive realization of this oneness: one cannot learn it from books, nor from teachers, one has to experience it. Erudite, romantic, unexperienced seekers of mystical insight would argue that the doctrines which establish the unity of subject and object (monistic Vedānta and other oriental schools, some heretical writings of Christian and Muslim mystics, the poetic sayings of Blake and others) are doctrines which have been generated by previous mystical, intuitive experiences of that oneness; only such intuitive experience can give intellectual certainty, the certainty which mystics own; now that we have that certainty, we understand the seemingly illogical oneness of subject and object, hence we must have had the mystical experience leading up to it. *Post hoc, ergo propter hoc.*

I have heard this argument from many people, Indians and occidentals alike. It is, in the first place, the official idiom of the modern Hindu who regards himself as religiously engagé; and it is the argument of most occidental admirers of oriental wisdom as they see it. There is an underlying, secondary argument, a rhetorical protasis as it were. The highly esoteric doctrines which teach the oneness of subject and object are very hard to understand discursively, rationally, because they are not logical, or they belong to a "higher logic," and ordinary, i.e. nonmystical minds, however intellectual, cannot understand what seems illogical to them; hence we have this understanding; we have it, not because we are just intellectuals, but because we are mystics. There is a highly depressing fallacy at the bottom of all this, which seems to have escaped critics so far. The idea that the subject-object identity is difficult to grasp, intellectually, is simply wrong. The fact is, it is rather easy to grasp in the perfectly ordinary sense of "understanding."

I asked about 100 freshmen and sophomores at several American universities if they understood the subject-object-identity teaching of the Vedānta: I had set it down in simple terms on one page, mimeographed it, and asked these students to reflect on it for one day. Only three told me they did not understand it at all. Now I can hear an indignant rejoinder from the illuminati: *that kind* of understanding is not what we mean; anyone can have that kind of understanding; it is the *intuitive understanding* that matters. But here, quite clearly, they are begging the question. Their claim to mystical knowledge rests on the assumption that they have understood the theory of the subject-object identity through mystical intuition, without which that understanding is not possible. Roughly one quarter of the young students intimated that this subject-object identity notion was interesting, fascinating, etc.; another half of them thought it was just one of the many philosophical ideas they had been glutted with, on a par, say, with idealism, solipsism, etc. And a very small percentage of the students welcomed it with enthusiasm; some of these were hippies and contemporary participants in the "mystical"-cum-drug scene; and they had been reading mystical stuff, pseudo-mystical stuff, Vedānta, Zen, I Ching, or Blavatsky.

As we shall see, true hippies or "freaks" were really closer to mysticism than the neo-Vedāntins, both in India and abroad. The Ramakrishna Mission has about a dozen centers in America and Europe; they are well established and stagnant; their clientele has not changed in twenty years, and the swamis in charge as well as their flock are profoundly against experimentation of any sort. One would assume that some message conducive to mystical practice would be brought home to the devotees, monistic Vedānta having been the official doctrine propounded by Vivekananda and the other disciples of Ramakrishna; and Ramakrishna Paramahamsa was the most powerful, as possibly the most pathological, mystical experimentalist of a century. But with monism on the official banners of the Ramakrishna mission, the patently mystical directive of that doctrine is being watered down into a respectable Sunday sermon: the audience is not only not encouraged to practice mysticism but, on the contrary, the swamis vie with each other to give establishmentarian, ecclesiastic advice, very much like most average Protestant ministers in the cities until thirty years ago. I have had long talks with Swami N., a direct disciple of Swami Vivekananda and president of the largest Ramakrishna Mission center in the U.S.A. He rejects hippiedom, he rejects euphoria of any sort, he would not even care to discuss the psychedelic situation. And when other Indian religious practitioners insist that the relation between drugs and spiritual practice is spurious, Swami N. denies that there is any connection at all.

The Ramakrishna Mission is the oldest, administratively and fiscally most securely established India-centered religious organization in the West. The Krishna Consciousness Hare Krishna people in New York City and California with their chapters in other American cities, are making themselves known, with saffron-clad, singing and dancing urban middle-class youths singing and acting out the Vaiṣṇava ritual of Caitanya.[2] Maharishi Mahesh Yogi's "transcendental meditation" chapters are all over the world. One would expect, then, that mystical experience was around the corner. So long as the young occidental is on his own—randomly reading Blavatsky, *The Third Eye,*[3] the *Bhagavadgita* and whatever else his eager eyes can get hold of in translation—he tends at least to try things which mystics have tried; he certainly stresses the experimental aspect of the quest, however unguided it may be. But as soon as his interest is subjected to eastern or western organization and management, the initial thrust subsides. The outward form of this come-down is fairly typical: no more drugs, no more overt sex, and a clean, good life seems to take over. The Maharishi Mahesh Yogi (whom this author knows from earlier monastic days in India, when M. was not known to anyone but his close friends and associates, and when even fewer Indian professional mystics took him seriously than now) disclaims psycho-experimentalism, which is and remains the hallmark of the mystical endeavour. The pietistic talk made by Hindu and Buddhist preachers in South Asia and abroad is antithetic to mystical success: do not indulge in things which have no moral backing; do not seek euphoria, and do not use it when it comes; do the things we tell you, which are to be good, sociable, neat, punctual—in other words all the things which the Protestant minister wants people to do. Many young people dropped out from this kind of establishmentarian soul-care to find something else; now they are brought back to it. The pop-gurus' chanting of OM and words in the unknown Sanskrit—these things and a whole lot of configurationally connected factors obfuscate the issue for the cross-culturally naive seekers of something different. Unless a young westerner takes the trouble to acquaint himself with primary sources—and this means the disciplined study of a primary language, the language in which mystics reported their experiences, and *not* translations made by people who did not share those experiences—he has little chance to distinguish what could be genuinely new and instructive for his quest. Their parents received the same hackneyed establishmentarian sermon from the local minister, though with no Indian accent, with no Indian robes and looks and, of course, with no Sanskrit words interspersed.

The matter is being even more complicated by another misconception among serious occidental students of oriental lore, as well as among the less erudite, translation-reading admirers of the mystic East. The confusion comes from Jungian literature and the blurring of *mythology* and *mysticism*. The language which reports mythology sounds recondite, detached, philosophical, and humanistic; so does the better informed talk *about* mystics and mystical literature. Joseph Campbell is one of the finest exponents of mythological and mystical themes; he collaborated with the late Heinrich Zimmer—that strange German scholar who, like his noble forebear Max Mueller, never set foot in India. (Readers will have noted a gentle rebuke at this point. I do indeed believe that living in the country of mystical professionalism deflates mystical zest, and that the keenness to be a mystic increases in direct proportion to the distance from India.) Now I do believe Campbell knows the difference between mysticism and mythology. He edited an interesting book,[4] replete with the enthusiastic writing of people of the *Eranos* circle: Jungians all, believers in hidden, universal profundities and in symbolism at any price. We read about the dragon, the mare, the snake, as pervasive symbolisms of all mythologies—and we read that these symbolic identifications are the works of mystics. But they are not.

The culturally-involved convert to oriental things sees them from inside and contrasts them with everything that lies outside, including science, sociology, the arts, etc. Thus "mysticism," "myth," and "mythology" become very much the same broth, although discreetly each of them is so very different from what the *etic* models and their proponents, i.e. the modern analytical researchers, do and say. Since none but a very small fraction of the young anti-establishmentarian, counter-culture seekers want to acquire the primary tools (Sanskrit, Chinese, and the other basic, boring, academic drills), most of them must choose to read and quote and admire the predigested works and words of anti-analytical scholars. In the communes in California, and among students and non-students around college campuses, we find few who are willing to conduct Asian studies seriously, with the linguistic prerequisites. But almost all of them have read, and they quote Mircea Eliade and Alan Watts, believing—wrongly—that these authors declare mythology and mysticism to belong to the same sacred, secret matrix.

Once I received this note from a young man in the Graduate House, Cleveland, Ohio: "Dear Sir—I have studied Jñāna Yoga of Padma Saṃbhava for over a year and now have need of a spiritually endowed teacher who possesses the Truths of Tantra. I would much appreciate any help you could give me in this regard.—sincerely, C.D." I knew what the young man was after. C.D. had read, not in the original Tibetan but in Evans-Wentz's "translation" (Evans-Wentz knew little Tibetan, having had to rely on a Tibetan monk who knew some English) the Padmasambhava trilogy, and the Book of the Dead. All this is out in paperback. And this, of course, is not sufficient qualification for the claim of having studied Jñāna Yoga or Padma Saṃbhava. There is an additional hitch to this. Jñāna Yoga is no term ever used in the Tibetan tradition, nor even in any established Hindu tradition. The term was coined by Swami Vivekananda, whose four little Yoga-booklets on popular Yoga and popular Vedānta have done a lot of harm to people. Written in a facile style that pleases the hungry in spirit, they provided a matrix out of which further quasi-mystical reading was to proceed during the next six decades. An almost pathological eclecticism permeates the entire counter-culture and it is the hallmark of the growing number of people in the western world who have "mystical" interests. I might seem unduly cantankerous: but I object to all these mixed bags being called mysticism—overloading a term means watering it down, and eventually depriving it of any communicational operativeness. I have pointed out that anthropologists use "mystic" as a synonym for strange, inexplicable, allegedly magical, etc.; in chapters to follow, I shall show that Christian and contemporary Indian uses of "mysticism" also strain the term. At this point I am trying to show that the young, counter-cultural neo- or quasi-mystic's amalgamation of wildly heterogeneous, unrelated sources creates further overloading, which makes the term as useless as a saturated sponge. But more importantly, my own experience has convinced me that the eclecticism by which the would-be mystics live—hippies young and old, middle-class Euro-Americans—is dysfunctional: it does not permit the individual to enter into the context of genuine mysticism; it remains pretext. Why so? Because in order to achieve the state of the mystic, a person has to follow a genuine tradition, whichever he chooses. He cannot do it by picking from what is popularly available here and there—some bad translations from one mystical tradition, some leader who has read and been impressed by similar eclectic readings and feelings. Talking, thinking, and writing about mysticism is not mysticism, just as talking, thinking, and writing about poetry isn't poetry.

Now this motley crowd think and believe that they do mysticism because they think about the mystical life: they read genuine and spurious mystics, and they become entranced by the visiting Asian charismatic; and, of course, they do some yoga, some meditation, "transcendental" or other, and the day comes, sooner or later, when these cognitive and affective acts culminate in self-appointed guru-hood. "Do you know what I am?" a young, sad-looking college junior with a guitar asked a

37

young, pretty college junior without a guitar, who had come for fun and sex. "Nope," she said. "I am an initiate," he said. "So what?" she asked. I was eavesdropping, went over and asked the young man "Initiate into what?" "Don't you know, man," he retorted, "an initiate—the white brotherhood, the sacred spirits of Mount Shasta, Shiva, Shiva—I am an initiate." Now this sounds silly, and it was. But between this sort of proclamation and the erudite writings and musings of a well-read mythologian, the difference is really only one in degree of learning. Neither is a mystic. In the first place, a real mystic has to say he is a mystic, meaning thereby that he is trying to achieve the unshakable numerical union with an absolute which he postulates in some theological framework; secondly, he should seek this union with discipline and enthusiasm in its most literal sense, by generating and utilizing euphoria. But the various kinds of people I have just mentioned do not satisfy these conditions: they may look for union, but they have adopted the puritanical vocabulary of the established churchman, modern Hindu swamis above all; or if they use euphoria, with or without drugs, with or without sex, they do not work toward that theological union but adapt and adopt eclecticism which aids ease and euphoria, avoids discipline, and rejects "numerical union" as it sounds too theological, un-euphoric, and dry.

So far I have tried to outline what the mystic does *not* experience; or better, I have sampled a few experiences which are not mystical, whatever else they are: erudite, mythological, eclectic, euphoric. And I have denied that they were "mystical," because if everything anybody likes at any specific time is called "mystical" because it fits his pious mood, of withdrawal, of dropping out, of fighting the church or the parents or the teachers, then *nothing* is.

Let me now proceed to report what I believe mysticism is, as experience. I shall use my own experience as a control point and as a point of departure. I am a mystic by profession—and as I do not mean this facetiously, this is all I can offer by way of declaring my qualifications. Who will corroborate my claim? Fellow-professionals in mysticism; some swamis, but not many. Let me add that I do not take the problem of legitimation lightly; and if I have to proclaim my qualification as a mystic so very brusquely, Indian readers will not be taken aback; occidentals will, unless, of course, they are familiar with the Indian mystic's traditional process of legitimation. Modern Hindus want a checklist of qualificatory items—in line with the pedantic taxonomies of some Indian traditions. The grassroot

38

Hindu had no such problem—if a man dons the garb, walks through the villages, says friendly words, talks religion, and goes away, that is his passport.

I was about eight when I got interested in India. There were many Indian medical students at that time in my native Vienna, which had a famous medical school in those days. I taught some of them German, they taught me Indian languages and things in return. Along with it, and perhaps even earlier, I had been engaged in youthful religious activism: an altar boy at St. Charles in Vienna, I planned to become a priest. Very soon, frustration with my Catholic surroundings set in—similar perhaps to those experienced by the youthful Aldous Huxley. By the time I was fifteen, I knew the alternative—it was bowing out of Christianity and opting into Hinduism. Scoffed at and admired by teachers, friends, and adversaries, I must have known more about religious things Indian than any other youngster in Central Europe at that time. I have given a full report about my career in my autobiography,[5] and will not repeat it even briefly. I must, however, single out the events which began to constitute my career as a mystic according to my definitions. They were not systematically arranged in the *Ochre Robe*.

One night when I was about twelve, it happened for the first time. I was falling asleep, when the whole world turned into one: one entity, one indivisible certainty. No euphoria, no colours, just a deadeningly sure oneness of which I was at the center—and everything else was just this, and nothing else. For a fraction of a minute perhaps, I saw nothing, felt nothing, but was that oneness, empty of content and feeling. Then, for another five minutes or so the wall with the *kitschy* flowers reappeared, and the fire crackled in the large brick stove. But I knew it was One, and I knew that this was the meaning of what I had been reading for a year or so—the Upaniṣadic dictum of oneness, and the literature around and about it. I did not think in terms of God, *ātman*, *brahman*, nor, strangely enough, in terms of having found some fulfillment—I was just struck by the fact that I had not known this oneness before, and that I had kept reading about it very much as I read about Gaul being divided into three parts, or elementary Sanskrit grammar. Then after some time, no longer than half an hour I would think, things returned to whatever had been normal before—but with a difference. Somehow, perhaps because I had not heard about the dark night of the soul and other yearnings, I did not doubt at all that this was to be my inalienable private knowledge, that it would come back—and I remember quite distinctly that I did

39

not worry at all, even for a moment, that it might not.

Years went by, and many things happened. By the time I was nineteen, I knew several Indian languages. Sanskrit was my referential center and India had become the cynosure. Between the *Anschluss* in March 1938 and my conscription into the *Wehrmacht*, I did what no one then did, though thousands of young and not so young people are doing it today in the western world: I practiced *yoga.* I read Vivekananda and everything else; gobbled it up. The fact that I now reproach people for doing the same does not confute the principle at all: I deliberately ignored these initial inspirations at about 20, proceeding to bigger and better things in the spirit. But the neo-yogis here and elsewhere do not leave off their pamphleteering, not even when they are past fifty when they should know better. That annoys me. Vivekananda, Ramakrishna, the *Tibetan Book of the Dead,* many gurus with the many similar words—they should be outgrown in good time, say, before one has reached the age of 25; for by that time, one must either have made it or one must have found better guides.

I practiced yoga by the book, and nothing happened. Being one of about four German male citizens under 60 who knew Hindustani, the *Wehrmacht* moved me (partly on my request) to the Free India Legion, a regiment of Indian soldiers who had been fighting in General Alexander's Fourth Division in North Africa, and had been captured by Rommel, brought to German P.O.W. camps, and spoken to by Subhas Chandra Bose (who had mysteriously vanished from house arrest in Calcutta). They had joined the Free India Legion to fight the British and be out of the P.O.W. camps. I was an interpreter, and I antagonized the German officers, not by doing anything to annoy them, but just by being there. One night, near Bordeaux where the Legion was stationed, I had a row with an officer and was shoved off into a cellar to cool down; there would be no action against me, because the officer was in the wrong and I had witnesses. But there I lay on my back in that small cell, and then the second coming occurred: very similar to the one I had experienced many years earlier, during my Vienna childhood. When it set in now, I immediately recalled that early night, but postponed comparisons so as not to come down. I was One, with all in me, but this time there was euphoria—not of the erotic, ecstatic kind I was to experience during my later tantric phase in India nor similar to my more recent experience here in America, reinforced by LSD-25. It was euphoria that was unsensuous. The certainty of oneness was there again, but the certainty was not important—what was important at that moment was that

40

it corroborated the canonical text which rang in my ears, quite loudly, as though I had said it to myself, but from outside—*aham brahmāsmi*, I am the *brahman*. When I reflect upon that experience now, over thirty years later, I often wonder why I did not think something amounting to "at long last" or "lo, here is the confirmation"—but then, I shouldn't wonder. The certainty of a mystical consummation entailed for me that the *scripture* was right, that it corroborated my experience.

When the Sikh sergeant let me out with a sympathetic grunt the next morning, I took a long walk along the Biscayan beach. I did not feel humble—that I seldom was so far as I recall—but I thought that I was really doing the opposite of what Christ had done. Whatever happened to him, he had to find some scriptural indicator to predict the action or passion; but when I was oneness that night, I felt that *I* had authorized the scriptural statement, *aham brahmāsmi*, I am *brahman*, and the other dicta which imply the same; that in an irreverently anachronistic fashion, I had authenticated the *Upaniṣad*. Many thoughts then crossed my mind, and not taking account of my strong linguistic penchant, I reveled in the thought that I was now a true Anti-Christ, as I had done the opposite of what the Nazarene had accomplished: the Scripture had authorized him, and I had authorized the scripture. For a day or two, I went about my military chores—guard duty, teleprinter duty—like an automaton; not better and not worse than usual, which was bad enough. Then the whole experience retreated into my own, well-remembered, well-recorded history.

In 1948, after the war, after captivity, and after some concluding work in Indology and ethnology at the University of Vienna, I moved to India to become a Hindu monk. All this went by an unwritten blueprint. I have reported it at length in *The Ochre Robe*; but I did not report in that book what I now regard as three genuine mystical experiences during my eight years of Indian sojourn. What I did report was the miraculous, as it were; some encounters with mythology, projected out of myself or injected into me from without. These were stunning, lovely, gently frightening, and euphoric in a very peculiar sense. They gave me evidence of my having "emically" entered the realm of Hindu *mythology*, but this is not mysticism at all, for so long as the gods and the goddesses of your cherished pantheon face you, meet you, make love to you, talk to you, give you advice, you have consummated your mythology, but you have not become a mystic unless you become these gods.

I was ordained a monk in the Sannyasi Order in 1951; and

41

in 1953, I underwent tantric training and obtained tantric
initiation in Assam. It was during one of the concluding
initiatory rites that I had my third genuine mystical experience.
I cannot disclose the exact circumstances, since tantrism
practised literally is anathema and criminal in India, and such
disclosure would jeopardize the functions and the existence of
one of the very few remaining centers of serious tantric practice.
But that experience occurred as the sun rose over the hills, and
after the practicants had disengaged themselves from their
female partners in the ritual. As I went to retire in the *ashram*, I
suddenly felt as though I was walking without making any
effort, very much as in a dream, with the orectic lines between
the will and the body disconnected as it were. I first ascribed
this to the fatigue of the night's initiatory phase, but then within
a few minutes something totally different happened. I did not
walk, but I was the universe moving in itself. I saw my legs and
all, but these were just two rather unimportant instruments
among millions of unseen instruments that made the universe
move; but I was the mover. Briefly, I recalled the night in the
stockade near Bordeaux, a decade earlier. Also, this was the
longest experience in duration—for that specific set of
instruments now called Agehananda somehow got to the
ashram, lay down on the cot, relaxed for at least an hour, and
then helped itself to a large glass of milk—it was then only that
the state came to a somewhat abrupt end, of the snap-out type
(I have always been suspicious of milk). This was it again, with
no real addition in value to the previous two, although with a
somewhat greater intensity than either, I think. By that time, I
knew that the state was achievable, that there could be no
doubt about its absoluteness; and as I was a fair philosopher by
that time in the technical sense, I was not involved in
ontological pretense, for then, as now, I believed there are no
ontological implications.

In 1958, during my first American year, as a Research
Associate of the Far Eastern Institute of the University of
Washington in Seattle in the marvelous Pacific Northwest, I
was one of the first people to experiment with that exquisite
product of Messrs. Sandoz of Basle, Lysergic Acid
Diethylamide, LSD-25. I believe Leary and Alpert had just
barely heard about it at that time. I have reason to believe that I
obtained material from the first batch Sandoz produced, and
quite officially transmitted to some medical and biochemical
research centers in this country. I had read the *Doors of
Perception*; I found some of Huxley's speculations about the
mystical quite delightful, but not too significant—and I was

under the impression that he did not really try to establish his mescalin experience as a mystical one, but as strongly hedonic.

LSD and other psychotomimetic drugs go badly, very badly, with set-up "clinical," laboratory-test conditions. They have to be taken with warm people, friends, and very preferably in the company of a person with whom the taker has a profound sexual involvement, not as yet curtailed by duration and routine. During my third take I was with a very beautiful woman. She was a nominal Buddhist, but not really concerned with religious matters. We took the drug around 8 p.m., listened to Bach and Purcell (whose *Ode on St. Cecilia's Day* with the Deller consort and the Ambrosian singers, on a Vanguard recording, is the most powerful psychedelic music I have known), and it was a highly pleasant, lovely experience, with incense, friendly people, no psychiatrists, and the proper paraphernalia around. The drug wore off on schedule, at around 4 a.m., and we went to sleep. As the sun rose, I woke up and looked through the window. I was clearly "down," with no optical distortions remaining, except that the green-coloured city bus which ran past the Lake below the window seemed to look more like a snake than like a bus. I turned to see if she was awake, as I wanted to tell her about the bus-snake or the snake-bus; but she was already sitting up in bed, looking out of the window. I began to make love to her, and as I kissed her body, I had a marvelous vision: her whole womb took on a bright golden hue, it looked, and this thought struck me immediately, like the *brahmāṇḍa*, the Golden Egg of the Indian cosmogony; and inside it, millions of entities, looking like so many fish, were copulating in fast, perfectly rhythmical motion.

Now, of course, this was simply a comeback of the drug, and I would not call it a mystical experience at all, a religious experience, a cosmological euphoria, or any such thing. But when this spectacle subsided and I withdrew from her, I was again all *that*, with nothing whatever excluded. The late Zaehner would have called this another "praeternatural" experience, an instance of "nature mysticism"—but again, that is his problem. There was no god to speak of, except myself. For a second or a fraction of a second, I feared that Matsuko was being left out, but as I tried to communicate this to her I noticed I couldn't, for she was *not* left out—she was me, or better, I was she, too. I did not recall Assam, nor the army cell near Bordeaux, nor the chintzy flower-paintings on my Vienna childhood wall; I did not recall India, nor any other history or geography. I was it—not *again*, but always.

When I now report about it, I must, by grammatical rules and by the rules of the language game talk about it in the past tense; and saying "I was . . . not again, but always," is awkward, though I have a hunch the spirit of Wittgenstein will forgive me. See the motto of this book *"das zeigt sich—das ist das Mystische"*—in paraphrase, what one cannot say, because it cannot be said within the rules of language, "shows itself—that is the mystical." So it is. I have been pondering about the effects of that last experience—did it do anything for me? Did it make me more certain of the possibility which *is* my reality—not in the existentialist sense, of course, but in the specific sense intelligible to the mystical practitioner? I cannot say, quite frankly, whether I have been more certain about the possibility of oneness after that last experience in Seattle, than I was, say, between the Assamese and the Seattle experience. I don't think it matters.

An aside: when I told Matsuko about it the next afternoon, she got a bit annoyed: "Why, if I was you, and you were also all other things, wasn't I then just one of those million things?" Yes, but so was I. LSD was the trigger—but so was the initiatory phase in Assam, and so was the narrow cell in the Indian Legion of the *Wehrmacht* near Bordeaux. It was not orgasm that triggered that last experience. I think between the snake bus and the last orgasm, some fifteen minutes might have elapsed, and between that and the mystical shift, at least half an hour. Yet, I think it would not have happened had Matsuko and LSD not been there.

Since about then, I have been a busy American university professor; I have been teaching large classes and conducting small seminars, have published a lot: (technical, jargonistic stuff), have sat on committees, written recommendations, and traveled a lot. The monastic status in the order of Sanyasins is a *character indelebilis:* only marriage or death rescinds it; marriage seems quite impossible, though death is probable. I have been performing my minimal observances—meditation and the practice of my *mantra* every morning except after the formal pollution of sexual relations. Now my daily contemplation centers on the mystical experience—that is what the official Sanyasa meditation is all about. The mantra which I was given by my *dīkṣāguru,* [6] the late Swami Virajananda, at Shyamlatal in the Himalayas over twenty years ago is the mantra which implies numerical oneness with the absolute, the brahman. But this experience never came in the wake of my regular meditation.

It has not come to me, and it has not come to any of the

many fellow monks I have talked to, heart to heart (for being the only monk-anthropologist, I have devised a way to elicit such candid monastic responses). In my monastic field-days in India, I must have spoken to over two hundred monks. Some dozen and a half were genuine mystics, by the definitions of the first chapter: persons whose self-appellation would be translatable into the English proposition "I am a mystic," and who have had, once, twice, or much more often, the enstatic, euphoric experience of numerical oneness with the stipulated theological ground, the *brahman*. Then at Seattle I worked with some of the most learned Tibetan lamas in the emigration. One of them quite obviously qualifies as a mystic; but the identificational process with Tibetan Buddhist specialists is more complex and roundabout: the utterances which would translate into "I am a mystic" would be much more complex than, say, the monistic Vedāntin's. The northern Buddhist key-*mantra* conveys the meaning "I am of the form of voidness" —voidness, *śūnyāta* (*stong pa nyid* in Tibetan) being the "theological" key concept.

No Buddhist concept refers to an ontological being of any sort. But that is no real obstacle to the experience of numerical union: mystical consummation is union with whatever is spoken of theologically, doctrinally, as the matrix, the ground, and it is quite unimportant whether this ground is conceived of as having ontological or epistemological status. In fact, it now seems to me that the Buddhists are easier off, as mystics, than others, for the mystic who derives his interpretational material from a tradition which postulates the ontological reality of a supreme being (God, Brahman, etc.) must *explain* the merger, or the oneness, of two very heterogeneous entities: that is, the merger of himself as something that has ontological status, with the divine, etc., which also has ontological status. And the exegetical burden rests upon him: he has to explain, to himself and to others, some way or other, that A becomes B, or that A is B, A being he himself, however conceived, and B being the real ground wherewith he merges. Not so for the Buddhist mystic: even if he admits some sort of ontological reality for his own individual person (many Buddhist schools do in fact admit this) all schools deny ontological reality to the Void, Buddhahood. Hence he does not have quite so hard a time explaining how he, some sort of an ontological aggregate of impressions referred to as "I," *is* actually the Void, Buddhahood, etc., the latter having not even that much ontological status. Thus, it seems to me that the Buddhist's apologetic is easier going than the Vedāntin's, let alone the

Christian's or the Muslim's. So far as the mystic's needs go toward the perpetuation of his experience, no exegesis, no apologetic is required. And all mystics I have known, in literature and in person, have tried to talk about their experience. It does seem to me that when we get down to explaining things that are strange to all but ourselves, we shall find it easier to explain how a person disappears totally than to explain how he changes into someone or something quite different, but equally real.

Let me now conclude my self-legitimation. After the Seattle merger, there have been occasions where I felt I was quite close to getting at it—and the older I get, the more I can control, during my regular observances and my matutinal meditation, the *certitude* of the possibility of merging. Now this will puzzle my Christian mystical friends: I do not hanker after the experience—it is non-addictive to me. This lack of yearning must be a personal trait, and is not directly connected with training or affiliation. There are and were many Hindu mystics, who got highly upset about prolonged non-occurrence: just think of Ramakrishna Paramahamsa, and of the sufi-poets assuming they really mean God when they talk longingly about their male or female beloved. In the Krishna-Radha complex of the Hindu Vaiṣnava tradition,[7] all the songs, the rhythms and the words represent the yearning for the beautiful beloved, who is God incarnate and God himself complete with peacock feather, flute, and the other iconographical paraphernalia. But then, there are and were many Indian mystics whose temperament, judged by the statements they made, was more serene and pacific. I am thinking of Ramana Maharshi, who died of a carcinoma in 1951. I visited his *ashram*, and as an ordained monk I was given slightly preferential treatment over lay visitors. I do not speak Tamil, and he did not speak English, but there were many interpreters around at all times. His devotees insisted that he was always in the state of *samādhi*,[8] that wherever he went—patting the cow Laksmi, talking to visitors, eating his austere, but tasty vegetarian meals—he was constantly experiencing oneness, in the manner, I was expected to believe, in which I had by then experienced it four times. Or was he?

I differ with my friends, the devotees of the late Ramana. Ramana had no doubt had the consummative experience of oneness, many times and for very long periods—ethno-science again, for he made statements to this effect. But during his daily chores, with the devotees, in the *ashram*, meeting visitors, he was, I think, "down" from the unitary experience, "down" without longing or yearning. Yet it was this lack of emotional display that seems to have made his devotees think that he was in the core state at all times, since he answered questions to that effect rather abruptly. When people asked him how hard his *tapasyā* (austerities) had been until he reached permanent *samādhi*, he said that he had not done any *tapasyā*: yet it was accepted by all that he had been living in a cave all by himself for years, where he would have died if some pious gentleman had not come and forced some food down his throat every other day; and where his legs became infested with vermin which had to be removed by a minor operation, as he had never left his seat of meditation for many weeks on end.

Now the modern Hindu, in line with the dialectic of the Hindu Renaissance,[9] reads this to mean that the saint thereby documents that he is constantly in the state of *samādhi*. This, *etically* speaking, doesn't follow from anything. Mystics are not always in the state of oneness, for during the periods, short or long, when they are in that state, they cannot function: they cannot talk and teach, take notes, listen to arguments and to petulant queries.

A famous photograph shows the great mystic Ramakrishna standing with his arms raised, in *samādhi*. His disciples surely learned something by witnessing the core experience, but it was not formal teaching, passing on of the lore. For this there must be words, in the proper order and well structured. So long as the mystic is in his core experience, he can produce no such thing. Hindu critics and possibly many Christian admirers of mysticism will claim that the great mystical teachers taught, in words as well as by example, as they were having the experience, the implication being that these masters never came down from on high. The critics are wrong. I dare anyone who has had the mystical experience even once, to tell me that he or she could have functioned discursively when in that state.

In Allahabad at the Kumbhamela[10] in 1954, one of the most profound, pleasant, and well known gurus was holding court in his tent. A German psychiatrist who had been converted to Jung, yoga and India sat in front of him and asked the great swami, "Sir, when you were in *samādhi* when you were young, didn't sexual thoughts disturb you?" The swami smiled (expected) and said "In *samādhi*, there are no sexual thoughts, so they cannot disturb you and me" (expected). There was a hum of admiration, a big collective nod, and the psychiatrist was silent, probably because he was flabbergasted, not having broken through the code of holy speech in India.

As so often in this study, I must adduce the psychomimetic

47

experience as a heuristic parallel, for this is precisely what it is, and the most adequate one we can think of at this time. In hedonic, erotically charged, musically supported, ritualistically informal LSD sessions, with unworried, concerned, mystically inclined people around, and with a dose of 200 micrograms of pure unblended LSD, the average taker enters the deepest place roughly four and a half hours after the take. This phase lasts about one hour, whereafter it ebbs off. During this phase, the taker is often removed from the discursive world of subjects, objects, and things. He could perhaps dial a phone number, or find it in the telephone directory, he could boil a cup of tea and do other easy things about the house. But the effort he has to put into such chores is enormous, and he usually does not feel like making it. But before and after that zero-state, he can and does do all kinds of helpful things for his friends and about the house. This is the parallel: the mystic teaches and looks after the things of the world at all times when he is not right inside the zero-experience. In it, he won't make the effort although he could, for the simple reason that there is no desire toward making any effort. I found myself very busy indeed before and after three out of the four mystical consummations I have reported; but right in them, there simply was no question about teaching or not teaching, nor even about such more important things as survival or dissolution—all these seem like remote verbal concepts, without any connection to what happens during that central phase.

I have now introduced the term "zero-experience." Toward this point of the blastoff countdown, all else has been preparatory in the Space Center. Less drastically, the term might have been borrowed from philosophical ratiocination: there is zero content of a cognitive sort in the experience. But I think the technological reference is more apt; for I would call any consummative experience a zero-experience, within each universe of discourse. Thus, orgasm would be the zero experience of the erotic situation, the solution of a mathematical problem in the situation of mathematical quest, etc.

Now the Indian mystic's answer to questions pertaining to his life as a teacher are coded stereotypes. Most mystics are ordained people, belonging to some monastic or paramonastic order however loosely organized; even the *svatantra* "independent" monk who lives by himself belongs to an order by virtue of his ordination. The one commitment which remains even when the person has severed all other ties with his erstwhile initiatory complex is the code of speech. He never

48

steps out of it; he never uses *etic* language to talk about mystical things; his reports are always well within the verbal code of the tradition.

This should not be cause for astonishment to western readers: Teresa of Avila, Suso, and virtually all Christian mystics talked Christian code when they talked about their experience, and whenever they deviated from the code they risked trouble for themselves, as did Meister Eckhart. Similarly, Mansur, al Hallaj, after pronouncing *an 'al haqq* "I am the Truth (i.e. Allah)," was impaled by the angry pious. Some western mystics would like to talk about the zero-experience in analytic detail; they would like to tell how it *feels*. Long before the coming of psychology and novelistic self-scrutiny, the mystics of the western world, Christians most, had been trying to speak about the experience itself; but they had to camouflage it, lest they should give dangerous offence to the ecclesiastic and the secular powers.

Today's mystics of the West, Huxley, Leary, Ginsberg, and possibly many thousands of the young who strive for vision, want to talk both about the experience and about a hidden theology. Yet they have no theology, save a Christian Protestant's eclectic packet. Those who do take the Christian background seriously do not often generate the attitudes that would single them out as mystics rather than as good, pious, contemporaries. In India, the situation is almost the reverse. The Indian mystic does indeed have a doctrine to back him, which propounds the zero-experience as part of its central doctrine, in the four great dicta of the *Upaniṣad*: "I am *brahman*": "Thou art That"; "the conscious functions are *brahman*"; and "verily all this is *brahman*." But the practicing contemporary Indian mystic, though seemingly aided by this scriptural fact, is at the same time operationally impeded by it, since he must regard himself, and can be regarded as a successful mystic, only when he talks in terms of having found and experienced that state. His code of transmission is rigid, stereotyped. He *must* tell his disciples that he is in the zero-state at all times, even as he talks to them. But he is not.

To trace this strange *emic* strategem, I must take a big step back into homiletic history. In the Hindu monastic tradition, the person who seeks the intuitive consummation, viz. the realization of numerical oneness with the absolute, is called a *jijñāsu* "one who is desirous of (obtaining) *jñāna* (intuition of oneness)"; and a person who has found it (who, in my terminology, has had the zero-experience) is called *jñāni* "a knower." These are narrow technical terms referring exclusively to the mystical universe of discourse, not to any kind of cognitive knowledge, scriptural or other. Now through a highly complex kind of dialectic which I cannot present here—a dialectic based on commentary and counter-commentary literature by the monastic and lay teachers between the 9th and 11th centuries—the status of the *jñāni* and that of the *jijñāsu* are nondistinct for all practical purposes. The normative implication seems to be that the layman should not make any such distinction, since he is not qualified to do so. Let us not forget that the Indian hieratic tradition has been, and is, highly authoritarian. But the layman should be informed that there has been an unwritten tradition among the gurus, especially the monastically ordained ones, not to make this distinction in their dialogue with the laity, nor in fact with each other. This must be the reason by the Indian mystic gives the impression that he can also function in all matters pertaining to everyday concerns. He says he has cognitive and conative coordination even when he is in the zero-state. For if he did teach "I can operate in the world only when I am not quite in the state, when I am out of it, though close to it . . ." etc., he would reintroduce the traditionally eliminated distinction between the *jijñāsu* and the *jñāni*.

When the mystic says "I function better in the world, as I have mystical vision, etc.," he means to say "having had the zero-experience (once, twice, often), I function better"; but he cannot mean "whenever I am in the zero-experience, I function better" simply because during the experience one cannot function at all. The analogy with love is not too far-fetched. A person in love may be more aware, sensitive, alive to his world. But in sexual intercourse?

The late R.C. Zaehner, the best educated and the shrewdest apologist for Christian mysticism, said "very many nature mystics have thought the same (i.e. that the identification of nature and God is wholly natural and self-evident) because they have been *deceived* (italics supplied) by the mere sensation of union or unity into the belief that the object of such union must always be the same."[11] And Swami Chinmayananda, the most fashionable among the English-speaking gurus of neo-Vedānta, said in a lecture "the dualists are animals—animals of the gods—and I would say, they also have the intelligence of animals. For how could a person who has meditated on divine things possibly think that the Self is different from God? My Vaiṣṇava friends here are raising an angry finger against me—but let me assure them, that when they will *go deeply into themselves and meditate more*, they will see that their dualism

50

is an illusion" (italics supplied). The passages which I italicized do not refer to any special contemplational process. They are, in Charles Stevenson's important terminology, [12] persuasive terms: they have the grammatical and semantic semblance of describing something, but they do not actually describe. Zaehner implies that he has had a zero-experience, if I am not wrong, and Chinmayananda, like all of my famous fellow-sanyasins, increase their audience by nourishing its assumption that they are having the zero-experience all the time.

"Nature mysticism" is a term of reprimand—a persuasive term again, not a descriptive one. For of course whatever we generate in ourselves is part of nature, since we are part of nature on anyone's account, pantheistic, monistic, theistic, or "pan-en-theistic," to quote Zaehner's pedantic term. Descriptively, therefore, "nature mysticism" is a pleonasm like Maharishi Mahesh Yogi's "Transcendental Meditation," or "mental telepathy." If you postulate that there is a God and that he is different from Nature ("When He created the world, he didn't even look at it" as al Ghazzali reportedly said) then every zero-experience that does not take cognizance of that separate God is "nature mysticism," since there is no *tertium quid* besides God and Nature. When I related parts of my Assam experience to an Indian Civil Servant, he seemed puzzled and asked, "But Swamiji, in all you saw and felt, was God not present? You never mentioned God—you talk only about *natural* things." As I was much less cynical then than I am now, I replied saying that I should have added that my experience, or rather, its contents, couldn't have been more *sat* ("Being"), more *cit* ("Consciousness"), and *anānda* ("Euphoria"), the three of which define "God." The man nodded and seemed satisfied: legitimation by scriptural quotation, of course, is known as both the scholar's and the devil's time-honoured device.

There are mystics who do not seek, know, or propound the theological concomitant of their experience. And it is not, as partisan expounders of mystical lore would have it, that an experience without theological reference is not a mystical experience but something else, like "nature mysticism." Rather, the mystical experience is far more central than either theological or non- and anti-theological interpretations of it, either by mystics themselves or by their apologist spokesmen. The minimal denominator of the mystical experience is that of numerical oneness—it is also due to its minimality that I call it the "zero"-experience. It is quite irrelevant to mysticism— though of course not to ideological afterthoughts of a theological or anti-theological kind—whether the experiment allocates the zero-splash to "nature," to himself as now integrated, or to deity however conceived and theologized.

If authors with theological investments pre-define a mystic as one who has certain experiences, and talk about them in the vocabulary of a specific theology, or in somewhat deviant, but theologically permissible marginal vocabulary, then there are no mystics outside the faith. When it comes to defining human artifacts, socifacts, and mentifacts the jargoneer-anthropologist has a prerogative before theologians and literary people. His job is, in part, to find the most general definitions for types of human behavior, for "cultural things," [13] of which religious behavior is an important segment. I claim the most general validity for my dual definition of a mystic and mysticism in Chapter I. If a sympathetic Christian theologian should suggest that "a mystic is a person who has what Bharati calls a zero-experience and who knows that this is what is meant by Grace, God, the Trinity, the second coming," etc., this would be a parochial overspecification and hence no definition.

The Hindu canonical scripture confirms "when one sees nothing else, hears nothing else, cognizes nothing else, that is the infinite . . . when one sees something else, hears something else, understands something else . . . that is the finite . . . the infinite is immortal, the finite mortal . . ."[14] I read this to mean that the zero-experience is not in any way subject to the mortality syndrome, whereas all other states, including those of the mystic when he has come down from the zero-experience, are subject to "mortality."

If I read the Dark Night of the Soul correctly, it means to convey the devastating anguish experienced by the Christian mystic who has had the zero-experience and who believes that its yearned-for recurrence depends on the goodwill of an agency he cannot control: God must show grace again, and why should He to one so wicked and humble. To the Nature-mystic, the person to whom any theological sanction is marginal or irrelevant, the zero-experience is one of complete autonomy. No God, avatāra, or devil can do anything to provide or prevent it. The mystic's own person generates it. And if it does not come about for a long time, it does not really matter any more than not being able to obtain a non-addictive drug like mescalin or LSD for a long time after having had a marvelous trip.

Here, for once, I agree with a central existentialist dictum: that possibility is more important than actuality. If I have my own very large bank account, I do not have to draw upon it at all. Spending from wages or other earnings, my account does not decrease, it is my own, it is something I can fall back upon at any time. But if the account belongs to my closest friend who has sworn allegiance to me and who has assured me that I can always draw from it, some anxiety is nevertheless bound to exist. Autonomy precludes anxiety; theologically structured dependence on an external Being generates anxiety. This may well account for the fact that there is very little anxiety-language in the reports made by people who have made the zero-experience ascribing it to any external entity. Śvetaketu goes on tending the cows and the buffaloes with a shrug, for another quarter century, as the guru keeps telling him that he isn't quite ready yet. The student or adept comes to the guru samitpāṇi—"fire-wood in hand"—for years and years, he tends the cattle, looks after the estate, and is instructed very gradually. Then one fine day he does obtain the zero-experience. It does not change him a bit; he remains very much the same as before, and goes on doing much the same things. If there is a personality change, it is not drastic. To use common American jargon—a man who doesn't have the real goods tends to be a put-on. I shall show that the genuine mystic as a person remains the person he was before—a king, a knave, a dentist.

In certain middle-class circles in metropolitan Tokyo, there is a rumor supported or invented by American Zen-converts, that the man who designed the Canon lens—better than the Leica optic, its German prototype—was a Rinzai Zen monk, who spent most of his time in satori [15] and made lenses, too. Now the more eager ones would probably claim that the most perfect photographic lens was designed while the monk was in satori. But if the story is true, it means that the monk has satori, and after that he designs lenses. He has his skill in making lenses not from the satori experience, but from being a fine lens-maker. And I must go further than that: the mystic who was a stinker before he had the zero-experience remains a stinker, socially speaking, after the experience. This, of course, does not mean that he cannot stop being a stinker; but for such change, he must make efforts of an ethical order, which have nothing at all to do with his mystical practice.

The apologists on behalf of the silent mystic majority (let us not forget that mystic derives from myesthai "to be silent") have a stake in claiming and believing that the mystic is ipso facto a sublime human being, a wise man, etc. This error I must dispel. It strikes me as rather odd, however, that the irrelevance of ethical to mystical behavior and vice versa should not have been stated with greater force than it has been. The Hindu speculative tradition, based on certain canonical passages, speaks of four "states" of the human mind; Swami Vivekananda and the neo-Vedantins between California and Calcutta have been reiterating these four states *ad nauseam*: the ordinary waking state *jāgarana*, the dreaming state *svapna*, the state of deep sleep *suṣupti*, and the fourth state *turīya*, "the fourth," which is the state of the zero-experience. Whatever the psychological merit or demerit of this somewhat rough and ready taxonomy, one thing is clear from it: that the teachers who established it also implied that *turīya* was different from the other three states. And from this it would follow that you cannot do in any one of them what you do in the other, especially not in the last, noblest, "highest," called the "fourth" to emphasize its difference from the other three. The mystical state, the zero-experience, *turīya* the "fourth," is something radically different from the others, and nothing that pertains to any of them can be pursued in the fourth. The ethical stature of a person surely must belong to the waking state, perhaps to the dream state, if we insist on quoting Freud as a latter-day witness to Vedantic wisdom; but it cannot belong to the "fourth," where there is nothing but oneness; and if Hindus insist on defining it, then this oneness is Being *sat*, Consciousness *cit*, and Ecstasy *ānanda*; but it is positively not moral behavior.

There is, however, another important point to be made as we analyze what a mystic says when he emerges from the zero-state: he tends to talk mysticism all the time. Literally, or obliquely, mysticism seems to remain his central theme—and the zero-experience lingers at the back of his mind and his speech. I believe it is precisely this that gives charisma to even the driest mystic. The themes may vary at the surface, and the topics chosen by the more learned among the mystics for formal communication may or may not be related to the religious and the mystical universe, but there is a hint, at all times, at what is supremely important in the long run: the zero-experience.

The fulltime mystic in India, i.e. the person who does not have to do anything else in the world but talk about the zero-experience, and directly orients his life toward it and toward nothing else, is a fool when out in the market place. But he is surrounded by a wall of devotees, of monastic institutes, of ecclesiastic functionaries or ashramites. The *swami*, the *sādhu*, the holy man—if he succeeds in having himself tagged as such he really does not have to talk or do anything else. This solves an apparent paradox: the mystic who does nothing else but wait for his next zero-experience tends to be incredibly naive and uninformed about the world; but this gives him institutional strength; he is looked after by his very own establishment. Once he moves out of it he must learn many other things. First of all, he must learn to camouflage the zero-experience in the face of the larger audience. Then he must learn a trade or a science which absorbs him so thoroughly that he does not worry about the possible non-recurrence of the zero-experience.

In addition to it, the worldly mystics have their private grudges; against bores, topical talk, and social duties. Why so? Because once the zero-experience has been had, the mystic's interests take a hierarchical turn: he realizes that some things are more important than others, and that he must learn to avoid the less important ones and isolate the persons who are unimportant to him. The mystic is *not* a samaritan. He can afford to like everything and everybody, if food, talk and people come to him, as in the monastic situation. But if he lives in the world he must develop strong and innocuous *dislikes*.

Trailinga Swami, a very famous mystic of the late nineteenth century, was a recluse. Had he so wished, the pious and the rich of Benares would have built him a castle of gold and marble. He did not choose it, but stayed by himself. He acted in an utterly obnoxious manner when people came to see him; he sent some away with profanities, and it is reported that he actually threw stones after people who were persistent in seeking his *darśan*.[16] He was quite fastidious about food. He liked *thumri*, the light sophisticated music in and around Benares, and he detested *khyāl* and *drupad*, the ornate classical style of Northern Indian music. Hindu and Buddhist hagiography, particularly the Tibetan *Jātakas*,[17] abound with narrative about the unpredictable roughness or tenderness of the Buddhas and the other mystics. Zen devotees in America know what terrible things the Sixth Patriarch did to his would-be disciples, "to test them," so they say and think. But that is only a small part of it: in reality, the mystic must cathect certain persons and things around him, and must strongly reject others, if he is to survive for further zero-experiences. Being nice about things and kind to all people erodes the mystical thrust. Mystics who do not live in sheltered surroundings are highly selective in their personal tastes and contacts. Mystics who make a compromise with the public's demand for nice and obliging gurus lose their poise, though not the public charisma. In India, as we shall see, charisma is a matter of ascription—*sādhus* are charismatics by appointment as it were, hence perhaps not genuine charismatics in Max Weber's sense.[18]

I believe the cause for the mystic's social selectivity must be sought in the need for sharp contours. Readers of this study know that the Zen master plagues his disciples by doing or demanding the unexpected, the traumatic, the seemingly and truly senseless—the clapping of one hand being the standard example. Zen and some of the tantric schools require and recommend traumatic conditioning to generate *satori* or other forms of enlightenment supporting the zero-experience and supported by it. It would appear that analogous traumatic conditions in the circum-mystical life, during the days and years without or between zero-experiences, are to be engineered by the mystic himself, to conduct an active highly cognitive life guided and goaded by his intellect; but this means a highly selective approach to objects and to people. Let me repeat that this restriction is significant only where the mystic does not choose, or cannot find an ashram-like institution to screen out the world; if he does find such a surrounding, he may or may not look for discursive divergence. He may remain a critic, even a cynic, very choosy about people and things—but he does not have to. I have seen monks and mystics of both kinds.

Mystical experimentation takes its clue from culturally concealed elements in the mystic's surroundings. He must cathect clues which non-mystics do not need—he must look for hidden meanings, but not in the pompous and often trivial manner of eclectic symbologists. His attitude must be empirical—it cannot be doctrinaire. This seems to fly in the face of what the swamis have been saying since 1900: all religions are true, all religions teach the same, etc. Swami Omananda, one of many "spiritual leaders" with an ashram in the Andhra country, has a swan, a rising moon, an OM and a cross as the emblem of his ashram and on the cover of his periodical *Peace*. The apologetic of Vivekananda and the post-Vivekananda swamis was formulated with some such intent: all religions are the same, but monistic Vedanta is better. Jesus and Mohammed spoke the same truth as Buddha, but in the end the monastic *advaitin* will have to punch the ticket for all who have seen his final light.

This is all nonsense. The mystical experience is monistic—but that does not at all mean that the philosophical monism of any kind, including the Vedantic, is a more refined creed than other forms of Hinduism, or indeed than Christianity and Islam. Advaita Vedānta and the Upaniṣadic core dicta historically propound the monistic experience as the ultimate official target—yet the authoritarian theology and the ideology that have clustered around it have alienated the Vedantic schools from the zero-experience about as much as have other

56

forms of post-experimental exegesis, in the Indian and the Mediterranean traditions. I recall Swami Chinmayananda who, when he was conducting his *jñāna-yajña* "wisdom sacrifice" in and around the salons of New Delhi, had himself propped up by his disciples and carried away from the microphone after his sermon. "*Samādhi* has overpowered him," a civil surgeon in the audience informed me; "his yoga experience is so strong, that his body cannot take it without support." Now, of course, the fact that Herbert von Karajan drills every stroke of his baton in front of the mirror makes him not a bad conductor but a vain man; and Chinmayananda's practicing all these histrionics does not make him a bad swami. He may well have had the zero-experience. But his sermons *interpret* the experience in the light of what is required by the neo-Hinduism of the urban, civil servant type—and that alienates the experience just as effectively as dualistic and theistic theologies do.

There are linguistic cues by which one who has had the zero-experience recognize another. Again, we have a good parallel in the drug scene: the hostile policemen and legislators, stupid psychiatrists and their funding agencies fight LSD and psilocybin and the people who experiment with these substances, and when they talk about psychedelics, they quite literally do not know what they are talking about. Even the most childish LSD talker can discern from a person's talk, however erudite and technical or however simple, whether he has taken the drug or not. So also there is a zero-experience language. Its lexical cues are multiple, much subtler than the LSD cues, but they form a *Gestalt*. Much of it is contained in the writings of the official mystics, and much of it, or course, is displayed in the writers about mystics, Jung, Zaehner, and many lesser ones. But the trouble is that theological and other interpretive lingo so dilutes the zero-report language that only a mystic will know if a writer on mysticism has had the experience, from certain additional clues which theological obfuscation cannot drown out. The cues are thin in statements by famous mystics: "This spiritual life is . . . unknown before the coming of Christ. Man is in a state of unconsciousness and his spirit still slumbers; it is an abortion . . . without form; the phantom self obscures the true self; man is already the son of God, but he doesn't know it."[19] If this is all Basilides meant, he was the first victim to the ecclesiastic powers. "This God," whom Basilides encountered in his most secret heart, " is the Gnostic God, a nothingness beyond thought."[20]

When Aldous Huxley reported[21] about the multifluorescence of his flannel trousers or the leg of the chair, it just wasn't his ordinary flannel suit or the leg of an ordinary chair— these were shorthand, poetically, consciously, or even unconsciously chosen words to hint euphoric content, maybe under conscious avoidance of theological terms. Zaehner wondered why Huxley did not mention God a single time when he reported about his mescalin experience. Huxley, like Zaehner, had heard words galore about the *brahman*, about the advaitic experience, about God. It was not that his experience was unrelated to these concepts, but he simply chose to use non-theological terms for, I think, pedagogical reasons. God-talk had driven him out of Christianity, God-talk later drove him out of Vedānta. Why should he perpetuate it when he really got on to something important? I believe his mescalin experience was the closest Huxley ever came to a zero-experience. When he spoke at Syracuse in 1967 shortly before he died, he gave me a blank look when I suggested this to him. But that look might have meant "yes zero-experience" or "no zero-experience," just as his core experience was every bit as "divine" as that of the saints and the more professional Christian mystics, except that for sheer surfeit he didn't talk God when he got close to, or entered zero-station. We have in Jaimini's comments on the canonical scripture this very important message: when the Veda, which is supreme knowledge, mentions the word "tree," then the reference can never be an ordinary tree; for such trees, Jaimini averred botany is the sole authority. "Tree" must be a code for a zero-experience or something close to it—for that is what the Veda scripture is about. As I see it, "chair legs" is much more complex and subtle than drugtakers' consensus would have it. A list of mystical merging expressions would be long and vacuous, because many of the idioms which constitute this code are shared by establishmentarian, ecclesiastic, and generally non-mystical parlance.

I have tried to show in this chapter what mystics experience partly on the basis of what they report and also on what their advocates say on their behalf. The main trouble about reporting mystical and meta-mystical language lies in the histrionic area. We know the Ganser syndrome in psychiatry: a person acts and talks as though he were insane, plays insane, until at one point there is no clinical distinction left between acting and being insane. Mystics in basically non-mystical, theistic traditions have had to talk themselves into theologically acceptable sainthood. Having had the zero-experience their theological culture prompts them to do and say the "right" thing about the experience. Those who did not quite grasp the theistic code were the deviants, or in Christian and Islamic situations, the heretics. Rimbaud didn't care a damn; he poses a problem only to the apologist for Christianity. It is quite irrelevant whether the word "God" or equivalent enters the statement a mystic makes about his experience; irrelevant, that is, to the mystical context, though it is highly relevant to the doctrinaire, ecclesiastical censor—e.g. the late Prof. Zaehner. The simple fact of the matter is that the mystic, the man or woman who has had the zero-experience cares not at all if some or all around him declare him "insane," "heretical," "nature mystic," or subject to "praeternatural experiences." Huxley's "flannel trousers" are as much code names for God, *ātman-brahman*, and the entire mush of theological language as Jaimini's "tree" was for some zero-experience.

To the mystic, temptation is desirable. To the theologian, it is highly undesirable, as the Nazarene indicàted in his chief prayer. The mystic plays with temptation because all temptation *reminds* him of the zero-experience; the establishment must dissuade and warn from temptation, and hence discourage the zero-experience. It often seems to me that the Lord's Prayer was the great repudiation of the zero-experience and its concentric derivatives. People have given esoteric interpretations to the *Pater noster*, declaring its words to be *mantras* with hidden meanings; but then one does not have to be a cynic to refuse being impressed by desperate attempts to esotericize the exoteric: the Lord's Prayer, the *Bhagavadgītā*, the *Dhammapāda*.

I would now say that most genuine mystics feel a lot but know very little. As a theologian, the mystic is just as good or bad as he was before he had his zero-encounter. As a prophet, he tends to make a mess of people and things—about which later. As a person, he isn't very nice unless he happened to have been nice before. The mystical experience is neither noble nor ignoble, it is not powerfully this or that, just very powerful and absorbing. "They are intrinsically ineffable experiences, as mystics themselves often allege," says Prof. Findlay,22 "while expressing them so richly and so eloquently as to demonstrate their extraordinary effability. They are also experiences whose expression delights to flout all logical rules rather than to obey them, and which accordingly admit of no logical treatment whatever." Such Pickwickian statements abound in the apologetic literature on behalf of mysticism, and I wonder if an actual mystic would write like this: for in mystical reality, neither the flouting of logical rules nor the poeticity of statements is important, unless the mystic happens to be a poet or an anti-logician for other pre-zero reasons. Surely a mystic, like any other person, may have a specific axe to grind, but he does this grinding not *qua* mystic, but *qua* axe-grinder.

Findlay, a scholar who takes himself seriously, dislikes W.T. Stace, who was no mystic either but who did not claim to be one; but Stace's treatment[23] is by far the most incisive by way of getting onto the mystical complex from outside. The apologists on behalf of the mystics constantly belabor ideological matters—should mysticisms be monistic, pantheistic, panenhenistic, theistic, scientific, anti-scientific, logical, alogical, etc.? A mystic pure and simple, if there is such an animal, does not care about all these matters one way or the other, since they are totally irrelevant, and totally trivial in the light of his main concern, the zero-experience. Yet the mystics I have known or read were not mystics pure and simple. They also happened to be theologians, ecclesiastics, musicians, scientists, and anthropologists. A person takes a stand about monism, theism, pantheism, etc.—not as a mystic but as a man engaging in extra-mystical activities. Zaehner's and Findlay's puzzlements are not the mystic's puzzlements, and the busy fears of the apologists as well as of the antagonists are no fears of the mystics.

People seem to think that the mystic's utterances about the zero-experience are somehow deliberately mysterious or mystifying, obscure and ambiguous, teasingly ambivalent, pedagogically anti-ecclesiastical etc. Has it never occurred to any of these authors that the mystic may simply be a clumsy speaker or writer? Lacking the forensic skills of professional talkers and writers, he makes statements which appear obtuse, ambivalent, or mystifying. There have been mystics who *also* happened to have writing skills, and some who had developed other skills which had nothing to do with mysticism.

Most musicians talking about music talk balderdash, but some musicians could and can talk about music—Richard Wagner was obnoxious but he said some fairly professional things about music. Similarly, some mystics were also philosophers, in addition to, not by reason of, their being mystics. I am thinking of my own ultimate preceptor, Śaṃkarācārya. That eighth century Nambudiri brahman who became a sanyāsi allegedly at the tender age of eight, was a mystic par excellence by both of my definitions. In the first place, he said he was one; in the second place, he was an enstatic monist. But in addition to it, he was also outstandingly well versed in the exegetical lore of his time, highly polemic, probably quite vengeful, highly literate, and a fair poet. Now his followers between 850 and 1970 A.D. suffer under the same confusion: they maintain that his mystical experience made him an eloquent philosopher. My own guru, a very saintly, kindly, and learned man, once told me when I voiced some such idea, "You see, when you ask the merit of the *ādiguru*[24] and of one who speaks in his own language and does not know a word of Sanskrit, their merit as *jñānis*[25] is absolutely identical; but their merit as teachers is very different indeed. It is like a flower on a simple meadow, and a similar flower placed in a marvelously wrought, expensive vase surrounded by a marble courtyard in a prince's mansion. People will tend to praise that flower due to its environments—they might ignore it in nature."

All mystics, I think, know euphoria, and all mystics know oneness, and I use "know" in the more intimate experiential sense. Some speak about it well, others atrociously, others again not at all. When St. Teresa of Avila talked about her experience, that aristocratic lady talked official theology in decent Spanish. If I were ignorant of the philosophical trouble invoked by making statements about other people's feelings, I would say "All mystics feel the same—but they say different things." As it is, I can only say that all people who have had the zero-experience talk about it as they must talk as members of specific linguistic and theological cultures and sub-cultures, not as psychologists who talk about their feelings. How they talk about what they feel will concern us in the next chapter.

Chapter Three

The Language of Mystical Experiences

"For where there is duality, there one smells another, one sees another, one hears another, one speaks to another, one thinks of another, one knows another; but where everything has become the self, then what should one smell, what should one see, etc. . . ." (*Bṛhadāraṇyaka Upaniṣad* II, 4, 40). The *Bṛhadāraṇyaka* and the *Candogya Upaniṣads* are the oldest extant texts dating to as early as 700 B.C., which talk unambiguously mystical language. There are several categories of scholars who deal with the mystic's traditional opus: philologically oriented Christian theologians; anti-Christian-oriented orientalists, and philologists inspired by Hinduism, Buddhism, Taoism, Confucianism, usually at an early age; the erudite collective-unconscious, group-soul sponsoring psychologists with Jungian trends, who see in the mystic a much more profound and clandestinely systematic wisdom than the mystic has, or needs to have; and most recently, we have the sociologists and the anthropologists who see in the mystic a rather quaint subject, the "philosopher" or "wise man" whom Paul Radin expected to find in every primitive community. The scholar *qua* scholar should not say, "the mystic seeks and finds union with God." Zaehner did that, he was a scholar, and he was wrong. He could have said, "the mystic has an experience, and reports his experience saying 'I seek and have found union with God'." Now the scholars and the Learys, the champions of chemical elixirs, unless they are analytical philosophers, constantly use *emic* language where they should speak *etically*. Erudite scholars who have made an enormous emotional investment in oriental thought find it difficult to accept that the genuine mystic may be neither a saint, nor a theologian, nor a humanist, but just a person who had the zero-experience and who happens to have been born in and surrounded by a culture which our scholar took many decades to study, and to identify with.

This is by no means the predicament of occidental scholars alone. Indian philosophers, viz. men who teach philosophy at

Indian universities and write books about philosophy in Indian English, share the plight. Prof. J.L. Mehta, now of the Harvard University Institute of World Religions, formerly at Banaras Hindu University, wrote the one important book ever written in India on Martin Heidegger. [1]

The Association for Asian Studies had its annual meeting in Boston, and everyone, including this author, was there. Also, some Sanskrit-learning genuine hippies made the scene. In the evening, Mehta and I had a long talk—and apart from reminiscing about old days when we jointly bootlegged A.J. Ayer, Gilbert Ryle and L. Wittgenstein into Banaras Hindu University, we spoke about mysticism, LSD, free sex, radical leftist politics, and the *Upaniṣads*. When I began research on this book a few months later, I found to my amazement that scholars with very different backgrounds share certain views about mysticism—R.C. Zaehner, J.L. Mehta, and about another half dozen I spoke to: they deny, quite vehemently, that ecstasy should be at the core of the mystical experience at all. They even deny that the mystical experience is euphoric; and they get quite annoyed at Huxley's and Leary's suggestions regarding the close proximity of drug-induced and yoga-induced experiences. Most of all, they really reject the idea that true mysticism might center on a hedonistic aesthetic experience. When I quoted the pleasure-scale from the *Taittirīya Upaniṣad* (*ānanda-mīmāṃsa*), Mehta got furious: this is not what was meant by it. And Zaehner, whom I have not met, disapproved of people claiming mystical experience when this experience is not checked through by the church and its overt and covert affiliates. No, mysticism cannot be pleasurable, orgasm-linked, flesh-linked. It must be something deeper, more hidden, more metaphorical; the scriptures and the saints cannot mean these coarse, simple things. They must mean something apparently accessible through a blend of reading, thinking, analogizing metaphors, believing, humility, patience. Mehta and Zaehner appreciate mystical *writings* in which erotics, drugs, ecstasy-metaphors abound, but they will not have drugs, erotics, and ecstasy. They seem to think that the mystical experience is something quite *different*: but different from what? I have a feeling that actual ecstasy scares them—they cherish written-about ecstasy, by the poets and mystics. I am certain that the erudite strategems of profound secrecy—theological codes, better literature, deeper speculation, etc.—are so many mantles protecting the anxious savant from the zero-experience. Why do they want to avoid the zero-experience, and why do they explain it away in others, by insisting that pleasure is not what the saints mean when they talk about pleasure? We have come full circle: without psychologizing these men, I do maintain that they denigrate the zero-experience because of their long-lasting, long-nurtured emotional and intellectual investment in circumvention and paraphrase in the academic, literary, scholarly life. This argument has been running for a long time; long before I started writing this book, I was carrying on dialogue with fellow scholars, in Euro-America and in Asia. At first I thought their notion that there could be no real, sensuous, ecstatic content in genuine religious experience might have been due to the pervasive Protestant ethic, that a thing can be right and true and good only to the degree in which it is unpleasant. "In America," said Allan Coult, late founder of the International Society of Psychedelic Anthropology, "you have to feel bad in order to feel good." What is it, I ask my conservative fellow-scholar, that makes an experience described by the canonical texts in terms of sheer delight, "bliss," *ānanda*, rapture, joy, etc., *not* directly delightful, blissful, rapturous? What is wrong with gaining such an experience without pain if it can be done? Now, of course, there are as many standardized and predictable answers as there are questions of this type: "Salvation cannot be ingested chemically." "If one could see God through drugs, then what would be the merit of the saints and the ascetics?" and, *pace* J.L. Mehta, "When the *Upaniṣads* talk about bliss (and a hierarchy of delights such as established in the *Taittirīya Upaniṣad*), they do not really mean the sort of euphoria hippies talk about." Why not? Precisely because "that would be too easy." The texts, so these scholars would then elaborate, state all the time that it is difficult, very difficult, that only one in a million succeeds, etc. But in the mystical segments of the canonical literature, even in the non-mystical pep talk of the *Bhagavadgītā*, the teachers say it is also very easy, a child's play. Then why reject the alternative possibility of easy rather than hard-come-by achievement? Because more passages in the texts say that the supreme achievement is hard, rather than easy to come by? No such count has been made; and even if it were, and the majority of passages were indeed shown favoring hard, unpleasant, ascetic procedures, it would hardly be to the point since the mystical experience is not amenable to statistical analyses. There are quantifiable standards of non-mystical religious behavior (congregational, devotional, etc.), but no such standards apply to the mystical.

I do not mean to say that mystical experience can be gained by pleasurable procedures only; whatever the processes, or whatever chance throws the person into the zero-event, the actions and passions that lead up to it, chronologically, in an individual's life are irrelevant to the autonomous experience, and this is what all mystics report. In Christian mystical language, it is Grace—and for the modern, theologically unconcerned or uncommitted mystic, it may well be "chance," good luck, psychosomatic readiness, and what not—but all these terms mean precisely that no determined set of actions, no planning for mystic vision, guarantees its occurrence. There may be theologians and mystics who believe that their good life elicited God's grace. Hindu sages and mystics like Ramana Maharshi made it abundantly clear to all questioners that their *sādhana*, their "spiritual exercise" to use the funny phrase of Renaissance Hindu writing in English, had no causal relation to the experience. My own guru, the late Swami Viśvananda Bharati, was asked by a fellow novice of mine, "If there is no connection between *sādhana* and *siddhi*,[2] then why do you, sir, and why do other saints make so much effort? We see you doing *tapasyā*[3] all the time—if these are not needed to achieve *samādhi*, why do *you* do them and why do you advise us to do them?" Viśvananda then gave what seemed to me one of the canned lectures which swamis in good standing share with good college teachers. The gist of it, however, does make sense: that people must do something, and that they will do the things they are wont to do. "Some plough the fields, some go to war, and some do *tapasyā*." This, of course, is in line with much of the official instruction of canonical and postcanonical Hinduism: that spiritual consummation can be achieved by everyone, "high-caste, low-caste, dog-eaters, nay, even women," as the *Bhagavadgītā* puts it so charmingly. As contrasted with the "Great Tradition" Sanskritic ritual, which can be performed only by male brahmins, the summum bonum, evidently, is theoretically open to all who try—though the pragmatic implication is that it might come easier to brahmins, since they are more professionally involved with the things, the people, and the texts that talk about the zero-experience. Now this has never been said, and it is important that I should say it here: *the zero-experience comes to those to whom it comes, regardless of what they do; it also comes, I believe, to those few who try very hard over a long period of time.* That is what the monastic life and the initiate's training are all about. There is no guarantee that the person who yearns for it will get the zero-experience even if he does those things which most traditions associate with the experience. *But that does not in any way lessen the possibility* that many people who don't try at all have the zero-experience anyway—I would think this covers about half of all mystics of all times and climes. And it is this fact which the scholar and the ecclesiastic resent. To them, this possibility seems improper and intolerable. When they talk to fellow scholars, and to people in general about esoteric things, they rub it in: genuine, *true* experience cannot come from infusing drugs—it cannot come easily. While this contradicts the facts as stated both by mystics whom they would regard as genuine and by pertinent scriptures, the scholars maintain their claim—and I think I have shown the two reasons why. I once asked a respondent who disliked Leary and Huxley and the tantrics, all of whom seemed to get to the zero-experience by some measure of fun, if he would resent two sportsmen, say, tennis players, being equally good, when one had been playing all his life five hours a day, and the other had just barely started, was practicing irregularly, and kept cavorting through the nights. My colleague said no, he wouldn't, but that tennis was not mysticism. The idea was that the mystical experience is so lofty and noble that analogies of this sort do not apply. But "noble," "lofty," "sacred" etc. do not describe anything; these are persuasive terms, telling the world something about the speaker's tastes, his specific proselytizing stance, but nothing about people and actions. Thus we have come to the end and the beginning of a large circle: good things cannot be achieved easily; the mystical experience is the best thing, the noblest, the *summum bonum*, hence it cannot be obtained easily. But it is known that quite a few if not most mystics really didn't do much to get there, and if they did lead austere lives they did so for reasons of routine, livelihood, monastic status, etc., not directly in quest of the zero-experience. So, the rule goes, if the zero-experience is to be good and genuine, it must have been come upon by hardship, not by pleasure; but "good" is not a descriptive term, so that the identification of "genuine" and "good" with "come by through hard work" is purely subjective, generated by moralistic ideology unconnected with mysticism. All sorts of fatuous arguments are marshaled at this point and in between: you cannot get a Master's degree in a day, you are not a scholar just by talking scholarly, etc. But the analogies do not hold, as the zero-experience, unlike scholarly knowledge, is not cumulative—it does not take time to aggregate it.

There is, of course, all the difference in the world between what the mystic says when he talks about his experience, and what non-mystics say when they talk about mystical experience. But it so happens that some genuine mystics must talk about *other* people's experience; and when they do, their speech is not necessarily more to the point than that of the non-mystical interpreters. There is good cause for this: when the person who has had the zero-experience wants to see it in the light of a tradition with which he identifies, he will tend to slant his report about his own and other mystics' experience so as to make it fit the convention. He has, in most traditions at least, a safeguard for integrity: he can fall back on the maxim that his experience is, in effect, ineffable; but what he reports about fellow-mystics' experience is what the traditions around him permit and recommend.

In interpreting the zero-experience the mystic may follow four consecutive phases in all traditions. In phase one, he accepts all interpretations of the scriptures and commentaries known to him (within the accessible system) as on a level, though he would often tacitly prefer one, quite often the less orthodox. In phase two, he espouses an unorthodox, even a heretical reading without overtly rejecting the others, thus creating his own "school" or scriptural jargon. In phase three, he shifts from one to the other, vacillating between them at different times; and in the last phase he has reconciled himself with all readings but he now no longer regards any one superior to any other. At this point, the mature mystic has developed his own private meaning as he reads and interprets the doctrine. I call this phenomenon "monolexis"—an individual code for absorbing and transmitting doctrine without risking dysfunctional conflict with his surroundings. There is a parallel in the secular world: scholars often latch on to a phrase to which they give their own meaning, regardless of whether it meets the originator's intention. Thus, Ruth Benedict, the anthropologist, had her monolectic reading of Nietzsche's Dionysian-Apollonian categories, and she applied them rather fancifully to the Pueblo Indians, the Plains Indians, and the Dobu Islanders.[4] More recently, T.L. Spriggs has given an excellent account of the philosophical possibilities involved in private meaning-ascription [5] and as I re-translate his statements for the analysis of mystical language, I find them quite fertile. What distinguishes the mystic's religious, doctrinal language from that of the ecclesiastics is precisely his monolexis: he uses words from the Writ, but he uses them in his own code. In fact, you can recognize the school of a mystic by the way its members use scriptural terms in a non-scriptural, esoteric sense, set by the mystical teacher through the process of monolexis. So, rather than quote the mystic's use of scriptural passages to illustrate the hidden meaning of the scripture, we should realize what his main intentions are, as distinct from the scripture and the ecclesiastics who are its trustees. "Peace" talk in the mystical idiom of Christianity has nothing to do with political and world-peace. Peace, to Jesus the mystic, seems to mean peace with one's own esoteric experience—or, poignantly in a strictly anti-mystical, dualistic tradition, peace between the official, contingent distinction between God and creature, high and low on the one side, and the zero-experience on the other. Non-mystically, Jesus says that he didn't bring peace but the sword: I read this statement as a rebellion against the encroachment of the zero-experience on the traditional rabbi that he was, up to a point. Observing that mystics are "peaceful" rather than violent, I think this is due to involuntary inertia and natural resistance: to hold the peace is less strenuous for the individual, and less distracting, than to be violent.

Hindus who have been exposed to Christian scripture tend to read Jesus's statement "I and the Father are One" as a monistic, *advaita*-type declaration. And if we recall our definition of a mystic, then the statement is indeed a tempting one. Now I am not sure that such was the speaker's intention. But I am quite sure that if there was internal conflict in Jesus between the mystical and the dualistic, the zero-experiential and the rabbinical element, the latter prevailed in the long run. Insisting on the dualistic, creature-creator language Zaehner launched a head-on attack against the zero-experience, calling it "nature mysticism," "pan-en-henic experience" etc., implying that these are not true mysticisms. The formal devotional syndrome which he predicates as the *sine qua non* for the true mystical experience confounds the issue and weakens the mystic's report, rendering it doctrinaire, ecclesiastic, camouflaged. I believe that Teresa of Avila, the German mystics, and even Jesus himself had the zero-experience, though some of them tried hard enough to explain it away with God-talk, echoed in later days by Zaehner, Underhill and Cuthbert Butler. The latter two knew next to nothing about Indian traditions. But learning or conversion is no excuse for slanted reports or analyses of experiences which intrinsically are not bound to any specific theological tradition. W.T. Stace has a relative advantage over Zaehner and myself, since he is not committed to any specific theology. Yet, I think there is a way of atoning for one's faith: one must radically criticize the doctrine with which one identifies, pointing out its weaknesses, its foibles, and the clay feet of its founders and sustainers, at every step. This I have done with Hinduism, incurring the wrath of the orthodox and the modern Hindu alike. Stace is right when he says that some religions do not deflect much from the mystical experience, since their doctrine supports it, or better, since the individual experiencing the zero-state does not have to do much interpreting when he reports his experience to his society. I am in a pedagogical quandary: I often wish I were not a Hindu professional—or even, not a Hindu at all, so that analytical minds would not need to have the uncomfortable feeling that I stress the monistic utterances of the Hindu tradition because I am a Hindu. This can't be helped. But the Hindu canonical scripture—part of it, that is—seems to describe the zero-experience as it is. "This *ātman* has been verily realized totally devoid of all cognition . . . it is free from the illusion of the manifold, it is non-dual, therefore, knowing the *ātman* to be just that, fix your attention on non-duality . . . and behave in the world like some inert object."[6] The last clause could mean "he behaves like some inert object so long as he is in the zero-experience," i.e. he really cannot act in the world. On the other hand, some think that the text recommends simply the quietistic, anti-ritualistic, and in Vedic days no doubt revolutionary mood of the first mystical rebels. They were probably like Tim Leary telling the rebels against ecclesiastic conventions, "turn on, tune in, . . . drop out"; don't *do* things. But whether we stay in, very actively, or drop out, quite inertly, is irrelevant to the zero-experience, as neither action nor inaction is dictated by the experience. One or the other may *seem* obligatory to most people who have had the zero-experience, simply because most people remain strongly ensconced in some ideological network. Most yogis in India have been following predictable patterns of exercise in the hope to repeat or stabilize the zero-experience. And yet, outside it, they have taught that their zero-experience entailed a specific theology and ideology, a specific type of action or inaction. They were simply mistaken. No specific theology, ideology, activity, follows from any specific spiritual training. But since mystics carry a cultural tie to some tradition, they feel that their zero-experience legitimates and validates the theology and the ideology with which they identified prior to or between their zero-experience, or else which they opposed. This is not some sort of a clever paradox: acceptance and opposition together constitute engagement in an ideology, the acceptance of opposition with indifference. I witnessed one purportedly genuine Black Mass with the head functionary actually impersonating Satan and entering the prostrate hierodule sexually. Now you have to be a Christian or an anti-Christian to do these acts consistently and with faith. Conceivably, some people may organize a black mass for the fun of it, or for show business or something in that genre—but that is as little of a black mass as a Te Deum conducted during a performance of Tosca on stage is a Te Deum. I do believe that a mystic could be indifferent and neutral about a theological and ideological system, neither identifying with it as a follower who would then explain his zero-experience in terms of doctrine, nor antagonizing it by playing up his zero-experience to prove the ideological-theological system false, hypocritical, etc. But it so happens that there have been few if any such mystics. And as most of us have not really heeded Sir Karl Popper's warnings against historicism in preaching, we somehow think that people who do not identify with or oppose a theological tradition are not really mystics. Huxley, Mr. "N" reported by Stace,[7] and some people I know are mystics on all counts, and certainly by my definitions; but since most writers about mysticism are historians of sorts, and since so many of them (not including Stace) entertain strong emotion for or against their theological environment and their background, no title has been found for those people.

I think the base for these confused definitions is the insistence, fanned by the historical concomitance of mystical practice with belief and ritual systems, that mysticism is somehow noble, dignified, marvelous, or indeed dangerous, heretical, perverse. This notion has diverted scholarly attention from what should be the basic concern—to discern genuine from spurious mysticism. Anthropologists have observed that only genuine spirit vision gives power to the Plains Indians of North America; pretended, spurious visions give spurious powers, and the native audience quickly uncovers such pretense. The person who has really had the zero-experience is the real mystic; if anyone has had a different experience which he subsequently makes fit descriptions of zero-experiences, he is a spurious mystic. Writers about mysticism have commented on the intensity of mystical experience, its relation to a theological framework, its nobility and purifying power. Mysticism is not important because it fulfills a previous prophecy, or gives a new lease to an old life, or makes people better. This belief is untrue, and bars the application of proper standards of evaluation and legitimation.

Mysticism is important to the practitioner. It may be more traumatic, more exciting, more powerful than other experiences in the mystic's life. But this is due to his specific value cathexis: he invites the experience as the most important. Objectively, however, the mystical experience is not any more important than, say, sexual, scientific, poetic, and other experiences which combine the cognitive, the orectic, and the affective. It is more important, say, than a culinary experience or a victorious run of eighteen holes, although, of course, even these trivial events might so engage the whole person that they take on a "mystical" quality; after all, the *Upaniṣad* equates man with food, with water, and consecutively with the other elements. Whether an intensive liking becomes an obsession or whether it is something noble and benign does not depend on any objective data, but on the nomenclature given to affects by the contemporary consensus. I would think that certain segments of human behavior tend to be more absorbing, hence more "important" to the individual by way of engaging his faculties, than others. Golfing, bowling, Sunday fishing, ball-games, and voting are immensely important and obviously absorbing activities to many Americans; but to me, an aggressively "hyphenated" American, some of them seem trivial and even stupid. But "stupid" and "trivial" are terms of persuasion—I do want others to share my tastes. It should be clear, however, that the mystical experience is just one among many total experiences, not more noble unless you call it so, not more pernicious unless you call it so—and all these are *emic* ascriptions. *Etic* statements about the effects of the mystical life are possible: one might argue, for instance, that the majority of mystics, most of whom have coordinated their zero-experience with a value system or a theology, were less sociocentric and more asocial in their ways than were the ecclesiastics; the mystical life tends to effect disengagement from society; it also has an illicit parameter which we shall have to discuss at a later stage.

The zero-experience is noble, sublime, etc. in *emic* talk; in *etic* terms, it is pleasurable, absorbing, genuine or spurious, by the given criteria. Mystics may talk about anguish and longing in their post-zero ruminations; but this is due to their post-zero and inter-zero ideological ascriptions and identifications. I watched two very young hippies in California take LSD for the first time. Their experience, judging from their reports, was very different indeed from the experiences of similar takers. Both of them received genuine zero-experiences, and neither ascribed it to any Judaeo-Christian ideology. These two young people reported the clear union experience, and along with it, they reported their pleasure (which was non-sexual or not directly sexual at that time), their being totally engulfed by it, their feeling that this was the basic state of things, but not the answer to their problems and questions. They did *not report* that they felt their experience was noble or morally good or bad until twenty-four hours later, when they had made love, had

71

reflected about what had happened, and had talked to other, senior takers, some of whom were spurious mystics, and all of whom were serious, senior hippies with records of at least one acid trip per week for at least one year. Their leader confided to me that he was not at all satisfied with the reports given by this young pair of lovers who had just walked in by chance; it did not fit the leader's variety of Zen mysticism nor the cosmic plans and models which he said are inevitable concomitants of the proper experience.

Ten years earlier, I had spent a day with a rather well known Jaina saint in the vicinity of Delhi. He had just returned from a visit to Dilwara, an important Jaina sanctuary in Western India. "I saw a man there," he told me, "who said strange things. He was a *digambara*[8] monk like myself, and he was well versed in the Jaina scriptures. But he said that when he meditated one morning near the big shrine, he knew that everything was really he himself. And he thought that this was an *anubhava* (experience) which the Niganthas [9] must be referring to when they talk about the state in which the *tīrthaṅkara* [10] finds himself." Then I suggested to the reporting saint that such unitary experience was not really what the highly atomistic, pluralistic, separatist Jaina doctrine taught. The saint thought for a while, and then he came up with an answer whose significance dawned upon me only years later, here in America, after I had observed that innocent young couple under LSD. "The scriptures fit all right," he said, "if you are ready to read them in terms of this *anubhava*."[11] Which must have meant that we should *not* read our experience in terms of scripture, and also something like this: "Yes, the Jaina scriptures teach atomism, separatism, multiplicity; but then they also teach *anekānta* and *syād*, 'multiple reference' and 'maybe'—that is to say, every proposition anyone ever makes can also be refuted by another proposition." In the Jaina dialectical tradition, the rule does not apply to Jaina doctrine itself—only to opposing doctrines, i.e. Hindu and Buddhist. This is an unwritten convention, and I believe the saint would have let me in on a secret: that the *anekānta* and the *syād* also refer to Jaina doctrine, corrigible or even refutable by the zero-experience which cannot be refuted—it escapes the dialectic.

One of the more insightful things Swami Vivekananda said or repeated was that Hinduism was "nonhistorical"; and he meant this to mean that the historicity of its founders was unimportant, that Hinduism is unlike Judaism, Christianity, and Islam, which would not "exist" were Moses, Christ, and Mohammed not actual persons in history. He should have left it at this; but unfortunately, he also insisted that the figures of the Hindu epics, the teachers of the Veda, etc., were all historical persons and that they lived many thousand years ago, which makes nonsense of the whole matter. Yet, we must take a cue here: the occidental insistence on *uniqueness* as a decisive factor in human and cultural history blunts the analysis of mysticism. Were it not for the notion that key-figures, inspired by the divine or incarnations of it, account for all events that are important in the spiritual realm, the study of mysticism might have been less opaque. Most critical and apologetic writers on mysticism in the West were Christians, some very few were Jews or Muslims. But all of them attached immense historical importance to the experiences of certain individuals, with unique experiences that reinforced the revealed truth, and just as the Prophets. It won't do for Huxley to have had an experience like Christ's. When we read the pamphleteering literature of contemporary Hinduism we get the same impression: that the acts and the feelings of saints and sages—Ramakrishna, Aurobindo, Meher Baba—were unique, hence uniquely important. This is clearly due to the powerful model set in the nineteenth century by the missionary to India, who unknowingly trained most of the Hindu religious leaders of the new India to think like himself about pure and impure, about good and bad, about true religion and superstition. Along with these strange, alien imports, the young college students in Calcutta and Bombay also learned history as a series of time-bound, dated events, history as the life stories of "important" men. And when all these ideas had been interiorized and become part of the modern Indian "scientific attitude, the way of approaching the local saints and sages more and more resembled these imports. No longer was it the holistic god or goddess or the total hero who was a mighty cog in the universe game that supreme divinity was playing to amuse itself. The texts that sing the names of the gods and the heroes in thousands of stereotyped panegyrics were still chanted, but in line with their European Christian model, events around the modern saints and sadhus lives became unique but portentous. The Ramakrishna and Vivekananda literature is replete with tales about the preceptor's feelings and conflicts. Even here, in the ashram in Thousand Islands Park in the St. Lawrence River, visitors are shown the room where Vivekananda had *samādhi*. It will be objected that India's shrines are shrines to the places of the saints' and seers' birth, death *and* their zero-experience; witness the *bodhi*-tree in Gaya and its saplings all across the world where there are Buddhists to plant them. But those shrines and places are formal, ritualistic sites; incantation, prayer, meditation are carried on there because these places exude power, because their *darśan*, their vision, conveys and bestows the numinous and, to those who are lucky, perhaps a glimpse of the mystic vision. For all that, it was the saints who were all-important, since they were divinity incarnate; it was not their experience which was unique or ennobling. Such a notion was a foreign import. No Hindu or Buddhist teacher ever wrote diaries and journals or reports about his progress, about the dark night of his soul, about his qualms and doubts. But since the turn of the century, this has changed. The late Swami Sivananda of Hrishikesh, to my mind the most grotesque product of the Hindu Renaissance, advised people to write their "spiritual diaries"; and in oral instructions, he told Indian and western disciples to write down how often they masturbated, and when they succeeded not to by using *japa*[12] and *prāṇāyāma*.[13] But in the orthodox monasteries of Hindu India there was little talk or instruction toward remorse, and there was that pleasant pedagogical shrug all over the place, which meant "nothing you do or don't do is unique—hundreds have done it before you and will do or omit it after you." No speculation, no rumination, no Kierkegaardian or Freudian self-analysis toward improvement.

It is beside the point whether mystics call their experience noble and marvelous, or think of it in some motivational terms and be inspired to great deeds. But the mystical experience has no merit beyond itself; assigning moral or other value to it is both logically wrong and dangerous. And the degree of conviction is no validation for its content. The fact that most mystics were saints or just good people, doing no harm or doing some or much good, must not deceive us: for with them, it so happened that they subscribed to a moral or a religious code which bade them do good deeds. But since religious codes equally often defy the sort of reasoning that leads to a liberal, individualistic, logic-based legislation, it is just as possible that the mystic, following some teaching which he wrongly holds, is authenticated by his zero-experience, may choose an ideology that kills and tortures. St. Teresa's code led her both to founding charitable institutions[14] and furthering the Inquisition.

Normatively, no ideology *ought* to be viewed as generating or as being generated by the zero-experience. To insure this, it is necessary to drop laudatory superlatives. It is and must be viewed as on a par with other personal achievements or endowments, particularly of the artistic kind. Societies should cease praising the mystic beyond his mystical prowess, and if he is to be praised for other achievements, they must be seen exclusively in their own right, unconnnected with his vision. If we praise Einstein for physics and for violin playing, we do not claim that his playing the violin is a result of his physics.

So long as nobility, sanctity, and supreme value are ascribed to the zero-experience, the thrust of the mystical will be thwarted. Mysticism, the zero-experience, together with the ideological accoutrements mystics have thought of as belonging to the experience, was given much status because of the ideological component ascribed to it. The zero-experience alone would hardly have elicited these value ascriptions. Christian apologists prate about the sanctity of mysticism. Again, Zaehner's is perhaps the clearest case in recent literature: the zero-experience may very well be sheer delight but it must also be holy and noble, as are the other teachings of Christ and the dicta of the Church. Zaehner seemed to fear the zero-experience alone, without these conventional attachments. Hence he and other Christian apologists for mysticism avoided declaring outright that a fakir's or a civilian's or a hippie's experience is inferior to Christian mystical situations.

Does this mean, then, that I identify mysticism with the zero-experience, and that the zero-experience is value-free, neither noble nor ignoble, just exciting, pleasant? It means precisely this. We have to learn at long last that the mystical experience is what it is. It is to be sought not because it is noble as wisdom or goodness are noble, but because it is an additional skill: a skill which confers delight. It also yields a highly pragmatic result, which again is value-free, it inures the practitioner against the vicissitudes of life, against boredom and despair, because all these can be viewed as silly and unimportant in the radiance of successive zero-experiences, or even of just one zero-experience properly remembered.

This, I am afraid, is an arid message to those who have expected to find the ultimate panacea of the religious and the secular life in the mystical. They are wrong, because they confuse the conventional doctrinal accompaniments of the zero-experience which do promise panacea, with the zero-experience itself which is really all there is.

The zero-experience is a peak experience, in one category perhaps with totally consummated erotic experiences, or with artistic and similar peak sensations. These experiences are valuable in themselves, and unless the surrounding world-view makes us look for something beyond them, something to be generated by them, they might just as well be left alone. Their value is intrinsic; it is not teleological.

Professor Findlay, a very serious man with serious Christian intentions, wrote something very much to the point: "To take this notion of an absolute seriously is further to treat the identity of everything, including oneself, with the absolute, as no mere remote intellectual conviction, but as something that ought to be capable of being realized so compellingly that it becomes a direct personal experience. Mystical experiences are not to be assimilated to queer extrasensory perceptions. They are the understandings of an identity as logically perspicuous as 'if p.q then q.p'. Only, while the theorems of the propositional calculus can be understood without passion being adjusted to our normal state of alienation, the theorems of mysticism can only be understood with passion: one must oneself live through, consummate the identity which they postulate. All mysticism involves a routine and a practice and any experience of ecstasy, and the experiential character of mysticism is simply a consequence of the meaning of the identity it posits, an identity in which the ordinary person is taken out of his alienation, and taken up, or partially taken up, into the ultimate mystical unity." [15]

Unfortunately, Findlay, like Zaehner, albeit in Protestant style, weakens this proper statement step by step as he subordinates it to his articles of Christian faith. The mystical experience does not remain autonomous; and it must not because the sheer autonomy of the zero-experience is value-free—and this is a possibility a scholarly gentleman who takes official Christianity more seriously than the zero-experience, cannot tolerate. At this point, something embarrassing emerges: when it comes to facing the mystics, both the Christian apologists and the modern Hindus, however antagonistic toward each other in matters of theological dispute, join hands in decrying the mystical experience and the mystic, when the latter does not assign religious, moral, or ideological value to the peripheral trappings of the zero-experience. Both the literate Christian sympathizer and the literate modern Hindu and Buddhist deny that the zero-experience *per se* is worth having. In the West we have the polite dialectic of hierarchy by which the unaligned mystics are given lower status than the officially condoned ones; in India today, and of course in Sri Lanka, Thailand, and Burma as well, the sheer mystic is termed a "loafer" in Indian English, a parasite or anti-social. The modern Indian, being a Gandhian in matters of interpersonal relations, of sex, ecstasy, and other things that count in the mystic world, will not tolerate sheer mysticism since it uses hedonistic language and even hedonistic principles for action. There is an old principle, shared irrationally by almost all literate cultures of the world, that really good things must not come easily. Modern religious leaders in India have been wont to adduce analogies from other fields of human action—the fine arts, sports, politics—to proclaim that if anything lasting and valuable ever came about, it was preceded by tough training and by long self-imposed renunciatory disciplines. Or they invoke a principle which is part of the fundamentalistic framework of their theology: grace for the Christian, Allah's special choice for the Muslim, a long series of ascetic and virtuous lives for the Buddhist and the Hindu. The latter two have a dialectic edge over the others: If a person seems to come by the zero-experience without any special effort, by taking a drug or just looking into the air, their argument is readily at hand: the man has accumulated merit in his previous incarnations, and this merit now shows itself. I have heard Swami Maheshvaranana, a rather learned monk in Northern India, muse about reports brought to him by some wide-eyed Peace Corps volunteers on zero-like experiences under hashish and LSD: he quoted the *Bhagavadgītā* which does indeed say that a man continues in his next life, morally and operationally speaking, exactly where he left off in his last. The Christian or Muslim has to find an explanation which derives from the inscrutability of God.

The genuine mystic tends to change or modify his corpus of legitimation, the sacred text or the preceptor's counsel. He is not always conscious of this strategem, and he doesn't have to be; but it helps to be familiar with linguistic analysis and ordinary language philosophy. The phrase "I know," in whatever language it is used, means many things to many people, and like all terms in ordinary language, its use in a new sense would raise little objection if that use seems to be justified for a person who creates standards for emulation himself, as prophets and mystics do. I shall discuss the crucial difference between the mystic and the prophet later, but they both regard themselves as authentic interpreters of the lore, over and against the professional ecclesiastics. Again the Hindu mystic has some advantage since canonical passages are, by definition, statements made by people who have had the zero-experience, for this is precisely what the *ṛṣi* "seer" is: he *sees* the *mantra*, the Vedic word, both in the sense that he is the receptacle and recipient of eternal revelation, and in the sense that he creates its hidden meaning. It happened in the last century that an Indian scholar *changed* the text of the Veda. Raja Ram Mohun

Roy, an early nineteenth century Bengali aristocrat and reformer who was greatly impressed by Christian writing, altered the monistic texts of the *Upaniṣads* to make them monotheistic. As soon as this became known among the learned, feelings polarized: those who did not object became sympathizers with his reform movement; and those who did, objected on the basis of his denial of authority (*adhikāra*); the Raja, the pandits of his day said, could not change the sacred text as he had not made it. Were he a true *ṛṣi*, he would pronounce truths that would not contradict or modify the sacred scripture, since all those seers who had formulated it in ancient times had done so on the basis of their direct vision. In more recent decades, people who enunciated monistic ideas were readily classed as *ṛṣis* (seers), fitting my criteria for a mystic. Ramakrishna was not illiterate, as some of his followers claim in order to play with paradox, but adequately well read in the basic sacerdotal literature. Yet there were highly learned men among his admirers, brahmans who literally knew the sacred lore by heart. He told many a parable, either of his own making or out of local folklore, but they were certainly not Vedic, as he claimed. Quite often, he preceded these tales by the words *bede āche* "it says in the Veda"; and I think the reason why even the most learned didn't object was that they tacitly granted him the status of a Veda-maker, a *ṛṣi*, on a par with the original compilers of the Veda. They did this because they were satisfied with his statements about the enstatic experiences he was having all the time, and with their display; the fact that some sophisticated urbanites from Calcutta called him a madman as some modern psychiatrists would have if they had seen him, established him more firmly, for the texts themselves often state that the man of total experience acts like a madman in the world. Even a lay Hindu immediately recalls the story of the Sage Bharata, who acted insane so people would leave him alone to his zero-state.

To formulate this a bit more precisely, we should say that to the mystic and his votaries, facticity is subordinated to intentionality. When a person ponders over some performed experience, and he reports about it, he tends to arrange all other events in a hierarchy of descending importance. But when the zero-experience is concerned all other things seem so low as to be trivial, or so trivial as to be unreal in comparison.

If there is some ulterior Truth somehow linked to the experience, we cannot know it. I think this could be tested, in theory at least, by questioning accomplished mystics: the zero-experience bestows the total conviction of unique reality, and the "real-unreal" terminology used by mystics is psychological usage, with no ontological reference.

This does not mean that the reporting mystic knows that his reference is psychological. He thinks that there is more than a psychological base to his experience of the supremely important as the only real, versus the to him ultimately unimportant as the unreal. The grading of reality was, in the history of thought, an eastern syndrome, not even taught in western philosophy. Grudgingly, this century's historians of western philosophy reported that the Indian had produced the notion of a graded reality, when Aristotelian and post-Aristotelian philosophy had never generated this fascinating notion.

The answer to the Indian speculative notion of a graded reality, as best and most radically elaborated in the monistic Vedānta, is rather simple. When Vedānta and other zero-based systems talk about a graded reality, they simply report and dilate upon the zero-experience of the founders and their successful followers. In the zero-experience, "reality" is so powerful and certain that extra-experiential items simply lose "reality" by comparison. The confusing diction suggests that reality *was* an objective implication of the zero-experience, which it is not. It would be preferable to say that the zero-experience itself is felt to *be* reality. The power of this experience is so penetrating that the semantics of comparison is replaced by the semantics of reality versus unreality. A psychological chain of events generates a set of convictions which can apparently be formulated in reality-unreality terms only. Many writers about mysticism think they are mystics, and some of them again certainly are. But both mystics and sympathetic writers about mysticism are just wrong if they think that there is a way of telling whether the other person has had a genuine experience or just pretends to have had one. Now, not being a poet or a literary critic I am not quite sure whether there are any subtle criteria for genuineness or fakery available to the poet and the critic. There are no such criteria between the mystic and the writer about mysticism.

Then there are scholars and journalists who do not claim to have had a mystical experience, but who report about what other people tell about theirs. I have heard people report about zero-experiences they have had, and their diction was such that it seemed almost an affront to the importance of the experience —dull, incoherent, unpoetical. On the other hand, I have heard several people describing with zest the zero-experience which they had not had. How did I find it out? By anthropological trickery: they told me so at some other time, either under LSD or under conditions of guided guru-disciple discourse. The experience is so incompatible with linguistic expression that the quality of that attempted expression provides no clue for or against the veracity of the statement. Whichever way we twist it, there simply are no parallels to other genres, no proper language. A man may write excellent love poetry without ever having been a comparable lover; it is the writer's skill as a writer that makes his words convincing, not his skill as a lover. The mystic's talk about his experience may be skillful or clumsy, but that does not improve or weaken his actual experience.

At this point I must offer another perhaps disappointing fact: all mystical writings say very much the same. Variations are few, and they are quite predictable once the jargon of the mystic's theological environment is understood. Mystics, like prophets, always say predictable things. Were I writing a full size study of mystical language rather than of mysticism, I could and would have to analyze expressions as to their literary merit and other merits not intrinsic to the mystical experience. The mystical experience does less to the mystics than the love experience does to the poet of love. The latter has his own idiolect, his autonomous guidelines, and if he projects surrounding convention in his style, we hold this against him, in modern times at least. The mystic's experience, were it exhausted in statements about it, would be a rather short and crude thing. It has little variation, since peak experiences do not have many variations. This seems to hold true in kindred fields. The supremely accomplished musical performances in the vocal arts sound quite like each other in their best performances. Caruso in his best days sounded almost exactly like Gigli in his best days, and Joan Sutherland, during her peak productions, sounds exactly like any other of the three or four best sopranos of recent days. When critics talk about individual styles and signatures they are actually talking about shortcomings, about performances below the peak. I dare any critic to tell me whether it is Casals or Starker, each on his best day, playing a Bach cello suite. "Style" is what makes people's performances different beneath the peak level of performance. On the peak, there is no difference. I interviewed wise women, asking them about their memory of the orgasms they have had; and all of them reported that the best and most beautiful orgasms they have had were identical; lesser orgasms were different from one another, the accompanying features were remembered and they seemed to linger in the memory.

This is most decidedly so in the case of the zero-experience. Its euphoria is strong, but the degrees of euphoria are not identical in all zero-experiences; there are some where there is hardly any component. The euphoria here plays the role, analogously speaking, of the "style" of artistic performances—it is not really central, however close it may be to the center. But the zero-experience is like distilled water, tasteless; hence there is little to say about it, and what the mystics talk about at great length, are the ramifying events, euphoric or visionary. Again, I think the Indian canonical language offers the most adequate reports in that it stresses the lack of quality in the peak experience—the terms used are adjectives of a privative kind, *acchedya* "unbreakable," *acintya* "unthinkable," *avāk manasagocara* "beyond speech, inaccessible to the mind," to pick a few. The positive terms of description are far less numerous, and there is endless repetition of terms connoting the light, brightness, lustre, brilliance, pervasion, penetration, bliss, and the whole euphoric vocabulary.

I am afraid that I cannot attach much value to the claim of lovers of mystical literature that mystical language is something grandiose, unique, supremely valuable; whatever is superlative about that language, may be so in terms of poetry and other artistic skills, or in terms of the passive aesthetic experience of those who enjoy poetry. I have looked through some forty volumes on mysticism during the past two years. Virtually all of them are anthologies of mystical statements: reports about zero-experiences, about camouflaged zero-experiences or about experiences which may or may not have been zero-experiences, but which projected the subjects into the world of mystical expression. There is very little non-religious mystical literature. Even Aldous Huxley let the religious intrude into his *Doors of Perception*; Arthur Koestler is perhaps closest to a non-religious diction of mystical experience. And there is a small number of honest, analytic studies, W.T. Stace's foremost among them. Here in the States there was, of course, the British-born Alan Watts. Here was a man who knew what he was talking about; I must confess that I was somewhat suspicious of him at first because of my orientalist colleagues' doubts about his scholastic skills—that he did not really read Chinese, Japanese, and Sanskrit; that he used ponies rather than primary sources. But we are talking about mystical language, not about scholarly tracts. Anyone who has read Watts' works and anyone who reads his journal [16] will notice that he hardly says anything new in the sense of adding new factual information on the basic experience. But Watts knew this very well; and as a pedagogue, his subtle repetitiveness is precisely the way of the mystic preceptors: he has to rub it in, there is no evading this instructional need. It is not only the hippies and the psychedelicists in this country who regarded him as an indisputable guru; some politically motivated radicals, not primarily interested in the mystical realm, "dug him too," they told me, because he exuded *autonomy*.

What the mystic sees, hears, feels, and cogitates about in his circum-zero-experience days and years may seem to relate to the world outside him, but the world outside him is not what reveals itself to his kind of quest. The Indian mystics and their western clients may say that there is no outside world and (since all that there is is within the mind of the mystic who *sees*) that the scientist is unwise, unenlightened. But this then becomes a linguistic problem: for if a person is prompted by powerful experiences which make the objective world appear unreal and trivial and calls only that world real which he experiences, then he extrapolates his world for his audience. This is a sort of solipsism.

I have long maintained that the mystic who happens to be a scholar must live and think in a manner which psychiatrists call schizophrenic. For the outside world seems trivial and chaotic to the mystic and yet he investigates this world as a scientist. Is there a contradiction which makes such involvement within both worlds a pathological effort? The modern mystic must learn what some very few mystics through the ages knew: *that the zero-experience does not and cannot confer existential status on its content.* From the fact that a person sees, hears, feels, or in any conjoint way experiences something which has been assigned a theological, philosophical, or other designation, it does not follow that this "something" has any ontological status. This rule may mean a lot of disappointment to mystics who are poor in mind. Only two mystical schools, one Hindu and one Buddhist, do not assume that the genuine mystical experience does confer existential status upon its content. Other than these, Hindu schools share the ontological fallacy with the Mediterranean traditions, for *śruti* (canonical doctrine) is what the mystics, the *ṛṣis*, the seers *saw*; and what they saw was not a congeries of sheer sense impressions but actual truths existing out there *and* inside them. It was only the Mādhyamika master Nāgārjuna (about 150 A.D.) and the semi-legendary founder of systematized yoga, Patañjali, who differed. Nāgārjuna, as a Buddhist, denied ontological status to any experience, but it seems that in addition he did not feel that the zero-experience could add anything to the experiencing person's knowledge about the world. Patañjali states that *īśvara*, i.e. the divine person or object contemplated upon, is a crutch, a construct, which may or may not be retained once the zero-experience has been achieved. Modern and ancient followers of Patañjali either missed this point completely, or else suppressed it as not in line with the surrounding ideological sentiments.

For the Jew, Christian, and Muslim, of course, this is bad tidings. Assuming that the report in the Old Testament was authentic, and that it reported a genuine experience, that Moses saw God in the burning bush, it does not follow that "God" exists. It only follows, or rather, it presupposes, that the prophet had powerful visions, visions which convinced him so profoundly that he took upon himself the job of a prophet. A prophet's job is to persuade himself and the world of the ontological status of whatever he, the prophet, has experienced. This distinguishes him from the mystic *per se*, the "silent one" who does not have to say what he experiences, nor, *qua* mystic, does he have to insist on any ontological corollary to his experience. The only clear demarcation between a mystic and a prophet is just this: the prophet who has had the zero-experience goes out and preaches ontological implications of his experience. What about the prophet who has had no zero-experience? He is a dangerous man, but I am not concerned with him. He reverberates moral convictions or, in a Durkheimian framework, he reiterates the ideal image of his society, using his charisma to make people act out the *mea culpa* syndrome and to implement his image of how things should be.

When the Prophet Muhammad saw the Angel Jibra'il, the latter gave him the Book to eat—and it tasted like honey. And everything the Prophet taught was in the book, and the book was both a synopsis and a new reading of *Al kitāb*, of the written canonical tradition given to the Jews and the Christians before him. It is ironic that the Muslim converters and converts in India raged against the Hindu pagans for this particular reason: that they did not have a *book*. But they had the Veda—four books at least, and the priests had been quoting it all the time. Could it be that to the Muslims "book" meant something written down? The Veda was regarded as so sacred that writing it down would pollute it. It was written down and published only in the nineteenth century. Other books, religious and secular, were and had been written down for ages before Muslim proselytization, but not the Veda.

From the Prophet's desert experience of Gabriel, the Book, and its taste, it does not follow that either the Angel or the Book existed, though its "taste" did. It is, of course, quite impossible to know whether the Angel, the Book, and Allah exist. But if they do, this does not follow from the Prophet's or anyone else's experience.

There *is* no outsider qualified to check and tell whether the mystic's experience is genuine or not; and much less so is there any outsider, human or divine, who could verify or falsify the mystic's report. This is what frustrates my Christian colleagues. Most of them tend to insist that the sentence "God speaks to me" or "God speaks to some Christians" is of the same cognitive category as "The President speaks to the Astronaut." With Karl Popper, I insist on the greater importance of falsification than of verification of a proposition. If Mystic X makes a statement of the form "I saw God" or 'Siva appeared to me with trident and crescent" or "I am the *brahman*" or "I am the one and there is nothing else," then there is no statement or question which could possibly falsify the implied experience as an experience, since nothing the questioner or the critic could possibly say or ask would undo the fact that the experience has been had. But this does not mean that the outsider cannot impugn the ontological existence of the object of the mystic's experience—God, the One, the absolute, etc. Further, the philosophical fact is that neither the mystic nor his critic can infer or deny any ontological status of the superhuman, divine, absolute object on the basis of any experience made or reported, since no such experience confers existential status on its object. Should I then modify my contention and say that the mystical experience "does not *indicate*" rather than "does not confer" ontological status on its content? I don't think I can do that, as many mystical experiences certainly do "indicate" such existence. Let me then suggest this final rule: No mystical experience confers existential status on its content in the manner in which one's experience of a chair "confers" existence upon it.

The big question which has been bothering all who are involved, the mystic and his sympathetic and non-sympathetic critics, is this: how do we, how does the mystic, and how does anyone know that his experience of God, the One, oneness, the Absolute, Siva, the Virgin, etc., is not *hallucination*? None can know whether this experience is a hallucination, a delusion, an illusion, or a something else. And just as the mystic's statements about the content of his experience cannot be falsified, so the contrary claim that one or all of these experiences could be hallucinations, auto-hypnosis, delusions, etc. cannot be falsified either, let alone verified. There are two kinds of mystics: wise mystics and unwise mystics. Wise mystics are those who are quite satisfied with the zero-experience *per se*, and with the things and thoughts that happen to them during, before, after, and between zero-experiences. They do not care at all whether or not these experiences indicate some objective reality. Patañjali was a wise mystic, for he made it perfectly clear that whatever the content of the consummate yoga experience, its ontological status is not the mystic's business. Those mystics who insist that there must be some sort of ontological reality to their experience are unwise mystics. They are men and women of busy fears: if there is no actual being that is being experienced, if there is no real Śiva both out there and in here who is being experienced in the zero-state, then the experience is of no real use, and then what is the use of undergoing all sorts of preparatory hardships, disciplines, renunciations? Well, for unwise mystics to become wise mystics, the advice can be just this: learn from the wise mystics that the ontological corollary of the zero-experience is totally irrelevant. Brahmin teachers like Vasiṣṭha, Patañjali, and Śrīharṣa taught that if anyone wants to know about the ontological status of divinity, or reality, of the cosmos, he must look for another source of information. That source is the infallible word of the Veda; but the zero-experience is not the locus where this certainty is generated. In this manner, Patañjali cuts through the mess other mystical traditions created before and after him, both in India and in other parts of the world. They were wedded to official theological doctrine and theorems; and their propounders thought that the zero-experience must somehow prove what the texts say about the absolute, the divine, etc. That is their problem. If others ask the wise mystic about God, Truth, and other ontological verities, he tells them, if he happens to be a humble man, to look up the Scriptures that will tell about these things; and if he is a snob like the Buddha, he simply does not answer at all, or rudely. My reading is that he kept silent because he did not believe that there was any validity to scripture, hence he could not possibly advise people about the ontological status of the world, or of transcendental things. He did know that nothing ontological followed from his experience—hence his silence.

The wise mystic, then, is not impressed by overt and covert terms of abuse such as Freudian and other doctors of all ages have made against the mystical experience: that it may be hallucination, auto-hypnosis, hypnosis, mania. The old-timers used humble-talk: Yes, we are truly mad in the eyes of the world, we are like pieces of stone, like imbeciles, like children. Thus they forestalled incipient and continuing insult and punitive recrimination. The modern mystic can marshal a far more powerful dialectic, he can show to the psychiatrist who dispenses labels freely that these—schizophrenia, paranoia, hysteria, depression, mania, catatonia and hebephrenesis—are so many *emic* terms, parts of a jargon of Euro-American psychiatrists who have never had the zero-experience and wouldn't see any worth and value in it, nor any meaning if it was reported to them, calmly and factually.

Chapter Four

The Question of Change

I have here a slender book by an Indian professor. *Mystics and Society: a point of view*,[1] is a concise attempt to state in positive terms what the mystic does to society, what society does to him, or better, what he ought to do to society and what society ought to do with him. He tells of the glories of non-instutionalized religion, of the mystical experience, of the supreme turmoil, loneliness, and rapture of specific mystics like certain western writers. He stresses the true but unaccepted reading of the religious doctrine of the land, and the manner in which priests and other religious establishmentarians conspired against the mystic until they saw the light and felt sorry. So far so good. But then, he proceeds to dilute the issue: the mystic is the true helper in need, he is the ideal man in human society, he supersedes the norms and rules of his tribe, he sets new norms or reinterprets the old ones so as to change the total ethical behavior and the moral perception of his people. And, if he survives in its memory, he will be the founder of a new religion, or at least a reformer of the old.

   All this is very nice, but wrong. My author twists and bends things to make a point that the mystic does things other people do, but better. The author digs up a passage where social virtues are extolled: "The elect do not avoid the crowd and remain in a chamber; there are people who act thus, they are called 'sick men'." Granted these are genuine translations from some primary text; yet, short of complete translations, quotations out of context in a language most readers do not read, slant the issue. Mystics and their interpreters say many things. But this should be clear through an honest and randomized reading of mystical texts: that by far the greatest portion of the mystics' report is of an asocial, even anti-social, autocentric, self-indulgent kind, marginally or artificially related to moral and social considerations. If modern scholars, concerned about the lack of involvement and of social relevance in the mystic's report, look around with the intention to find passages where a mystic does say sociable things, and if the scholars then adduce all such found passages, and stack them up against passages which do not bespeak such concern, it is quite easy to make the large laity believe that mystics were indeed as much concerned with the world and with their society as with their own experience, and at least as much so as their nonmystical contemporaries.

But all these ventures seem to me intellectually dishonest. I can fathom the ennui which scholars, infected with the Protestant Ethic, must feel when they thumb through hundreds of pages of mystical effusion without finding reference to the world outside the mystic's chamber; and I sense their uneasiness with the paranoid self-interest the mystics often display. One does not have to be taking sides with the people and the priests, or with the mystics against the people and the priests, to see the obvious: that "nature," including the flowers, beasts, gods, stars, and even the people that the mystic talks about are constructs filtered through his highly selective high-strung consciousness. Even the most unsophisticated hippie knows that the girl and the chair and the pizza and the stereo-set, even the Bach, the Purcell, and the Beatles as they get inside him when he is four hours high on acid or mescalin, are not quite the girl and the chair and the pizza and the stereo-set which he knows and uses before and after the session. Now, of course, the cleverer hippies generate their rebellious world view from precisely these experiences: if the girl and the pizza and the music are ordinarily part of the game other people play, then by the standards set by the experiences they shall be exalted in the future. One might then think, reflecting on this novel analogy, that perhaps the mystics did see different people and plants and gods through the power of their zero-experience. This may or may not be so. The fact remains that the mystic does not deal with these subjects in a manner different from other people, before or after his zero-experience. If they are more to him than they are to his unadept fellow men, they are more to him only so long as he sees them reflected in his experience, which they do not share. It is not people *qua* people whom he appreciates, but people *qua* zero-experience; and herein lies his being anti-social.

In the realm of the mystic, we have mystics who are just that—they talk to and instruct only a few fellow adepts whom they have sought out, or by whom they have been found, in the often highly ritualized processes of guru-quest, so well documented in Indian literature and in the neighboring literatures which took their lead from India, particularly Tibetan. But then there are mystics who are also part of the religious establishment, of the ecclesiastic bodies; there are monks, priests, even bishops, perhaps a pope or two. In India certainly the most highly regarded mystics at all times were extremely well-established monastics; and even those who were not regular monks in the sense of being affiliated with a monastic order had the full status of those who were, since the term *svatantra* "independent," when referring to a holy man for his status-identification, carries the same honor as affiliation with a monastic order, because technically anyone who obtains initiation by a monk of any order is forthwith a monk of that tradition, regardless of whether he attaches himself to some monastic institution or goes on living by himself, as a mendicant or as a settled hermit. True, many Indian mystics underplay or camouflage their initiatory background. Ramana Maharshi was an exceptional mystic. It is possible that he did not formally accept the monastic initiation, *sannyāsa*, which is a very simple ceremony, from an ordained monk; but his numerous disciples never bothered to find out, since it is really quite unimportant. Ramakrishna, the famous Bengali saint of the late nineteenth century, did take formal *sannyāsa* from Totapuri, a naked ordained monk—not because he thought he needed this initiation for higher spiritual achievement, but probably because it seemed to him more fitting to be an established *sannyāsi de iure*, lest people should keep complaining that he was neglecting his wife (taking ordination means formal severance of the matrimonial commitment).

The fact remains that mystics in all traditions have often straddled the fence: they were established members of the available ecclesiastic organizations, and there were few who went it all alone. Virtually all of the great central European mystics of the Middle Ages were priests or monks in various contemplative orders. Yet mystics have tended to disavow such liaison, or where it was evident or known, to play down its importance.

Suppose the mystic is a priest, established shaman, or some other specialist. He is suspect on both sides—to the ecclesiastic establishment which harbors him, on account of his covert or overt claims to religious individuality and to the lay mystics for his entrepreneurial ways, for his being part of the establishment. As in the case of the professor who becomes a dean, who "joins the power structure," but tries to retain his academic, non-administration "ideals," the mystic who might conceivably tread the zero path (which, as we know from the *Upaniṣad* and from Somerset Maugham, is as narrow as a razor's edge) often prefers to join with the forces where the traditional view of things religious is in permanent storage, albeit covered with the dust and dirt of a dormant pollution which is thought of as an inevitable accompaniment of organized religion. The mystic who is also part of the religious establishment *is*, after all, part of the society which he affects in his potentially asocial or anti-social way and he must therefore hold back some of the spiritual goods which he controls. This accounts for the cautious language Christian and Muslim mystics used in talking about their experience. The unattached mystic can afford to polemicize to his heart's content, the only risk he takes being that of martyrdom, which many saintly people and many mystics have regarded as about the best thing that could happen to them. We have here a dichotomy of affective types: how the mystic is changed through his experience depends not so much on the experience (the power of change inherent in the zero-experience is insignificant) but on the social-institutional allegiances which surround his experience. The allegiance, of course, is not his choice. People came by the zero-experience after having been members of a formal institution like a monastery or an ashram. People at all times join a religious organization because they hope to gain what their religion promises as its highest good; and however that highest good may be conceived in different traditions, the mystic's promise is always at the back of it. Whether a creed talks about salvation, *nirvāṇa*, or any other kind of permanent emancipation, blissful or neutral, the genuine seekers are alert to the language the mystics use, even when—or perhaps because—the official doctrine criticizes or condemns the mystic for his non-alignment.

Typical of a certain apologetic is Jacques De Marquette's *Introduction to Comparative Mysticism*,[2] a series of printed talks on Hinduism, Buddhism, Islam, Christianity. He shows he knows what mysticism is, when he writes "the fundamental idea of mysticism is that the essence of life and of the whole world is an all-embracing spiritual substance, which is the reality in the core of all beings, irrespective of their outer appearances or activities."[3] But he immediately weakens this insight by adding that mysticism is also the true knowledge about the individual's relation to other people, to society, and about the "two natures," reducible to the true and the false, the perennial and the ephemeral, or, in sermonistic parlance, the good and the bad.

The literary apologetic for the mystic is dreary, monotonous, and vast. The counter-culture in America and Europe adds to the measure. All of it boils down to the wrong assertion that the mystical life makes people better—as citizens, as thinkers, as spouses, even as rebels and revolutionaries. The insistence on a necessary correlation between mystical practice and the good life is fascinating and silly. It does not seem to suffice that mysticism is quite valuable all by itself, as a highly structured pursuit of experiential maximization. The improvement of the human race is something that must be achieved by means other than mystical. I mean this as a challenge: show me one single case in the history of mysticism where there is evidence beyond folklore and panegyric that a mystic was made a better and greater man by his mystical experience, *and not by totally different factors* of a social, moral, or idiosyncratic provenience. On the other hand, I have witnessed, with much initial dismay, that some of the best mystics were the greatest stinkers among men. Self-righteous, smug, anti-women, anti-men, politically fascist, stubborn, irrational. Somehow, the historical, intellectual investment in the stipulated sequence from the mystical experience to the better life is so strong that the perfectly commonsense, non-esoteric daily evidence against such actual relationship has been ignored, and I mean to expose it, not in order to annoy mystics and moralists, but for the sheer joy of factual reporting.

A young South Indian leader, a staunch Gandhian, son of a State Minister, said to me a day before his final examination in mathematics, "Oh I wish I were a yogi like you—then I could pass the mathematics exam without having to prepare for it." This notion, quite pervasive in India, is not derived from some magical imputations or from a belief in osmosis; it rests on an old confusion of a textual sort, passed on by orthodox scholars to the non-learned laity over hundreds of years. There is a statement in the canonical text which says that the knower of *brahman* knows everything; *brahmajña* and *sarvajña* are synonyms. Literally, of course, *brahma jña* "brahman-knower" and *sarva jña* "all-knower" sounds like the definition of one term by another. But this is not at all the scriptural intention: rather, *sarva* "all" is a theological synonym for *brahma*, the Absolute is the All. But *sarva* does not mean "all objects of knowledge" as modern Hindus and their forebears think it does. In other words, by knowing *brahman* one does not know anything but *brahman*; not physics, nor mathematics, nor the stock-market—else the monastic profession in India would be much more affluent than it is. The naive assumption is that yogic vision, the zero-experience, also brings about knowledge of all things to be known. This is nonsense. The implication is quite clear: that the knowledge of the Absolute, the mystical knowledge, the zero-experience, is of a precious sort all of its own and does not generate other types of knowledge.

Jaimini, an almost mythical brahmin teacher, said that religious texts must not be interpreted for use in non-religious contexts; that when the word "tree" appears in the Veda, this cannot denote any real tree, since real trees are dealt with by botany, not by the Veda, because the Veda deals exclusively with definitions and injunctions about the contemplative universe of discourse, about the achievement of zero-states. Let us take a cue from this: we do not learn mathematics, physics, and stock market behavior by crossing our legs, withholding breath and sperm, and taking other yoga poses, but by proper secular studies.

As we cross back into the West, we find an amazing parallel developing right under our own eyes. Paradigmatically, let me adduce the phenomenon that was Alan Watts. A British minister originally of the Church of England, but with Buddhist interests since his early and precocious boyhood at Canterbury, he became the foremost popular exponent of Eastern mysticism to the English-speaking West, and in translations, to the remaining part of Europe. His books number close to twenty. He wrote powerfully about meditation, man, woman, and sex, about relaxation, about letting go, about the manipulation of ecstasy; and he told about his own hedonism. Once he addressed a packed audience of Syracuse University students. It was hot, there were hundreds of bearded, barechested young men with their beautiful coed mates, and many large dogs milling around. He told them what he always told people—let go, take it easy, don't cling. A buddhist message in a hedonistic frame. After the talk, dozens of young men surrounded him. "Have you read the Urantia Book?" "Have you seen the Book of Klamdesh?" etc. He hadn't. But neither did he have to: one of the signs of the young seekers of mystical vision, on and off university campuses, in the U.S. and Europe and Asia, is that they do not read except for inspiration. In the quest for the ultimate wisdom, there is the pervasive notion that much reading is bad, and that if the one work that has everything has been found and absorbed, nothing else need be read.

This is another field where the political radical of our day and the mystic in the West meet on common ground; they do not like to read, and some have conscious or unconscious affinities with medieval and post-medieval book burners, East and West. Student protesters at the University of Michigan placed some non-negotiable demands before the administration; these were granted. Later, the library was broken into, the index cards torn out and scattered and some 20,000 books were torn up and thrown out into the road, and a bonfire was started, but extinguished. The following monologue was overheard. The speaker was a bare-chested, bearded mystic with a genuine *rudrākṣa* rosary[4] around his neck. "You read all these books, man, and you like to see movies with plots; we don't need that anymore—words after words, sentence after sentence, just words and plots . . . who wants them; we want to meditate and be free, man." This is very much in line with the young men who approached Watts after his lecture, asking him if he knew the Urantia Book[5] and the Book of Klamdesh. There is a strong sentiment against scholarly books in general, but quite particularly against serious studies of the religio-mystical situation. When yoga and things Indian became the vogue, far beyond the little old ladies' circles around the Ramakrishna Mission monks in America, aided by LSD, political disaffection, and sartorial negligence, I and my orientalist colleagues thought our very special day had come, that the department of Indian studies, Sanskrit, Tibetan, would forthwith bulge with eager students. Nothing of the sort has happened. Of about five dozen young men and women who came to me thinking and hoping I was a busily initiating swami, two went into serious orientalist studies; one of them left after a month of Sanskrit declensions, the other one has done very well indeed so far. If anything, the number of serious Indologists and other orientalists has decreased since the adoption of Asian sounds, smells, sights, and pretensions became part of the mystagogic counter-culture. Some good reasons are being given for the decline of oriental studies; lack of funds from foundations and the government, the Vietnamese involvement and its costs, India's disillusion at Kissinger's "tilt" toward Pakistan. But I have a hunch that the causes lie deeper: the mystical culture, which is anti-intellectual and powerful today, is drawing away potential students of genuine Asian lore. Judging from my own childhood and adolescence, had there been LSD, willing maidens available for all experiments, plenty of Indian LP records, incense, etc., I might well have chosen those rather than seeking out, with Teutonic doggedness, the few sources that were obtainable in pre-World War II Austria and Germany: university libraries, a few departments and seminars of Asian studies, and, of course, the Vivekananda-type pamphlet literature.

Unless the mystic chooses sophistication along with the zero-experience—not because it enhances or improves the

93

experience, which it doesn't, but so as to fill the inter-zero gaps with interesting and pleasurable pursuits which require a different kind of intensive cultivation and discipline—he will be at one with ideological totalitarians of all hues including the political: he will want simple total answers, nothing piecemeal, nothing partial. Learned books, whether well written or not, make no difference to the typical mystic; his discursive faculties do not usually impel him to read, either about his own "field," i.e. mysticism, or about kindred things: philosophy, religion, ideas. In fact, some of the greatest mystics quite emphatically dissuaded their disciples from reading. Swami Sivananda, a pseudo-mystic, deceased, an erstwhile medical doctor, fat and smiling, with roughly two million followers all over the world, taught: "Read, Govinda,[6] the *Bhagavadgītā*, Govinda, and the *Upaniṣads*, Govinda, and the works of Swami Sivananda, Govinda; do NOT read, Govinda, Herbert Spencer, Govinda, and Karl Marx, Govinda, these will make you, Govinda, an atheist, Govinda . . ." Conversion mania has been studied by psychologists and anthropologists. Even milder forms of conversion symptoms do not commend themselves to the intellectual hedonist and the humanist: the central expression of experienced conversion always suggests the notion that the person has no more problems, that they are all solved, and that the unsolved problems are unimportant. Now in canonical and poetic contexts, such statements are beautiful and inspiring: "the knots of the heart are torn asunder, all doubts cease for him who has seen the supreme," the *Upaniṣad* says. The late M.N. Roy, no doubt one of the greatest Indian political thinkers, told me that when he became a communist, he went through all these feelings of doubtlessness; and I myself recall most vividly, more so now as I report it, that nothing mattered at all during and shortly after my own zero-experiences. I recall that in one instance, the one in India, I said to myself: "If prayers had an object to go to, I would pray that this present certainty, that nothing else is important at all, might last . . ." But it didn't and in fact most of the post-experiential cries, hopes, prayers, or simple ruminations seem to center on the hope of retaining this state of supreme non-caring, and of recapturing it when lost. The pompous diction of the oft-quoted "dark night of the soul" has always annoyed me, but I know that it refers to this lapse or lag.

I think I have shown why mystics are likely to be anti-intellectual and anti-scholarly. Now of course, there have been mystic *authors*, Indian and Christian, who were fine scholars in their field: doctors of their respective theological and specu-

94

lative traditions. I am a bit more doubtful about the likelihood of a mystic being an intellectual, or remaining one after going through numerous occurrences of the zero-experience. I doubt, for instance, that I would have kept relishing as I do, the sharp, critical, often reckless intellectual games occidental intellectuals play if the zero-experience had happened to me, say, several hundred times as it did to Ramakrishna and to Ramana Maharshi—two persons whose reports I tend to take verbatim. Intellectual mystics, people like Arthur Koestler, the late Aldous Huxley, some Indians whose names my readers cannot know, and myself, may well be people to whom the experience did not occur often enough to alienate them permanently from their other interests. You must bear in mind that my definitions of a mystic do not include frequency of occurrence of the zero-experience as a criterion; mysticism is like virginity—you either have it or you don't; there are no intermediate degrees. It seems quite possible that the reason for not being intellectual, or being anti-intellectual, may have to be sought in a field to which this study does not apply, i.e. the frequency of zero-experiential occurrence and the psychological changes that may (or may not) occur in a person when the experience crowds out other possible interests by sheer repetitive force. The only thing I can report is that the famous mystics I knew in person or have studied at a distance remained what they were before they had their experience, or experiences—nice people, impossible human beings, good or bad public relations men, etc. Mystical fame and the frequency of the occurrence of the zero-experience show no correlation. I know that this realization would be painful to both the simple-hearted mystics and their not-so-simple-hearted apologists—but their discomfort would be due to the emotional investment they have made in this correlation under ancient tutelage which has never been questioned until now. The argument for such correlation, however fictitious, runs along these lines: "if the mystical experience does nothing else for the mystic than being just an individual event—nothing for his morals, nothing for his knowledge, nothing for his wisdom—then it is not worthwhile." This is one of history's perennial *nonsequiturs*. No one has ever said "what's the use of good music if it means only enjoyment for the music-lover" or "what's the use of sexual intercourse if it means only pleasure for the participants." Such arguments have been made—and have been at the heart of much technological moralizing. But there is no necessary connection between these sheer experiences and their postulated extra-experiential adjuncts, and no need for such a connection. Here is the difference between professionals and dilettantes among the mystics and their sympathizers. Just as we have selective autonomy in the scholarly and scientific disciplines, where people know how far afield they can ramble without opting out from being scholars in their fields, we find mystics who tend to be quite satisfied with the zero-experience, with imparting to their disciples the skills which they assume lead up to it, and with leading lives and doing things to keep clear the road and fill up the intervals between the zero-experiences. These are the professionals: for them, the experience is sufficient and whatever else they do is much like so many hobbies to them. But then there are mystics who concatenate a whole world of irrelevant things with mysticism: they must be leaders of mankind, reformers shaking up the world or at least the present state of religion, they must be benign, wise, they must be charismatics, and they must sermonize for or against the current theology and about things one relates with mysticism, theology, sociology, and other content.

There is a distinction between the mystics and genuine, non-apologetic scholars about mysticism. The mystic, like most revolutionaries, wants total solutions; but serious scholars eschew total solutions. The scholarly apologist for the mystic takes a mongrel position: as a man of learning he cannot, of course, espouse total solutions; and if he talks about them, he must do so *emically*—quoting other people, mystics for instance, as recommending total solutions. Yet it seems to me that many serious scholars who have done research in this field were motivated in the first place by a desire for total solutions. Among social scientists we now have a clear polarization— there are some who would reduce their findings to some underlying totem, and would advise others to look for total solutions, casually or teleologically couched in such terms as "the primitive," "economic man," "*homo faber*," "culture," "the unconscious," and there are others who reject such universals as romantic, and probably wrong, and who ask people who investigate mysticism and other phenomena in the world of comparative religion to proceed on piecemeal, non-reductionist, and descriptive lines. Yet scholars who study mysticism rather than, say, ritualistic themes, shamanism, comparative belief systems, ecclesiastical or hagiological history, may have been prompted toward such choice because they want their object to be of the total solution type, for which mysticism provides a cogent example. Much literature about mysticism is erudite, diffuse, and comprehensive, detailed, with the proper footnotes and scholarly apparatus. Yet this literature

96

is strangely reductionist and totalistic. Indian authors like S.N. Dasgupta,[7] S. Radhakrishnan,[8] and V. Raghavan,[9] marshal a large amount of literary and historical material—yet all of it is subsumed in a single recommendation: that Advaita Vedānta, the monistic form of learned Hinduism, is the final truth, borne out by saints, thinkers, and mystics alike. Western writers like Zaehner, Underhill and Cuthbert Butler [10] inevitably revert to the *una sancta*: that there is no true mysticism, unless it assumes the ultimate rightness of the established Roman doctrine. Now, of course, many or most of the Christian apologists for mystics are intellectually sincere and believe that mystical experience inevitably leads to the realization that what the official doctrine says is true, that experience corroborates Writ. The Indian tradition followed the obverse course: what the mystic experiences creates the Scripture; its genesis and its corroboration lie in the mystic's experience, not the other way round. For the doctrinally oriented Jew, Christian, and Muslim, as well as for theistic sectarians in India, the transmitted word is so important that the individual's experience must either bear it out or be rejected. An ontologically conceived god, one that exists independently from experiencing beings, cannot afford to lose his status to people who might deny either his importance or his existence; hence basically, as we read some ancient Christian teachers of modern apologists like Zaehner, what concerns them most is the purity and untouchability of the God who must exist ontologically. Prof. Ninian Smart has shown [11] that the history of Indian thought tells a contrasting story: here, the stronger the theistic bent of a school, the weaker was its philosophical argument. The most highly refined, sophisticated schools of Indian thought, the *mādhyamika* Buddhists and the monistic Vedāntins, succeeded in stigmatizing all straight theism as rustic and childish. This never fazed the devotional teachers of mysticism in India: Ramakrishna once said, "I want to eat sugar, I don't want to be sugar," a direct swipe at Saṃkarācārya and the monists, whose experience Ramakrishna shared for a while. Sociologically naive writers seem to think that because a man has converted himself to something else, or because he "saw the light," and abandoned one way of thinking for another, the latter way must be superior to the former, since *ipse dixit*. From the fact that Ramakrishna moved away from the non-dualistic to dualistic devotional experience, it does not follow that the latter is superior, even if we grant that the man was taking a step forward: for if he did, that step was his own step. Directions of individual mystical experiences are not normative, and not universalizable. We are not talking about the dialectic advantages of one doctrine over the other now. The zero-experience is non-ideological, for its links to one or another doctrinal, moral, or social system are adventitious, resulting from the mystic's unfamiliarity with critical argument and his aversion against it, reinforced by affiliation with theological, anti-intellectual, holistic doctrine. We can thumb through reams of religious literature and we will hardly ever find a pleasant word about logic—the true logic being that of fools or children.

I think it is now easy to explain why writers about mysticism and some ecclesiastical mystics are so keen on proving that the mystical experience makes a better man out of the experiences: by historical accident, the first writers, speakers, teachers, and other specialists deployed by society were priests, prophets, or other people with a sacerdotal marking. Since scholars tend to talk about everything and since there was little topical specialization in early days, those people slanted their statements about everything else in an arcane, "religious" direction: the good man was not just a man who did things well and who was at ease with himself and others but he was good because he was pleasant in the eyes of whatever superhuman agency society stipulated. You couldn't just be good in a secular fashion, because there was nobody to define the secular and pronounce about sheer goodness or brightness, about positive characteristics unrelated to the superhuman. This must be one of the reasons why the first secular moralists, the teachers of Athens, were suspect and hated—very much as intellectuals are suspect in western countries in our own days. But once superiority, goodness, emotional and intellectual skills have been referred to the supernatural for a long time, the person who has no sacerdotal commitment finds it hard to speak with authority about experiences which have been the domain of the only vocal people there were, the priests and prophets.

One would expect that in our own age secular people other than psychiatrists would have talked about peak experiences in non-poetical language. But this is obviously not the case: most people who write about mystics do so under some theological auspices. Many psychiatrists who are professionally anti-theological and anti-clerical do not seem to be able to talk descriptively about the mystics either, but relegate them to the realm of psychopathological patienthood.

I believe that scholars, gentlemen, and mystics of the future will be contented with the knowledge that the zero-experience and the actions stimulating its repetition are all that there is to mysticism, and that changes of moral quality and the addition of skills may or may not follow upon the mystical experience.

Love between man and woman, centering on sexual congress, is similar to mysticism in that many things happen between acts of love or in the expectation of it: people become poets, musicians, artists, philosophers, even saints in the quest of the beauty which is the beloved. They may at times become felons, too. Love may change the lover, or it may not. The parallel to mystical experience and change should be evident. A good carpenter might say that he feels a better man, a better husband, a better citizen when he has done some fine work in his shop; and the successful stock broker may rub his hands and be nice to his wife and kids after clinching an especially good deal. I will admit that the zero-experience occasionally prods such changes in daily routine—but it does not generate moral splendor, scientific grandeur, or any extra-mystical excellence.

What does the zero-experience do to a person's view of himself? Here, the answer is radically different. As the zero-experience is a specific kind of cognitive process, we must attend on the mystic's own statements about changes that have occurred to him. The mystic regards himself as a new man, as reborn, as dead to the old world, as no longer quite human but as somehow divine, or *truly* human; in short, as something very different from what he was before the zero-experience happened. We might even say that the perennial mode of the mystic's self-report is that of change. The sheer force of such expression leads the apologists to think that "change" would also have to mean social change, moral change, change in skills, all-embracing change. Now unless a person is trained in the methods of analytical sciences like pyschology and social anthropology, he can hardly emancipate his diction from the communication patterns around him. The Christian mystic, until this century, could not possibly isolate his zero-experience report from other Christian talk, since such isolation was totally alien to the analyses and reporting strategies. Today the mystic who happens to be a social scientist can feel reasonably certain that future mystics will learn to reject the stylistic shell of their environment when they report their zero-experiences.

Let us apply common sense to the fact of personality change due to the zero-experience. It makes a person feel that he contains something he has never realized, something else than he has been taught to think. It would hardly impress him with marvelous visions and insights unless its unheard-of visions and dreams come through as new information. The person feels he has changed since he knows more; he changed because he grew. If the zero-experience did not generate growth in the ecstatic knowledge which a mystic experiences as change it would not mean much more than, say, a proper orgasm, or a very fine aesthetic experience. It would be perhaps a lasting memory, but it would not be the gigantic event it is. I think it is quite futile to speculate about *how* the zero-experience engenders all these *post-facto* riches. Exegetical literature and hagiography have tried this all the time. It should be possible to explain the yield of the zero-experience in psychological terms: changes in the view of self, in self-esteem, security, etc. If my readers were novices and I were the abbot, I would probably ask them, at this point, to put the book away and to read mystical reports, poetry, religious tracts about mystics for two years. But with the necessarily abrasive method we have to use in an *etic* strategy, I can only say that we know these two facts: 1) that the zero-experience invades the person's ego-perspective, changing him in few ways not predictable from his previous career, though his style of reporting may be predictable from antecedents in his culture; 2) that it does nothing to the person in his interactional patterns with other people and with human society at large.

The Yogavasiṣṭha,[12] an eighth century A.D. scholium in the monistic Vedānta tradition, contains what some people regard as a disturbing statement: the state of the *mukta*, the redeemed person, or, in our language, the person who has had repeated consummatory zero-experiences, is "like unto a stone" (*pāṣāṇavat samam*). If salvation means "being like a stone," then it can not even change the person as an individual, make him richer, more perfect unto himself. Then why meditate at all? Why bother? I do not see why the diction of the Yogavasiṣṭha and similar statements in brahmanical and Buddhist India should give cause for concern. Even when I abstract it from all ideological and traditional accoutrements, there seems to be nothing wrong with perfectly deep sleep which, to the person who has just woken up from it, was a marvelous experience. Suppose I match this experience, the "memory" of not being at all, as it were, with experiences of an ecstatic kind which I have also had, the more euphoric zero-experiences, certain drug experiences, or those supreme orgasms with expected and unexpected sexual partners. As I reflect on this comparison—being at a safe distance from any of these extremes at the moment—I am at a loss to decide which of the three seems preferable *in the long run*. For while I may want

100

to have an orgasm with Miss Universe during the next three months or years, I do not think I would want to choose this alternative over the "stonelike" zero-experience if it were guaranteed over a much longer period of time; as to the zero-experience, I wouldn't want to have it at this time at all, since I have certain deadlines and other highly secular matters in mind, far less absorbing in the cosmic situation perhaps, but quite important to me at this moment. St. Augustine might have been in a similar quandary when he said, "O Lord, give me chastity, but not yet." In conjunction with the "hierarchy of pleasure" (ānanda-mimāṃsa) of the Upaniṣad, discussed in an earlier section, one might well read the situation in this manner: the mystic has his vision once, twice, or very many more times. Sooner or later, the novelty of the experience wears off, and only the fervent theologian and the fervent apologist on behalf of the mystic wants to believe that there is absolutely no other interest left to the mystic except his experience, or his God, his divine contemplation, or what not. I do not think that this is borne out by the mystic's reports—and I do not find it borne out in my own experience. Other interests come up again, and the interval between the experiences is not filled exclusively with yearning for the next occurrence unless the mystic has no other skills—intellectual, aesthetical, or of any other order. Could it be that the mystic who has no other resources than his experience and the theological system he has learnt to abide by, fears boredom and calls it the Dark Night of the Soul, or gives it other poetic titles as he talks about the intervals between his visions? I think that this is worth considering. The mystic who has other resources—knowledge skills, artistic skills, even erotic and other ecstatic skills—is not likely to go through these specific depressions. I say this on the authority of none less than Saṃkarācārya, founder of my Order, a man who could not have possibly been bored since he had many things to do; not just little routine things like washing his begging bowl and his robe, but disputing and defeating opponents all over the land, founding schools and monasteries, meeting lots of people, plus a good deal of sorcery and anti-sorcery. Correspondingly I say this on the authority also of Thomas Aquinas, whom I do not regard as a mystic, but whose writings do not strike me as those of a man who got depressed or bored, and who was upset by the Dark Night, however long it lasted. Most cogently, I say this on the authority of my own experience—I have never felt any boredom, fear, or apprehension about the zero-experience returning or not returning at all; I teach, write, make love, annoy Hindus, travel, listen to music, meditate, and am rather curious to see if some time the zero-experience may return. But it doesn't bother me, as I do not think it bothered Śamkarācārya. Yet it obviously bothered some who were truly poor in spirit, like unto the children; but since they were not children, they suffered depression—and they had no means to defeat it since they knew little and could do so little except pray, perform austerities and be pious. The upshot of this seems to be that "change" applies to the mystic's rhythm of doing things—he arranges his deeds and thoughts in a hierarchy, at the base or at the top of which stands the zero-experience. All other actions of his, potential or actualized, are arranged in a descending scale of importance, and failures in their achievement do not count for much. But when the zero-experience does not recur for a long time, then hierarchical rhythm ceases to operate and the man is lost, in darkness with nothing *important* to fall back on.

There have been mystics who were good carpenters, but there have been much better carpenters who were not mystics; there have been mystics who have been poets, but there have been a great many better poets who were not mystics; and, most vexingly, there have been mystics who were theologians, but most of the greatest theologians were no mystics, though some of them whimsically wished they were. There have been many saints who were no mystics at all; their visions were no visions of oneness, and their raptures were saintly raptures, but not mystical ones. Which takes me back to the main point of this chapter: mystical practice affords no self-improvement outside of itself. Others are better in the moral field, the field of skills, the theological field, Meister Eckhart, Angelus Silesius, Jakob Boehme, and Blake were mystics and poets, but only Blake wrote poetry that is still alive. "Swami Vivekananda," a famous Indian historian of our day wrote, "was a master architect as he had the combined insight of a sociologist, a scientist, a historian, a philosopher, a psychologist and a mystic." Assuming that Vivekananda was a mystic he certainly was a poor sociologist in any sense "sociologist" is used now, and, of course, there were many better historians, philosophers, and psychologists than Vivekananda [13] in his day.

Swami Sivananda Sarasvati, [14] who died not long ago, was easily the most successful swami in his day. He started as a medical doctor in Malaysia, but returned to India in mid-career and set himself up as a "saint" (remember that this is a purely descriptive, professional term without any moralistic overtones). His "Yoga Vedanta Forest Academy" is an extremely well run institution; the Divine Life Society, created by the late Swami, has some 200 centers in India, and another 200 around the globe—with about three dozen highly active chapters in the United States and Canada; even Santiago di Chile and Lima have centers. A German woman who took ordination from the Swami has been running a successful campaign in Germany and the other German-speaking countries, and Swami Sivananda Radha, another German woman living now in Canada, has scored well with a varied, though highly predictable audience: not intellectuals, not college people, but also not carpenters and truck drivers; lower middle class and middle class people in American sociological terms, and some "professionals" of the lower order: dentists, some physicians and lawyers. Swami Sivananda wrote, edited, published, and distributed some forty full-size books; he wrote two hours every day, come heat come monsoon, and the books are readily available; they were all written in Indian English. the dustjacket of one of his books, *Conquest of Mind*, [15] reads as follows: "Born on the eighth September 1887, in the illustrious family of Sage Appaya Dikshita and several other renowned saints and savants, Sri Swami Sivananda had a natural flair for a life devoted to the study and practice of Vedanta. Added to this was an inborn eagerness to serve all and an innate feeling of unity with all mankind." Another passage says he was a "radiator of Peace and Unity." [16]

Now Sivananda called himself a mystic; and there is no reason why he should not have had the zero-experience. His disciples swear by his sanctity, his holiness, his divine faculties, etc., and it is unthinkable to say anything critical about him in front of them. There is in the Indian tradition the notion that *guru-nindā* "criticizing the guru" is a thing that the disciples must not tolerate; and they don't. I met a more secular Sivananda as I came down to Hrishikesh very thirsty, after a long trek to the *terai*, and mildly hungry. It seems that some of the guardians at the gate must have espied me, for no sooner did I enter than a right royal welcome was ready for me. Two foreign disciples—Germans to judge by their cameras— pounced upon me as though directed by some superior force, and then with a benign smile Sivananda came out from a door, very much like the Speaker in the *Magic Flute*; he greeted me politely as a junior fellow monk. The Swami was really a very practical man; a fair diagnostician and physician, quite domineering in interpersonal contacts, and though he never came down from the sermonistic rostrum, things went very well indeed around him. For years, he made it known that he would visit some of the Society's European and American institutions;

103

he never did, but the tension was kept high. I cannot go into any details, but I saw that the man was clever, orderly, a managerial Tamil gentleman, brahmin, and physician. His disciples praise him for his superhuman deeds and feats, but these when listed and analyzed amount to twenty years of average, helpful, but quite non-extraordinary public work, medical and social. His teachings are incredibly naive and even more fundamentᴀistic than those of the earlier Vivekananda: ladies (Indian-English for women) should not compete with men, they should be mothers, and if they do study, they should be nurses or lady doctors; don't eat meat and fish and eggs; don't have sex at all if possible, and as little as possible if impossible; don't eat rich and spicy food; pray many hours a day; make a list of transgressions and spiritual successes (or, as one male disciple told me, "make a list of number of times when you use hand for pleasure, and check it like double book keeping against number of times when you renounced use of hand . . ."), don't go to movies, not even "religious" movies which abound on the Indian screen, for in reality they are just as sensuous, under the guise of being religious; don't read books of controversial nature; this meant Herbert Spencer— Spencer being about the only nineteenth century thinker Vivekananda mentioned in his writings, and Sivananda having read Vivekananda, singled out Spencer as one of the writers one shouldn't read; one should read the *Upaniṣads*, the *Bhagavadgītā*, and the works of Swami Sivananda.

As I said, I assume Sivananda had had the zero-experience, and it might have prompted him to abandon his medical practice and become a monk; but then it might not, for knowing English and medicine makes a monastic career a more charismatic business than setting up a medical practice in Madras or Delhi. Be that as it may, if we grant that the zero-experience had made him change his status, that was about the only change I could discern between his way of handling the world and the way of non-mystics and non-monastics with the same qualifications and background.

Sri Aurobindo was no doubt a very different kettle of fish. The erstwhile Bengali terrorist who hardly knew any Bengali, who thought and wrote in stilted English all his life, and who became a saint by default, as it were, escaping the British to the then French enclave of Pondicherry in the early 20's, saw the mystic light, and began to write and talk about it. His writings are different indeed from those of the older Vivekananda and the younger Sivananda. Aurobindo might not have been a good poet, but he was a poet; he might not have been a thinker in any professional sense, but he expressed fairly sophisticated theological and ideological views about virtually everything. His ashram attracted people from all over India and the world, very different people from those who frequented Sivananda. Aurobindo was joined by The Mother, the French journalist who died in 1974 at 95, and who ruled the ashram with the strength of a medieval patroness-abbess. Aurobindo's thrust was yogic, experimental, and certainly in line with the less moralistic, less banal, and less sanctimonious teachers of traditional yoga in India. I do not agree with much of what he said; and I believe that his *Life Divine*,[17] a large two-volume book which has been imprinted and translated dozens of times, could be condensed to about one-fifth of its size without any substantial loss of content and message. He did write about union, identification, and all the classical mystical nomenclature, but it seems that he saw himself, and wanted to be seen, as a total innovator. He presented his specific aesthetical dualism, a set of dyadic statements about inside and outside, above and below, total and partial—quite tedious reading for all those who have done mystical and religious reading all their lives, but fascinating and full of proselytizing vigor for those who haven't, who want something of the spirit, and who are impressionable.

In the last decade of his life, Sri Aurobindo gave *darśan*[18] only three times a year, sitting in yogic posture on a dais, the "Mother" behind him with searchlights trained on them, a huge audience filling the hall. He did not speak any more—it was just *darśan*, and this was enough for the believing audience. He had said and written all there was to be said and written—now he just sat there, three times a year.

When he died, his devotees thought his body would not decompose as it was "full of electricity"; hadn't the master himself talked about a metamorphosis of the body into something perfect? Well, this did not work; Pondicherry is a tropical place, and the body was cremated after about three days.

Modern Indian hagiography fills many volumes of eulogy, with no analytic attempt. I chose Sivananda and Aurobindo as two famous mystics. What I report about them illustrates my conclusion that the mystical experience does not change the person except in his own self-image. The changes that occur to his environments and to his devotees are changes created by them, not by the mystic. Their interpretation of his every act, gaze, movement, and word creates a semblance of change: it creates the impression that the mystic has changed himself along with his surroundings. Hagiography is compiled and intended as reportage about saints, but in truth, it is reportage about the reporters. I think that the Buddha, Jesus, Mohammed, the early Christian and Muslim saints, and the Hindu and the western saints of our own days—Gurdjieff, Bennet, Alan Watts, and all the charismatics of the Spirit, are human beings with compassion and with clay feet. I believe they all have had zero-experiences, and that these experiences altered their self-image. But the legend that goes around them, the mythology, the tales that make copy, are not part of their own personalities, but ascribed to them in a patterned fashion. These men are not without responsibility. For legends to be spun, the subject of the legend had to consent.

The question now arises why the mystic should want to be the center of the legend, the subject of hagiography. Why shouldn't he? He is not free from vanity. If vanity is a vice, the mystical experience does not extirpate it. Many mystics no doubt were not vain, and did not want any publicity. I am thinking of Baba Mukunddass, a fine mystic whom I knew in the District of Almora in the Central Himalayas. The man was about sixty. People around him, both urban sophisticates from as far away as Delhi and Lucknow, and the more bucolic denizens of the area, had created a veritable wall of legendary dissimulation around him. He was, so they claimed, seen to levitate every *ekadaśī*, [19] at night. This, I said to myself, I had to see. As I got there in time for the show, some four dozen people had assembled. There they all sat, and I among them, for the better part of the night. I then fell asleep. In the morning, some men who had also been sleeping asked me how I liked the Swamiji's levitation this time? When did he levitate, I inquired, fearing that the event might have taken place when I had dozed off. But no, they said, hadn't I seen him levitate at least four yards above the ground from sunset to sunrise? I hadn't. This perturbed me a bit. Now I know that "seeing a saint levitate" or witnessing a yogi do any superhuman feat, is an *emic* statement from within that part of Hinduism which I call committed, free-wheeling, and non-scriptural. A saint levitates by ascription, he masters the seven great magical powers by ascription, he has perfect knowledge of everything by ascription, and what would be called an empirical display to prove it, in an *etic* sense, just does not fit the scheme at all. Had I objected to the men who had "seen" him levitate, they would simply have said that I was not pure enough, not enlightened enough, or too nervous. At a large monastic assembly about a year later, when he was not surrounded by his lay devotees but by highly institutionalized fellow monks, in a sort of professional convention, I asked him about his levitation. "I never levitate," he said quite seriously, "nor do I do any of the feats told about me. It is the *bhaktas* (devotees) who say these things." Perhaps I should have asked him why he didn't stop them from doing so.

The mystics' consent to legend about them is a complex matter. In the first place, mystics identify with the mythological if not the ideological themes which surround them before their zero-experience, and after. Society, both lay and ecclesiastic where there is such a dichotomy, reinforces the mystic's identification with the mythological themes since his reports are so out of the ordinary that mythology remains the only comparable sphere. The mystic has made his zero-experience, society makes him want to express it in terms of some supernatural realm it envisages. His general euphoria supports his notion that the mythological or the heroic language of his society adequately represents his feelings. More and more, he persuades himself that he exemplifies all this. If society provides a messianic slot and theme, he acts the savior to himself and the world until he *is* the savior. Quite soberly, we must define "being a savior" as "being proclaimed and accepted as a savior by the society whose savior X wants to be." This accounts for Jesus' constant quoting of Scripture to support all his movements, and eventual agonies. Much more recently, we have the Hindu saints of this century, and the hippie saints such as Tim Leary, and a host of neo-mystics whose names are not known to any except their own small crowd of votaries; if they succeed in generating a large audience, they will then prevail as gurus, saviors, prophets, etc.

This self-propelling mood is shared by all but the most critical mystics. It is remarkably similar in cultures without mutual contact and diffusion. It takes the form, "he who understands my (the mystic's) true, heroic, divine nature, really understands me." Again, we know how Jesus commended Peter for saying just that; Peter's support made Christ declare him the rock upon which his church was to be built. Nineteen hundred years later, young Naren Dutt, the later Swami Vivekananda, was asked by Sri Ramakrishna what he, Naren, *really* thought of him and Vivekananda, certainly not cognizant of St. Peter's well elicited eulogy and its reward, granted that Ramakrishna was the incarnation of the Divine. Ramakrishna nodded enthusiastically and said just this: "You have truly understood me." And Vivekananda became the torch-bearer for Ramakrishna, or for what he thought Ramakrishna's message had been.

" 'You are God, I know it, Mr. Finkle.'—'Yeah, yeah, I know,' said Finkle with a twinkle." The hippie in New York who sang this to his own tune hit the nail on the head. He had got the idea for this song, he said, as he watched some people gaping at Maharishi Mahesh Yogi as he performed in the large city, at the height of his career, when the Beatles and Mia Farrow had not yet gone to India.

We tend to be dismayed as we witness the blatant, stupendous commercialization of some mystics' establishments. Mother Anandamayi, a charming Bengali lady saint was seen— and photographed—walking on clouds across the globe. She knows nothing about the Hindu scriptures and never claims she does; but great pandits and scholars come to consult her about fine points of theological disputation. It is not easy for an ordinary Hindu to get near her, for her ashrams are visited by Governors, Generals, Food Ministers, and very rich men. Monastic and lay managers flit around busily wherever she is in residence. People—including this author—asked her quite often how she could put up with such discrimination around her, for the benefit of the rich and the powerful. "I am your poor daughter," she told me (she was about 30 years older than I; but that's the way lady saints [professional] speak to male saints [professional] in India). "I do not know about these things." "Isn't she great and marvelous," a Bengali devotee of hers gasped. "She always hides her greatness. Great scholars and pandits have come to her, asking her about this and that meaning in the scriptures—but she always hides her greatness." " 'Why do you ask me these things, I am your unlearned daughter, I do not know about these things,' she tells them." The Bengali devotee, paradigmatic of all of her thousands of devotees, does indeed believe that she knew "all these things," all the scriptures and the philosophies, she really knew that the rich and the powerful came, and that the poor and powerless didn't find it so easy to have her *darsan*; but that, in her infinite wisdom, she arranged all these things in the proper way, for the benefit of all concerned, including that of the poor and the powerless. She did not tell people what to do, how to manage their and her affairs, but her spirit was so strong that people do her will anyway. That the poor could not get to her was due to their *karma*, they simply did not deserve the riches and the power which those people had who could get her *darsan*, and every human being has his or her specific, karmically defined *adhikāra*, the capacity and the qualification to hear a particular doctrine, to work out religious things from his specific stage of inner development.

108

I am often asked, both by believing Hindus and by interested aliens, whether I had met truly great saints, and which of them I had come to regard with the reverence they wished for themselves. I did meet some very few, but only one of them is well known. He was Ramana Maharshi of Tiruvannamalai in the State of Madras. He is the one who used to say "I did not do anything at all," when people asked him how he came by his powerful experience of oneness. As a youth he felt so afraid of death that he lay down on the ground one day and "practiced" being dead, imagining being wrapped in a shroud, taken out to the cremation ground and cremated. Thus he lost all fear of death (a fair psychotherapeutic procedure). He left home all of a sudden, to the great grief of his relatives, just like the Buddha 2500 years earlier and Śamkarācārya 1200 years ago. He went up to the Arunachala shrine, where Śiva reigns in the form of fire, as one of the five "nature-lingas" distributed over the Tamil land. Then he sat down in a cave and went into *samādhi* [20] until vermin began to eat his flesh. Then a sympathetic gentleman picked him up and put him where he was to remain for the rest of his fairly long life, and began to build a simple ashram around him. At this point, though legend does not cease to work its web, there begins another, more worldly phase. Devotees, pilgrims, and influential people began to flock to the ashram; books, booklets, and pamphlets about the master and his words were published, and about twenty years later the first foreigners came to pay homage—Harold Osborn, Paul Brunton, and then many more. By 1945 the ashram and the master were well known, his relatives and his more managerially minded disciples having created substantial public relations. Unlike Sivananda's writings, which are as grotesque as they are volumimous, Ramana's own words, collected and edited by his disciples, encompassed about three slender volumes of an aphorismic kind. They all teach straight advaitic monism. Of all modern mystical literature Ramana's words reflect the most direct uninterpreted zero-experience—a relatively simple matter for the radical monism of the Vedānta, where the orthodox scholastic formulation happens to coincide with the uninterpreted content of the zero-experience. By the time I visited Ramana's ashram about two months before he died in 1951, the place was reeking with management. There was a constant throng of visitors, Indian and foreign; they were given food and shelter, but some were treated coldly and not given shelter if they came unannounced and if they were not known to the management. Ramana reclined on his couch for many hours a day; his *darśan* was not theatrical at all, unlike that of Sri Aurobindo, and most of the inmates saw him almost every day. Fine Sanskrit chants went on most of the time, with incense burning, and there was indeed a palpably numinous atmosphere about the place. But the various cliques and the minor and major battles within the managerial hierarchy were known to every perceptive visitor, and long-time inmates were part of the factionalism. Quite often Ramana was asked why he put up with all this nonsense. It seems he never replied directly: he simply ignored these questions or he gave answers of a didactic sort which defy further probing. This much is quite sure, however: of all the professional saints and mystics I visited in India he was the one who had most clearly not changed at all, socially speaking; or his personal transformation had happened so early that no one witnessed it. There is reason to believe that he remained very much the same person between 17 and 70. The legend around him was not the story of his life, but a ritualistic tale of hieratic events. As always, people began to report curious therapies and wonderful at-a-distance experiences connected with him—the hagiography was complete and has been steadily augmented since his death.

Being a legend is like "being popular," linguistically speaking: it is not something the saint or the mystic is himself; it is a description of how other people talk and feel and think about him. Ramana Maharshi and Aurobindo were "saintly" to the people who thought them so. "Mystic" and "mystical," at least in the manner I suggest in this book, *are* descriptive terms —a person who has a certain experience and identifies himself as a mystic is one. And when an Indian introduces himself as a "saint," this, too, is an *etic* term, descriptive, for it states a quasi-professional, full-time engagement in certain activities: meditating, preaching, wandering, fasting, abstaining from sex, wearing some monastic garb, etc. But the western language adjectives "saintly," "holy," or "spiritual" in Indian English, are persuasive terms, terms describing the mood of the speaker, and not the person intended.

Hagiography is an inextricable blend of statements about the zero-experience *and* of legends superimposed by his audience. The zero-experience cannot generate sanctity, extra-mystical skills, wisdom, academic qualification, political leader-ship, or even charisma, any more than orgasm can generate good citizenship, good parental virtue, or even love in the romantic-erotic sense. This is an important analogy, since many people in the western world today have come to believe that proper sexual consummation yields all these goods directly, or elliptically in the manner that sex-and-marriage manuals indicate.

110

We would have to use a proper quaternary sampling procedure and see how many people with the zero-experience did well in other matters such as moral living, charismatic power, political leadership, scholarship, holiness, etc., how many mystics failed in some or all of these, how many non-mystics achieved these human ends, and how many non-mystics didn't. Those who still insist that there is a causal nexus between the mystical experience and the other events—a nexus applying to the mystic, not his audience talking about him—have to bear the burden of proof, and show the connection as necessary.

When modern Hindus of neo-Vedānta proclivity are asked their opinion about Christ's teaching they are likely to quote his words "I and the Father are One" as his central statement, and as proof for his being a good monist in the Vedānta tradition. Few Christians interpret it that way. Even if Christ's own exalted experiences and transfigurations, carefully culled from the New Testament, were put together and presented as the core of the Christian *dogma* and *kerygma*, with nothing else added—no moral teachings, no descent to hell, no sacrifice for humanity, no mysteries of transubstantiation, no passion—it would not attract many Christians. For these experiences only, central though they may have been to Christ, Christianity as a faith would not have been generated. At the back of all enquiry into mysticism there is an unspoken "why bother, if it is only that." My argument is secular and *etic*. It must do without special intuitions and without grace; if special grace is needed for mystical intuition then we are, of course, back to the proselytization game of old days. If there is good faith in this analysis, we have to agree on using the same tools. These are of the empirical sort. Someone might argue that a man has had one or more zero-experiences; this gave him tremendous self confidence, he was elated and converted; and it made him act better in society. But this is a very different matter from claiming that the experience made the man what he was. This cannot be proved even theoretically, for it would mean that unless man has had the zero-experience, such superbly positive social behavior would not be possible; and this is patently wrong, for most of the world's greatest and purest never even claimed that they had had mystical experience.

111

Chapter Five

The Mystic and his Methods

"Methods of communion also vary, from the use of certain drugs and other physical means of ecstasy, to concentration on bright objects or on symbols, formulae, or ceremonies, auto- or hetero-hypnosis . . ." [1]

One would wish that the author, an Indian intellectual and a scholar of status and a powerful academic administrator, had said this and let it stand. Mukerjee is less of a puritan than most of his contemporaries, thanks to the cultural symbiosis of this century's Bengali intellectuals with Rabindranath Tagore and the aesthetic renascence ushered in by the poet. But in the end, he follows the all-Indian apology. Indian writers of this century cannot let pleasant things be as they are; ecstasy and delight may be phases en route to religious consummation, but the ultimate rule is asceticism. The pamphleteering of neo-Hinduism is deeply anti-hedonistic; the quest of pleasure is condemned. That pleasure can be the means to religious consummation is borne out by passages in the canonical texts, but these are either ignored or metaphorized away.

In this chapter, I shall analyze the methods of the mystic. It is quite unimportant how the mystic comes by the zero-experience; if observation shows that the zero-experience is triggered by meditational procedures, by drugs, by orgasm, by fasting, or by anything else, then moralistic assessments about its genesis are out of place.

The respectable and orthodox do not like to hear about people who have had mystical experiences after taking a psychedelic drug. R.C. Zaehner, in his introduction to *Mysticisms Sacred and Profane*, actually tells us that he wrote the book in order to rebut Huxley who claimed to have had mystical experiences under the influence of mescalin. On a crossing of the British Channel a young bearded Pakistani psychology student got into a conversation with me. The talk turned to drugs, and when I suggested that some Muslim saints, some sufis, had talked about *gāñjā*,[2] he burst into an angry tirade against "loafers who do not understand the meaning of

112

mārafat; [3] *mārafat* is very high and holy thing, not for these useless people"; and then he proceeded to metaphorize the sufis' use of *gañjā*, applying the dialectic of all non-mystical apologists for their own specific mystical tradition: when saints talk about the pleasures of sex, the beauty of a woman, the intoxication of wine or *gañjā*, they don't mean sex, women, and *cannabis*, but something much loftier, subtler, more ethereal, totally unphysical, something which has nothing to do with the (bad) ecstasies derived from these bad things; and that they have to use such metaphor so as to either impress the potential adepts or to deter the audiences that are not yet ripe for such higher wisdom.

Let us inquire into the causality of the mystical act, the occurrence of the zero-experience, its repetition, the proneness of some persons to have it. Professor Zaehner, who believed in God, thought that God meets the mystic half way, that God makes the first step, and that the mystic makes his experience, if it is the real thing, by God's grace; and of course, grace-language goes a long way to placate inquisitive people on the fence of faith. Astrologers would say that the stars and planets associated with the birth of the person caused the zero-experience. For the literate Buddhist, Hindu, Jain, and more recently, for the Euro-American converts to Indian doctrine, the *karma* answer is the proof. A man gets what he deserves, and even the worst translation of the *Bhagavadgītā* says it quite clearly: the yogi starts where he left off—so if a man has a zero-experience and enters the mystical life without any preparation in this life, it simply means that he brought all the readiness along from his previous careers, because the karma doctrine does not permit a *tabula rasa*. But then, there is a mixed scientific explanation, an explanation which cannot give much satisfaction to any of those who seek an intellectually adequate cause to an emotionally overwhelming experience. The scientific, boring, *etically* valid explanation runs somewhat like this: a certain psychosomatic readiness was there—perhaps by inheritance of a conducive physique; more likely by environmental syndromes of conflict and cohesion. A thought-chain occurred which the thinker *felt* as meaning "you are the All, I am the All, I am whatever divinity there is." There is a fair chance that this thought-chain occurs to many more non-mystics than to mystics, that it might conceivably occur to the majority of people either when they are very young, or when they are under stress—but the difference between them and the mystics is that they do not heed it, that they brush it away, nip it in the bud, push it out before it can mature

113

sufficiently to create the sudden attention which is needed to stabilize and reinforce the experience. I have witnessed a few cases where a person had incipient zero-experiences, but refused to let them take shape and mature. He got scared, he felt physically uncomfortable, and did one or several things to obstruct, impede, deflect, or weaken the experience. "Snapping out" is a fine art according to therapists and worried parents, but "snapping out" may also mean preventing the zero-experience from crystallizing, or from recurring when it has happened. And, "snapping out" is relatively easy. It can be accomplished by a series of rapid bodily motions, by abruptly leaving the site of the occurrence, by talking to different people about indifferent matters. The opposite of "snapping out" is staying in, and this is quite often all that is needed when the zero-experience occurs. It is very much harder to *recapture* it through one's own effort, by meditation, drugs, continence, controlled ecstasy, and prayer. The Christian or Muslim saint's "waiting for grace" expresses this phase. This wait is shot through with a large number of bodily and mental postures informed by a set of rules accepted by the saint or mystic.

People who are unfamiliar with the hidden self-evidence of sociological statements might now grumble and say that my "explanation" of the origin of the zero-experience and the inception of the mystical life in an individual is not only dry and arid, but no explanation at all, that it is just a statement of things happening. Precise description, however, is causal explanation in the social sciences. If causality could only be understood in terms of a one-to-one temporal sequence as in a simple Newtonian universe, then no social phenomenon could be discussed at all, since no social or individual event can have just one cause. Thus, in statements like "the man died from a bullet through his heart" or "from incurable cancer," there is at least the semblance of a one-to-one causal nexus, elliptically stated. But the psychoanalytic statement "he committed suicide due to severe depression" should not be intended as a one-to-one causal statement, since "depression" is not a single event. If one insists that precise description, based on complete observation, temporal sequence analysis, and acquaintance with past individual and environmental events, is not an explanation in the causal sense, then by the same token there can be no explanation of the origin of the mystical, except *emic* explanations based on articles of faith, God, *karma*, constellations, etc. A non-believer cannot accept such explanations in the long run; *emic* talk is fine for literary purposes but an *etic* explanation will be required in due course.

114

As an anthropologist in an African or Indian village, I may be satisfied with the villagers' explanation that the excessively large number of stillborn children is due to witchcraft, and in my ethnological report, I shall bracket these notions under the chapter on the Supernatural. But if I am called upon to do something about remedying the situation, I shall have to draw on the *etic* part of my assessment of the trouble, get medicines, or report the matter to the local health authorities. Analogously I refuse to accept article-of-faith "explanations" as causal, in matters of mystical experience.

Mysticism, as I said before, is also a skill. Skills can and must be learned; I am extremely skeptical about "talents." There are people who just grab a tennis racket and win a game without practice, but these successes have no predictable repeatability. No doubt, some people like Mr. Custance [4] hit upon the zero-experience without any preparation, and without further interest. They do not identify themselves as mystics, nor do they interiorize the experience as one of cosmic union. A man tells me about what might have been a zero-experience that happened to him and he sounds like the properly married business executive who picks up a whore once in his life in some city where no one knows him and where he is not going to go again: something for his own private record, but nothing to set a standard for his further actions. As a rule, people with some sort of religious interest seem to welcome the zero-experience when it comes out of the blue, as it were; the "typical" businessman, broker or medical man tends to reject it. I am not talking about the new seekers, the young people of the counter-culture who court the experience ardently, nor about societies where it is part of a total, modal concern as in India or pre-Chinese Tibet. The North American Plains Indians' spirit quest, much mentioned in anthropological literature, is no doubt such a modal readiness for the zero-experience, whatever local interpretation it acquires. I have found that the average Protestant clergyman in the western world is positively afraid of the zero-experience; he tends to advise against its pursuit very much like the secular man of the world. The zero-experience poses a very direct threat to the man's profession: for after all, his job is to worship God with profit and to make his congregation do the same, not to be God. The coffee-cake Protestantism so prevalent in American cities and suburbia is inimical to the zero-experience, which erodes the ecclesiastical structure.

The causal explanation of the mystical event is an analysis of training. The German idiom *"der Knopf geht auf"* (lit. "the

115

button opens") conveys the point: it is the result of some sort of discipline. The phrase is used by coaches of football and by mathematics teachers. The student fumbles, tries again and again, and then, all of a sudden, he gets it. The most important step has been made, and from here on it is a question of slow refinement and perfection. In the case of the zero-experience which first occurs without planning, the pedagogical element, of course, cannot be said to be there at the outset. Yet such explanations as *karma*, or more recently of "being hip" or "being high" are helpful as *emic* crutches to *etic* causal explanation. All these terms are tautologies; for if I say that a person does something well because he is a genius at it, then this is just another way of saying that he does it very well indeed. Still, once the zero-experience has been made, and the person *wants* to live the mystical life, wants to have repeated experiences, wants that this should do something to his view of himself, of life, and of the people around him, we have a simple explanation in terms of learning, just as the statement "he plays his piano well because he works a lot at it, practices two hours every morning, listens a lot to good piano playing, etc." is an explanation of his playing well. The *Bhagavadgītā* puts this quite squarely *abhyāsena gṛhyate* "you hold it through practice." When implemented, it is the explanation of the mystic's ways. As to the first, unsought occurrence, there simply cannot be a scientific explanation, since the possible psychological, psychosomatic, physical, social, historical concomitants are so numerous that there is no way of selecting any of them as causal elements. There is no way of explaining why the tenor was superb during last night's performance of *Aida*; for such explanations as the condition of his throat or he was happy because he knew he would make love to a new woman after the performance, and she was sitting in the house," cannot be pinned down as causal and the same explanations could be invoked if he had sung badly that night.

Although I denied causal status to *emic* statements about mystical events, we must deal extensively with the various *emic* strategies which the insiders use. We must talk about grace, *karma*, drugs, etc., since they are part of the mystic's training, irrespective of their objective existence or relevance. Just as Kant's division between analytic and synthetic truths seems absolute only at one specific period, with the possibility that what was seen as a synthetic truth might turn out to be analytic with more information turning up, so the *emic* and the *etic* status of research strategies vacillate over a sufficiently long stretch of time. It is quite easy to show, for instance, that the psychiatrist's concept of "deviance" has always been *emic*. It is not easy to show that what was believed to be an *emic* statement turns out to be *etically* true. A woman I knew in India was possessed by the spirit of her dead mother-in-law. She got cramps, fever, and all sorts of catatonic fits. Then came a famous exorcist, who persuaded the mother-in-law's spirit to leave the woman alone, and the woman was cured—no more fits, no more fever, and normal functioning in every way. This was an *etic* happening, so to speak, and although it is doubtful whether any spirit was really exorcized, it is quite clear that the sort of very personal attention given to the patient, the central place which had been assigned to her in her husband's household, which was alien and hostile at other times and constantly curtailed her individuality, had helped her in psychological and biological ways. "The spirit has let her go" is *emic*, no doubt, as a statement of successful therapy in that Indian village; but so is the psychiatrist's statement "Mr. X has finally been cured of schizophrenia," a Euro-American metropolitan psychiatrical *emic* utterance, in which "schizophrenia" has the function of "the spirit" in the Indian village context. Schizophrenia and the whole array of diagnostic terms in psychiatry do not refer to any disease at all in the manner tuberculosis or broken legs do. Mental illness in the classical Freudian sense is a myth, as Thomas Szasz has shown;[5] and I would add, from a crosscultural perspective, enlarging Szasz's statement, that schizophrenia and paranoia are just as much or as little of a myth as ghosts and possessing spirits. Thus, just as psychiatric terms and terms denoting similar phenomena in regions where there is no psychiatry are either *etic* or *emic* depending on the status of research and the advancement of therapy, "unscientific" statements about mystical genesis and development may well be *emic* statements made by the initiates, their followers, and indeed by a whole tradition which has concerned itself with mysticism over a long period of time. This ethnosemantic stratagem gives us great relief: for we can now investigate *emic* causal explanations of mystical events.

Let me refer once again to the Ganser syndrome. For reasons presumably known to him, a person pretends to be "insane" (or depressed, paranoid, schizophrenic, etc.), perhaps in the manner Shakespeare intended the Prince of Denmark to act. If, again for reasons still known to him, the person continues these histrionics, then a time may come and, according to some research, must come, when the person actually is insane (depressed, manic, etc.) and then we can no

117

longer say "for reasons best known to him." I tend to believe with Harry Stack Sullivan[6] and the Chicago psychiatrists that there is no real division between acting insane and being insane. You can pretend to have a cold and cough and clear your throat and spit, and you still do not have a real cold; but if you keep acting insane, that is precisely what is meant by being insane. Here, human language and "clinical" fact coalesce, for a change. In Buddhist countries, where people are much more cautious about calling people by punitive names, a man is said to be insane if he reviles the Buddha. This does not mean, as a naive professor of psychiatry visiting me in Thailand averred, that "if a man keeps rejecting the super-ego of the society, he will eventually become psychotic." If you revile the Buddha, you *are* insane—reviling the Buddha being the criterion of the mental deviance which that Buddhist people designate by a term which translates "insane."

A person has zero-experience, enjoys it, and begins attending to it by way of hoping for its recurrence, and does things and thinks thoughts which his society has long ascribed to people who were mystics and saints. Then, whether the experience actually recurs or not, this person will keep acting, playing with the deeds and thoughts which his society identifies with proper mystical or saintly behavior. Someone may say "I know the bloke better; he pretends to do saintly things, he pretends to be charitable, he makes believe that he is meditative and prayerful—but in reality he is a crook, he wants to persuade his neighbors of his sanctity, because he wants his pious uncle to bequeath him his fortune." But if you pretend doing odd actions, thinking good thoughts, preserving a meditative pose for a very long time to the exclusion of opposite actions and attitudes, then you are doing just those things. Whether the mystic "pretends" to have zero-experiences, and keeps pretending to do appropriate deeds, or whether he actually does these things, is quite irrelevant in the specific context of events. I assume the zero-experience must have occurred at least once for a person to want to be a mystic, though he might have become attracted to the mystical life merely by hearing someone talk about it, or by reading about other people's zero-experiences. The person then has to do certain things, as prescribed by that segment of his society which deals with the holy and the esoteric. Or if you prefer, he has to pretend doing these things. He has to do them, or pretend to do them, for a long time until he feels convinced that he has made it. We have to rid ourselves of Judaeo-Christian moralisms with regard to the assessment of actions and attitudes pretended. In terms parallel to the Ganser effect, the mystic now cathects objects and quite common events, in the light of the newly found directive; he ignores commonsense explanations of events if esoteric explanations are available; he acts as the saints and the other mystics do. And in due course, forgets the difference between playing at being a saint and being a saint and a mystic. "Playing at," "pretending to" have to be understood neutrally, non-moralistically, in the technical sense of doing, or acting out. As we analyze the language by which we can talk about mystical experiences, we see that in order to be a true mystic one has to act like one—and "acting like a mystic" means precisely to imitate what one knows about saints and mystics and their actions. It is one thing to act morally, respectably, pay one's taxes, take the children to the zoo, go to church or, in the Hindu scene, feed the poor on occasions. There are public criteria for the actual completion of these deeds. There is no such checklist open to this sort of public inspection of "mystical" activity. All the adept can go by are poetic, pious, dogmatic, and other impressionistic hints given by saints and mystics, and he mimics what he thinks they conveyed. The very Christian term "imitation of Christ" means precisely "pretending to be Christ," to do things the way the pious consensus enjoins. Since no one knows how the well known mystics actually felt, prayed, meditated, and lived, it is transmitted words that shape the imitation. Their emulators must do what they understand the mystical teachers to have done without any warranty of verisimilitude. It is for this reason that mysticism has been mysterious. A time may come when mysticism will be recognized for what it is, a skill which can be learned, and an achievement which does not confer any supernatural, or superhuman status at all, nor any moral excellence beyond what can be acquired through accompanying efforts of a non-mystical kind: moral, artistic, intellectual.

The mystic, who has had a zero-experience, has to keep on believing that the cognitive content of the zero-experience is permanent, that it is the true, unassailable state of things, that the objects, persons, and ideas which take over when the zero-experience recedes are either less real, or at least less important, and not to be heeded with the intensity of the newly intuited reality. Not a reality like the second law of thermodynamics, but a reality privately certified by the impact which the zero-experience wields on its subject. Although the zero-experience is not there any longer or not yet again, the mystic has to be convinced that what he has experienced is valid at all times. I am not sure whether this is what a pious Christian or Muslim simply calls "faith," and not concerned. "Faith" is a Judaeo-Christian *emic* term, whereas "being convinced" is *etic*, hence more suitable for description and analysis.

The Christian act of Grace is, I think, by far the simplest *emic* explanation. I do not claim to "understand" Grace or its workings in the sense of being affected by it, converted by its impact so as to admit its workings. I do not know if an apostate, a radical critic of Christian doctrine, would qualify for an act of grace by a Christian God. Logically, this seems quite possible, as the more liberal theologian might say that whatever positive interaction there is between divinity and the individual, an act of grace is involved even though the non-Christian does not recognize it as such and the non-Christian teachers did not discover it in their vision of the deity. I recall the late M.N. Roy telling me about his escape from the enemy, through the Gobi Desert, where it never rains. The trucks could not possibly have passed through the dry sand. "Then, Swamiji," Roy said with a serious face, "God helped me." Now Roy, mentor of Mao Tse-tung, was one of India's few professional atheists. Richard L. Park calls him the "secular brahmin." Roy was being facetious. But apart from that, his diction was elicited by a reflection on an impossible situation: it never rains in the Gobi Desert, but it *did* rain on that one day, the sand compacted, the trucks could pass. "Pure chance," "a rare meteorological combination," etc., might have been perfectly good verbal accompaniments of the report. But the sheer implausibility of the event warranted a statement that was not only quite atypical for the speaker, but also impossible by his own rules. I think "grace," to the Christian insider, means *emically* precisely what "God helped me" meant to Roy *etically*: the statement of a *quia absurdum*, conveying something quite different in type both from "pure chance" and from traceable events. There are some Protestant teachers who say that grace can be understood rationally, cognitively. Paul Tillich told me just that: it is not that Grace is something mysterious in the manner in which the Eucharist or the Resurrection are; rather, he said, it is like a sudden successful mathematical solution. Here he used the phrase *es geht ihm der Knopf auf*, "the button opens"; he grasps suddenly, not through a gradual process of cognitive adaptation. The mathematician has behind him many years of training and practice. Unlike historians and some natural scientists, the training and practice specific to mathematicians is of an intuitive order: the quantity of his reading has very little to do with his success. Similarly, Tillich thought, the religious expert, the reflectively pious man (*der denkend fromme Mensch*), grasps "grace not by an accumulation of theological knowledge, nor by prayer and meditation, nor of course, by good deeds, but by coaching himself for a readiness similar to that of the mathematician. Then, when grace comes, he knows it, and it solves his religious problem, just as the mathematician's intuited solution solves his mathematical problem. In this conversation, which took place almost two decades ago, I failed to ask Tillich questions which I would now ask him: Did he imply, then, that understanding grace *was* an intellectual act? How far would he press the mathematician analogy? For surely, with all the intuitive quality of an aesthetically elegant solution, one would still think that the mathematician's effort was primarily intellectual. How about grace? If it is "understood" by a Christian, and if he reports his understanding, or his having experienced it himself, and if some patriarch who has formulated the notion of "grace" not by intuition but dogmatically, then agrees that the person has indeed understood grace, what sort of "understanding" was it? Also, intuitions may be wrong, innocuously as in the case of following a hunch on the wrong horse, or very dangerously as in the case of Hitler who intuited the supremacy of the *Herrenvolk*. If by intution the learned consensus means "intuition granted especially by God," then this begs the question, for such intuition is already a part of grace which has not been explained. Is understanding grace then perhaps a crypto-intellectual act? I think this is what Tillich thought it was: intellectual, but not of the syllogistic kind; perhaps very subtle yet intelligible by processes of ratiocination and discursive reflection.

Now to the insider, the believer, this does not pose any problem—when he feels Grace he knows that this is it, and he really doesn't need any further corroboration; nor are there any possible arguments to make him change his mind. Seen thus, grace works in multiple ways: an old lady, walking across the Forum in Rome with me in a party randomly assembled by American Express, said "These old things prove to me once again that God has done wonderful things." Now I thought I should argue that it was the Romans who had made it, and at a time when the Christian God had not yet been invented or discovered, or when the Romans dished up Christians to lions. But if she meant it elliptically, "God does great things, he created great people long ago, and great people create great things," then of course this was just a Glory-to-God statement. I did not say any of this to her, but I did ask her why she thought that these *heathen* things were somehow closer to God's genius than, say, a little Christian church just about 200 feet away? "It is through God's grace that these things happen," she said. What things? "Things I can appreciate." We have to span a wide gap here: when M.N. Roy said that God had helped him to cross the Gobi Desert, and when the lady said that God had shown her grace for appreciating that such marvelous things came about in olden days, one statement obviously was that of a non-believer, the other of a believer.

What does that do to grace as an explanation for the origin of the mystical state? There is of course a logical possibility that there is a God and that he sometimes ingresses into the minds of human beings. I do not think this is very likely. Also, most of these things can be explained without God. I think that William of Occam, that learned monk, was really a clandestine viper in the fold—for Occam's razor, *etically* applied, cuts right through all theology: *entia non sunt multiplicanda praeter necessitatem.* If entities are not to be multiplied beyond heuristic necessity, grace, among other things, does not have to be adduced to explain the zero-experience and its sequels. If all genetic and environmental causes could be known God's intervention would be superfluous, even if it is claimed that for this sort of supremely important feat God's presence is that of a catalyst, i.e., it would not happen without his interfering grace; or, as Christian theologians tell me, if something of the sort happens without grace, it isn't the real thing, even if it looks quite alike. This is a bit like saying beer cannot be as good as in Munich, even if it tastes exactly like Munich beer.

However, Occam's Razor should not be brought into the fray when people talk about grace and the mystical in *emic* terms. Explanations which are redundant in an *etic* context may be felt necessary in the *emic* stance of the believer. Indian farmers when given American wheat seeds, German fertilizers, and Russian tractors, still claim that the *roṭi* made out of Indian wheat "tastes sweeter" than the *roṭi* made of the *etically* superior American wheat. When Zaehner or any other orthodox Christian thinker assigns genuineness, value, or demerit to mysticism partly or wholly accounted for by God's grace, putting Hindu monists and Buddhist contemplatives down the totem pole, then this is a close analogue to the Munich beer drinker. Differences between zero-experiences do not lie in the theological doctrines that cluster around them, but in the intensity, quality, feeling-tone, degree of emotional involvement, degree of euphoria. Some doctrines recommend one type of experience over another and their spokesmen would tend to subdue or to reinterpret statements that do not seem to fit into the accepted style, but this, again, is quite incidental to the experiences. Zaehner and other writers on mysticism, not knowing the *emic-etic* model created by modern linguistic anthropology, simply confuse the *emic* and the *etic*, regarding specific (*emic*) theological diction as essential and on a par with the zero-experience itself. If Zaehner found two mystics who reported exactly the same experience to him, one of whom identified himself as a Hindu *sannyasī*, the other as a Trappist monk, then Zaehner quite certainly would have claimed that the latter's was a higher, more genuine, truer, more ultimate experience; and he would claim that the other's experience could not have been quite the same *because* it lacked the accoutrements of grace and Christian insight.

Faith and love are many splendored things, but their dictions are *emic*. Grace as an *emic* instrument of causal explanation of the mystical act is not, of course, a Christian monopoly. In several traditions of Hindu India and Northern Buddhism we have very similar notions, so similar in the case of the Mādhavite school of Hinduism[7] that some Christian Indologists of the last century thought that Madhava must have had some Christian contacts. He flourished in the thirteenth century, and by that time there had been Syrian Christian settlements in his general area for some centuries. There is nothing in the teaching of Madhavācārya which indicates Christian inspiration; but the concept of *anugraha*, "divine favor, divine selection," is comparable to grace. Madhava and other *bhakti*[8] teachers usually quote a passage from the *Bhagavadgītā* and from one *Upaniṣad* which says that he only can reach the goal whom divinity favors or selects (*ācchādati* "to cover," but also "to elect"). In the Pure Land School of Northern Buddhism, the Buddha is the giver of grace to those who worship him faithfully, with very little attention to the highly individualistic, speculative, and affect-less meditations which go with the Theravāda and with many Māhāyana schools. The Buddhist term is *karuna*, which means "compassion" in the older, more general Buddhist context; but in the devotional schools of Northern Buddhism this term takes on quite a different quality. It moves from the ontological in Tantric Buddhism[9] to the soteriological in the Pure Land and other personalistic, grace-oriented sects of Northern Buddhism. In contemporary Japan, we have the highly politicized *Soka Gakkai*, the "rushing of the gods," with a fanaticized version of the teachings of Nichiren, a Japanese monk of the eleventh century. The formula chanted is *namu myohorengekyo* "obeisance to the lotus of the true law"—this being the Sino-Japanese rendering of the *Saddharmapuṇḍarīka*, an important Mahāyāna text. It evokes strong emotional responses among its followers. The Buddha of this school is simply a divine being who bestows grace upon his followers, and every success seems to depend on it—a far cry from the speculative, intensely individualistic guidelines set down in the Pali and Sanskrit Buddhist texts. I would be prepared to construe millenial cults of this kind as potentially mystical, without blurring the semantic demarcations of "mysticism" which I have set. Anthropology has produced a very large number of studies on revitalization movements [10] and millenial cults. Some of these cults are indeed mystical since their objectives entail identification with a larger, cosmically conceived entity, variously referred to by the name of the tribe, some tribal deity, the land, etc. Undoubtedly, Hitler's ramblings contained a mystical element—the *Reich*, the *Volk*, the *Vorsehung* ("providence")—these were non-descriptive terms in his perorations, entities with which the initiate, the party member, must identify; not by any rational process, but by such millenial procedures as chanting (shouting), rhythmic and thespian movements (marching), and, of course, very loud and rather well performed ritualistic music (marching tunes, with an occasional *Meistersinger* overture thrown in). Mystics can be saints, they can be vicious tyrants, or anything else. The fact that literature has so far talked only about saints, or saints-to-be, as mystics, is due to the *emic* frame of the authors, who were bound by homiletic and exegetical allegiance to one theology or the other. In the millennial-type mystical movements, grace—not usually called by this term—plays an important role not only as a state of things to be hoped or worked for, but also as an explaining, quasi-causal factor, issuing from the charismatic figure who functions like God or any divine entity in the theistic forms of mysticism. There is a very important difference between individual mystical experience and the millennial situation: in all genuine mystical traditions, each individual can find mystical consummations; in the millennial movements it is only the charismatic who has found oneness with whatever principle or divinity he invokes. In this situation, the people and the followers are spectators; in the genuine mystical traditions there are no spectators—there are only mystics and non-mystics. I think that the feeling of being chosen *now*, the feeling some people in the theistic tradition have when they encounter the zero-experience, is one of institutionalized gratitude: since there can be no true gain

124

without grace, there must have been a supreme act of grace when the experience occurred. Where the mystic is not quite sure, where the experience is not strong enough, or perhaps too strong, and where it does not seem to jibe with doctrinal prescriptions, he feels grace is still missing, or worse, that some other force has occupied his soul—the devil, some demon, or something that was not the agent of grace. If the feeling is quite right, if there is not too much ecstasy, no wild visions, no inflation of the senses, but complete satisfaction, then that was true experience, but since it is believed to be the result of grace only, grace it must have been. If the experience was not quite right (and many *etic* things account for that, including a sore throat, an acid stomach, or some emotional upset) it was not grace. Mysticism in the Mediterranean idiom is a result of God's grace *emically* speaking; *etically*, mysticism is the experience of oneness. Its causes are multiple—idiosyncratic, social, historical, and probably more than we yet know, nutritional. The Hindus had a good hunch at it: in the *Bhagavadgītā*, there is the notion that some kinds of food aid spiritual experience, others obstruct it. The Indians, with their great love for taxonomies, had to assign the dullest things of the kitchen— milk, sugar, clarified butter, fruit—as promoting mysticism; the interesting foods, spicy and full of various flavors, were said to prompt passionate, heroic, but not religious action. There are marginal schools, the Tantric tradition foremost among them, where the effects of these substances are inverted; but typically, light white food with low proteins is godly, in the minds of most Hindus.

Long before physicians and psychiatrists began to bracket certain clinical phenomena as "psycho-somatic," mystics realized that any conceptual division between body and mind had to be abandoned when it came to achieving states of union. In theory, a person may cognitively entertain such a division between body and mind but it makes mystical discipline difficult. If we pick up a Hindu or Buddhist report about mystical practice, and then a Christian report, chances are that the latter will contain confessions of agony, anguish, and general discomfort except in the statements of consummation— bliss, *visio beatifica*. Hindu and Buddhist reports, on the other hand, have something matter-of-fact, something technical, but at the same time something painless about them, even when some of the uglier methods of asceticism are being reported: Jaina monks exposing their bodies to living vermin so as to feed life by life; Hindu pilgrims measuring the road to the shrine with their bodies, entailing many thousand prostrations until the shrine is within sight; or some of the better known forms of self-torture—standing on one leg for a month, clenching one's fist permanently, sitting on nailboards. Many of these feats were displayed for show and for wages, but there are texts in the tradition of the *Gheraṇḍasaṃhitā* (about fifth century A.D.), where such measures are recommended to the mystic in quest of the zero-experience or its repetition. Yet, these reports have an aura of detachment, of personal non-involvement. The Christian mystic's rejection of the use of drugs and sex, and his habit of self pity stem from the axiomatic mind-body dichotomy. Once the two systems coalesce, such body-using and body-directed procedures as sacral sex and euphoric drugs lose their stigma.

This is borne out by cross-cultural observation: those schools in the Hindu and the Buddhist traditions which do regard body and mind as fundamentally distinct entities—and this is the case with virtually all Hindu reform movements of the nineteenth century and later, created upon exposure and in reaction to Christian and Muslim proselytization—do indeed echo painful lamentations similar in style and tone to the Christian corpus. Swami Śivananda referred to himself as a non-dualist, a follower of Saṃkarācārya, but the suggestions he gave to his numerous Indian and international disciples were very different indeed from the traditional monistic counsel of the orthodox monasteries. I would go even further: wherever a meditative target is conceived of as anthropomorphic, but not subject to physical change, or in other words, where divinity is contemplated as having unchanging physical features, self-pity and lamentation seem to be the order. The Christian monk's target figure is Jesus Christ, distinctly perceived as a human being in agony. The late Trappist mystic Thomas Merton once told me that he personally disliked the orthopractical advice to meditate on Christ's passion, and that he preferred the few available alternatives: the Virgin, the risen Christ, the heart of the saviour, etc. In India, the Vaiṣṇavas contemplate Viṣṇu adorned with exactly prescribed emblems, and with detailed descriptions of his looks, his smile, the posture of his body. Compare this with the Tantric schools, both in Hinduism and in Northern Buddhism. Here, the shape and the features of the target divinities are also enumerated, but they fluctuate: they change their hue, they generate other forms out of themselves, they present different emblems for progressive entry into their being. Thus, the primal goddess in the Hindu tradition is known and meditated upon in fearful guises as Kālī, Durgā, or even less pleasantly, as Chinnamastā—the goddess holding her decapitated heads in her hands, drinking up the blood which gushes forth from her headless trunk. Schools which posit these fluctuating, protean targets for enstatic meditation, present easy-going, agonyless reports in a detached, objective style. This also accounts for much of the great popularity these better known and better propagated forms of Indian meditation have achieved in the young counter-culture in the West. The hedonistic element is an integral part of the quest of the seekers of emancipation withheld from them by the "people over thirty," the churches and all the Sunday school catechisms. The *Tibetan Book of the Dead*, badly translated by Evans-Wentz, [11] is attractive to them because its uncanniness, its "way-out" message does not reject sex, it does not forbid pleasures.

Alan Watts once suggested that in another fifty years or so, people in India will drive around in cars, live in suburbia, and play baseball, whereas people in America will sit in caves in Oregon and in the Rockies and meditate on their navel and on *ātman* and *nirvāna*. This was meant to be a facetious, but forensically useful exaggeration—still, the trend is certainly there. Nothing annoys and frustrates a modern Hindu more than witnessing Europeans and Americans grow beards, wear beads, and do yoga. At my university, an Indian scholar was hired a couple of years ago to teach a course on India's ancient history. Toward the end of the term, three students came to him and announced they would be going to India shortly, to visit the holy city of Banaras, and the yogis in the Himalayan foothills. Prof. G. got quite angry. "Why you want to visit at those dirty places? Why do you not visit Bhakra Nangal Dam and Damodar Valley and Bhilai Steel Plant?" The boys replied that there were oodles of steel plants and power dams in the States, but there were no temples and yogis, and there was no quest for *nirvāna* in America.

This discussion epitomizes a trend. The modern Indian has problems of self-representation and cultural self-assessment. He knows that the West, in the anti-war and anti-establishment strivings of its youth, is turning for guidance to the East. He also knows that those in real power in the East cannot give such guidance, since they reject the yogic ways as superstitious, responsible for India's backwardness. Yet the modern Hindu stresses the uniqueness of the Hindu tradition, including yoga. Over the past forty years or so, modern Hindus have developed a strange dialectic of dissimulation. They claim, and perhaps believe, that all the hardware, the technological equipment and the scientific know-how of the West was not western in origin, but was Indian, many thousands of years ago. They adduce the

127

Rāmāyaṇa, the Mahābhārata, and other ancient texts which do indeed mention strange contraptions flying through the air, and weaponry that kills thousands at once. All this is then said to have happened 20,000 years ago, and archaeological arguments against such a possibility are summarily rejected as misguided occidental propaganda. Modern Hindus tend to admire Hitler— first, because he was a leader of the Germans, who have the closest link with India's legendary past; second, he spoke of Aryans and selected the *svastika*, a sun symbol of great sanctity in all indigenous Indian religious traditions, as the emblem for his party; next—this sounds funny to orientalists and Sanskritists—the Germans supposedly know Sanskrit much better than anyone except the Indians themselves (Sanskrit is thought to be taught in high schools and German, as a language, is closer to Sanskrit, they believe, than any other non-Indian speech!) *Etically*, all this is incredible nonsense; but *emically*, it is now part of a defensive parlance in India.

There is a widening gap between the actual mystical efforts of the more *engagé* cultists in occidental countries and the actual efforts of modern Hindus who articulate their concern with religion and its workings for the individual. If we sample the student population of an Indian university, and the student population of an equally large American or European university, it will be seen that there is a considerably higher percentage of Euro-American students who actually do engage in yogic exercise. Indian students of orthodox background, rural or urban, perform some minimal religious observances during their college days. Meditation in the mystical context, however, is supererogatory from the standpoint of the official religion; and this holds true for the Judaeo-Christian-Islamic as well as the Hindu world. The matter is different with Buddhists, since in theory at least there is no observance other than meditation aiming at mystical consummation, *nirvāna*. This is one of the more irritating things in modern Hindu discourse with other people: *yoga* and other esoteric wisdoms are talked about, the monks and the other gurus of the Hindu Renaissance are listened to and quoted, but their votaries do not really meditate. They *talk* about meditation. This also holds for modern monks whose professed job it is to meditate. When I was a novice at the Advaita Ashrama, the publication center of the Ramakrishna Order in the Central Himalayas, I noticed that only two out of roughly a dozen fellow monks and novices actually meditated in the mornings, the official time for meditation. I took this part of the monastic life very seriously, thinking that this was what I had come for. Yet it was resented by my fellow monastics. The matter is very different in the orthodox monastic orders—I have seen literally hundreds of monks of all ages in the monastic centers in India, who spend roughly half of their waking time—half of twenty hours, that is, since they sleep only four hours a night—in solid meditation. The paradox is complete: American and European youngsters who have been attracted to Indian and other Asian contemplative lore—albeit through bad translations, itinerant yogis, the drug culture, and sexual freedom—often meditate. Few of them have been to India to obtain formal training and initiation. Some have been given some sort of *dīkṣā* [12] by ordained monks in India. Not more than a dozen genuine Indian monks who traveled in the West have been giving *dīkṣā*, but those have been very successful in spreading their skills; witness Maharishi Mahesh Yogi's "transcendental meditation" with classes in virtually all larger American and British cities, and with chapters on all the university campuses I have seen over the past several years. All this illustrates the paradox facetiously presaged by Alan Watts: it is the young occidentals who do the meditation; among culturally concerned, motivated Hindus, meditation itself is not practiced to support the pep talk, "the East is spiritual, the West is materialistic."

A person has now had a zero-experience, or he has heard and read about it and is impressed. What does he do? Very different things. There are different schools with rules of various degrees of rigor. Meditational traditions which prescribe a gradual, well defined set of physical and cognitive activities, and which provide highly formulated guidelines for peripheral behavior—food, dress, sexual demeanor—and which reject attempts at sudden advances toward the zero-state are aesthetically the least attractive. They seem to appeal to the greatest number of people, since most people are conformists, and accept supererogatory behavior as representing orthodox behavior. Why are the most laborious, intrinsically unpleasant, pedantic, joyless methods the orthodox ones? Because "important things are hard to come by; real consummation is the result of real effort," etc. None of these explanations has ever convinced anyone who did not want to be convinced. The reasons for the symbiosis of orthodoxy and orthopraxis seem to lie deeply embedded in ideology and in *power*. At a time when a religious system has reached its plateau, when its clergy or its ecclesiastic institutions are firmly ensconced, it is the professional spokesman for the system whose voice is most audible, since it is he who has access to the people (even though a village may have its special village saint or rebel). Gradual, strenuous, orthopractical training is the least likely to rock the boat. The processes of gradual training toward mystical ends are so time-absorbing, so highly formalized, and so schedule-bound, that the disciples have neither the time nor the energy to get funny ideas. Danger to the religious establishment comes from heretics, from people who dispute the official claim that the laborious way is the only one, or even the best. When I learned Latin and Greek as a lad in the Viennese *Gymnasium*, I often wondered why they fed us the most incredibly boring texts. In later years Latin scholars explained the persistence of Caesar in the face of less pedantic, more pleasant alternatives: Caesar is important, tough, historical, serious; he inculcates virtues a young man must have. The *Priapica* of Martial are lewd; they would ruin the young man's mind as lewdness had wrecked the Roman Empire. So, the religious establishment, where it recognizes mysticism, prescribes tough, boring, gradual, laborious, inspectible methods. I recall a heated conversation with Prof. V. Raghavan. I was then just getting interested in Tantrism and in the short-cut or "leap" types [13] of mystical behavior. Raghavan said no, there is no short-cut; a man must perform his prescribed daily ritual, must keep pure in mind and body, must eat the proper diet, must follow the prescribed lengthy meditations—and then, without any additional doings, he will find eschatological fulfillment at the end of his life and not be reborn. The implication was that even the orthodox Yoga, to which we shall turn later, the Patañjali system of meditation and ecstasy, are not really welcome, since that too teaches a short-cut.

Similarly, Christian doctrine that permits mysticism emphasizes the hard way. Whether we look into an old monastic *regula* or into the works of Zaehner, Underhill, and other apologists, the hard and long way, the publicly inspectible way is the good way. Where mystics have come to terms with the official powers controlling religion, and use ecstatic simile, it is quickly pointed out that their talk about ecstasies and delights is metaphorical. Why is it that neither rabbinical nor Christian sermon ever uses the Song of Solomon as a point of departure? The official metaphors, the beauteous woman being the Church, the lover being Jesus, etc. are far-fetched. It is so much safer to schedule uncontroversial passages. The Father in Heaven bestows compassion upon the people, he issues rewards, but just what the rewards are is not pointed out, and if the point is pressed, the answers are banal: peace on earth, good family relations, but not things the mystic thinks about and advocates when he relates ecstasy and when he lives it. The official teachings of the world discriminate against sex, and most of them discriminate against woman: none of the extant religions with a written tradition has priestesses. With an amazing diffusion among otherwise very different world views, the distrust and the patent suspicion of woman as the paradigm of sex, as the giver of extreme delight, pervades all ecclesiastically sanctioned methods of mystical intuition. There are recognized woman-mystics in all orthodox traditions—Gārgī in Vedic literature, Mirabai in historical, late medieval India, and Teresa of Avila. But once these ladies achieved zero-condition, they immediately rejected their feminine domain and reiterated the male value system, the male mystical language, aiding and abetting systematic suspicion against woman, not against men who would, one might think pose the same threat to a female ascetic. Ramakrishna constantly chirped that the two central impediments to spiritual progress were *kāminī kāñcana* "woman and gold." I think the gold part of it did not really bother him, since there was not much of it to go around anyway—it alliterates nicely with *kāminī*; but it was woman that bothered him. Some of his wilder, more hip disciples emphasized his non-orthodox practices, the tantric phase of his career. But a thorough study of the literature about him (all *emic* literature compiled by his disciples and admirers) leaves no doubt that he supported the hard way eventually—asceticism, chastity, intensive alliance to the theological norm as he understood it.

The orthodox methods of mystical effort are easily enumerated. First, there is the insistence on physical discipline and on theological study. Second, there is the ruling of social selectivity, which means either withdrawal from society in general or restriction to a specialized sub-society—the monastery, the *sangha*,[14] and all sorts of *retraits*. Next, as a corollary to selective withdrawal, there is the injunction of sexual continence. And lastly, there are certain dietetic rules. "Physical discipline" in the first clause does not mean sexual continence and dietetic rules, which had to be listed separately; it means quite literally a physical posture, highly regularized daily routines, fewer hours of sleep than common people, the seeking of bare minima for physical support, the renunciation of comfort—a hard cot rather than a bed, the forest rather than a lavatory, the ice cold river rather than a warm bath. Yet discipline does not mean the practice of sports or other formal physical activity of that genre. In some para-monastic institutions in India, we find regular gymnasia where young men do pushups, knee-bends, and other calesthenic exercise.

Some of them may belong to an ascetic organization, and there is an overall notion in India that traditional gymnastics—which exclude tennis, golf, hockey and imported sports—aid spiritual growth. But these apply to the sacerdotal rather than to the mystical segment in India; the brahmin caste *pahlwān*, the wrestler at the court of the Maharaja of Banaras, is honored by people as a good man, even as a potentially saintly man, but he does not have the charisma of the sadhu, the monk, whom popular opinion identifies with the mystic.

Despite the diffusion of meditative techniques we should still think in terms of Indian techniques and Judaeo-Christian techniques as the two technical extremes. Islamic *sufi* meditation holds a middle position. No mystical technique today is so unique that it can not be placed on a continuum between Indian yoga techniques and Christian historical contemplation—a term which I shall explain in the sixth chapter. The various techniques, with minor modifications, are applied on any of the methodological matrices—orthodox ascetic-gradual to *laissez-faire* indulgent. Once again we encounter the erroneous, habitual ascription of one technique to one particular matrix: for at least two and a half thousand years, yogis, mendicants, and mystics have thought that the specific technique they used and transmitted to their disciples was necessarily bound to the style of life which they led and which they recommended. Again, they were and are wrong: any technique can and is used along with any style of religio-mystical life. The most arduous ascetic rule goes with *laya-yoga*, the technique of merging an imaginary secondary body inside the contemplative with the theologically stipulated godhead or absolute; and the most highly eroticized forms of lefthanded tantrism, whose followers consume spicy meat and who copulate with hierodoulic partners, apply a very similar, if not at times identical, technique of "merging." The pervasive, hitherto unchallenged, notion that a particular contemplative technique must be generated by or generate a particular life-style is as fallacious as the earlier discussed, equally pervasive notion that the mystical experience generates morality, skills, specific philosophies, and other extra-mystical qualifications.

Social selectivity is the second cross-cultural rule of all hardline, ascetic, orthodox systems. This, of course, must be the root of monasticism: a person who wants out cannot stay in. The quest for solitude is not necessarily a quest for being totally alone; in fact, the single recluse is rare in the mystical world. But it certainly means withdrawing from the market place, the assembly of men. Most important, it means with-

132

drawal from woman and children, and from parents, that is, from people who get to you systematically. Withdrawing from them cannot be done inwardly, mentally. Some Indian texts speak about and eulogize saints who contrived to live in the world, surrounded by their families, or even by regal splendor, yet remaining untouched. The "in the world but not of the world" sermon is precisely only a sermon. We should not be too impressed with modern Indian and Japanese mystics' claim that the truly great mystic is he who can move about the market place and be alone nevertheless. We have here a confusion between what is desirable and what is feasible: it would be great, no doubt, if a person who has had the zero-experience and who wants it to occur again, could go on acting as he did before he had it, or before it began to affect him. But there are hardly any mystics who do in fact go on as though nothing had happened. Some mystics dramatize their importance to society by saying that they are still with it, since it is desirable to be part of the society which harbors and feeds them. Yet the secular and the ecclesiastic-establishmentarian agents of his society are not impressed. As one whose ultimate purpose is to merge with any entity which is far removed from the concern of the non-mystical majority, the mystic cannot win them over, even though they may be listening. The Buddha, most radical of all mystical preceptors, made no compromise with society at any time. Every single one of his speeches starts with *bhikkave*, "ye begging monks"; he never addressed anyone who wanted to stay out.

The official homiletic usually holds that all men are equally entitled to mystical experience, and this would seem to imply that the mystic should be available to all. The paradox, however, is of such long standing that scarcely anyone ever challenged the saints' behavior. Monks live by themselves and to themselves, recluses live alone, and spiritual teachers are surrounded by their disciples who ward off intruders. And yet these teachers are benefactors of mankind, they are supposed to be accessible at all times like the Hebrew kings. This is a systematic confusion between the "is" and the "ought." Mystics and their disciples in unofficial reality are not available and accessible, and hagiographies from Asia and Europe are replete with tales of the ingenuity of would-be adepts who finally got to their elusive teacher. Kabir was Muslim, a low-caste weaver. He had singled out a famous brahmin mystic to be his teacher, but the man did not even let him come near, for fear of pollution by contact. So Kabir placed himself horizontally on one of the steps of the ghats in Banaras, at the hour when the saint and his disciples came to take their dip in the river; when the teacher's foot touched Kabir, he had to accept him by the complex Indian dialectic of pollution and purification. About five hundred years earlier, the South Indian brahmin saint and mystic Rāmānuja, against the advice of his guru who had impressed the secrecy of the *mantra* upon him, ascended the steps of the great shrine of Srirangam and chanted the secret *mantra* loudly, beckoning all those who would hear to join him—and they did. This and scores of similar episodes have created the notion among the apologists for mysticism that the great teachers did mix and mingle, that they were not apart, that they cared for all human beings. Again, this is wrong. The orthodox teachings, promulgated by an established, pro-mystical segment of the official agents of religion, require selectivity, even though other teachers, also established in the official tradition, speak against such seclusion. The mystic follows both these injunctions serially. When he espouses loneliness or selective contacts, he listens to those who ask him to do so; when he has achieved mystical safety, those people no longer speak to him, and the others, whose mission entails criticizing selectivity and eulogizing gregariousness, become his new guides. In the traditions known to me, these shifts occur informally. As if to compensate for this lack of official assignments, we find a large number of make-believe hierarchies and successive initiations into ever greater mysteries. This is the case with such very different organizations as the Freemasons, the *bkah rgyud pa* school of Tibetan Buddhism, and certain sectarian groups in India. Such fakeries of this century as the White Brotherhood in the Himalayas, invented by Blavatsky the arch-witch, have become more real to many hippies and to many non-hip seekers of ultimate wisdom than the actually existing, but somewhat unexalted monastic and contemplative organizations in India or the Tibetan monks accessible in Europe and America since 1960.

The most fascinating problem about orthodox mysticism in the cross-cultural setting is its strictures on sex. Here, remarkably similar if not identical arguments are presented by otherwise totally heterogeneous traditions. I can phrase these restrictions in a manner that would be acceptable to any of the official, hardline mystical formulae anywhere in the world, and during any era including our own; more than that, I think I could so phrase it that no proponent of any of these traditions whould notice that they were not written by a spokesman of his specific school. Here is such a perennial formulation: "Sex is necessary for mankind, since it is the way in which mankind replenishes itself. For the mystic, however, it is to be avoided totally, or restricted to the bare minimum in case he or she has yet to beget or bear children to fulfill society's behest. But sex is spiritually debilitating, it weakens the body, it weakens the mind, and it weakens the meditative thrust which gets the mystic to his spiritual consummation. Chastity is obligatory, in action, words, and thought."

None of these premises has ever been challenged by orthodox mystics and their mentors, or even put into doubt by the literary, philosophical, and ideological apologists for the mystic. Those who did criticize and eventually reject the postulate of chastity were votaries of unorthodox mystical methods which we shall discuss shortly. The simple test for hardline attitudes toward sex is the official reaction toward infringement of chastity rules. Other transgressions are pardoned, by and large, when the proper dialectic supports the defense. Mystics have been punished and pardoned for sloppiness, lying, even for stealing or hurting other people. But sexual acts are not forgiven, unless they have occurred in the acknowledged service of a further consummatory goal. The Egyptian Mary—who may or may not have been a mystic—offers her body to the oarsman to take her across to the holy site; her action is justified. Yet this tale is a rare one, not paralleled in Christian hagiography. A Chinese woman-bodhisattva [15] observed the overriding importance of compassion by immediately responding to all sexual advances. Hers is probably a non-orthodox case and one would have to tabulate orthodox Chinese Buddhist response to this story.

Let me add at this point that the founders' documented attitudes are not decisive in this situation. Buddha said to the monk who asked him what he should do if a lovely woman got into his view. "Don't look at her," the Enlightened One replied. "What if I have already looked at her?" "Don't let your mind hover around her body." "What if my mind has already hovered around her body?" "Don't let your body get near her." "What if my body has already gotten near her?" "Don't embrace her." "What if I have already embraced her?" "Don't ejaculate." "What if I have already ejaculated?" "Don't look next time." Founders tend to be more liberal than their official votaries in later days. Jesus talked to all sorts of strange people, the woman at the well and other people with problems; and he never raised a moralizing finger at the numerous whores and bores he talked to. But it is not the founders who fortify the ecclesiastic institutions; men of lesser mystical prowess and

greater managerial skills do that. Managers must be moralists—
you cannot hold the shop together if people go off on a tangent,
meditating, fornicating, taking drugs, and doing other things
which make them autonomous rather than cooperative. It is a
long way from a usually kindly, non-punitive Christ to a stern,
obnoxious Dr. Calvin who forbade women in Geneva to have
more than one dress. Ideally, mystics should be founders as
well; but aware of the tedium that goes with organization and
management they do not create institutions and fail to interfere
wth the managers even though they seem to condone the
travesties of institutionalization and commercialization.

The dietetic rules for the mystic are not properly universal
sanctions since they are self-imposed and idiosyncratic. The
Bhagavadgītā, in what I regard as its silliest portion, establishes
a taxonomy of foods and what they do to a person's spirit.
Milk, sugar, ghee (clarified butter)—in short, all the heavenly
dull things—give *sattva* or luminous, brilliant, pious,
meditative power; meat, spices, hot stuff, curries—all the more
interesting things the Indian cuisine has to offer—give passion,
heroic powers, physical strength, anger; and stale, putrid
things—which would probably include camembert and
gorgonzola—make the mind slothful, the person lazy. Instead
of veering away from this pedantic tract, modern Hindus make
it a point to call it "scientific," and I have had to face literally
hundreds of protests against my un-swami-like tastes in food
and drink in India. The hip culture in America insists on having
the proper amount of *yin* food and the proper amount of *yang*
food; one consists of nut bread, nuts, and other cereals, the
other of juicier things. Then there is the macrobiotic and other
diets, some of which are potential killers, others more or less
harmless nuisances. The *etic* fact is that food and drink do not
do much to the mind, unless of course one thinks they do; for
then psychosomatics take over and the nutriment intake does
affect people. I am talking about food and non-alcoholic
beverages, for it goes without saying that getting drunk does
not aid meditation and the mystical experience.

I now turn to the less rigid but also less orthodox methods
of mysticism. Between the two extremes—total orthodoxy
and total heresy or heterodoxy, signified by experimentation
without reference to, or often in defiance of any textual or
traditional guidance—we have a large number of intermediate
methods.

From its original home in Southern Central Asia, the
Naqśbandi sect of Muslim sufism spread well into Northern
India within a hundred years of its inception. The orthodox

'ulema circles of the Muslim population rejected and rebuked the Naqśbandi sufis for the sin of laxity, of not performing the prayers regularly, and worse, the setting up of partners for Allah in the process of achieving identity with the divine. But the Northwest Indian Muslim population and many village folks in what is now Afghanistan and Baluchistan took to the Naqśbandi mystics as kindly tellers of stories, singers of songs, and religious entertainers, who gave reprieve and respite from the stern commands of orthodox Islam. The Naqśbandi mystics smoked *cannabis*—but this was the lay style of the area, and it was only the outsider who took notice of it. In Northern India, where Hindus had been eating and drinking *cannabis* quite openly on certain festivals like Holi, and for more general relaxation, the sufis' way of taking *cannabis* appeared as strange at first. Until the sixteenth century smoking was identified with being foreign, Muslim, hence ritualistically polluted. Indians prepared *cannabis* as a decoction and churned it with sherbet, milk, or other drinks, or else ate it with *pān*, the ubiquitous betel leaf. The Turk rulers of Delhi and the later Moghuls fortified their alcoholic beverages with hemp derivatives. This, thought the Hindu at and around the Muslim rulers' courts, accounted for their wild, rapist attitudes.

If we look into Naqśbandi literature, and listen to the present-day heirs of the tradition in Sindh and in the Multan District of West Pakistan, a totally different story emerges. It is true that the Naqśbandi mystics, so their followers say, flaunted their independence from the official narrow rules of Islam, and shocked the orthodox with unorthodox talk and behavior; they spoke about sexual love as similar to divine love; they spoke about the irrelevance of formal prayer and of food restrictions, but without actually breaking the Islamic food laws. And they did smoke hashish—but so did other Muslims, perfectly orthodox people in the area. The Naqśbandi mystics, who had reached the highest state of ecstasy, *mārafat*, felt they were no longer bound by the strictures imposed on the laity, and they said so. It was this that people resented. Also, the *murīds* and *mursīds*, i.e. the initiates and the initiands, kept some of their disciplines secret—not because there was anything obscene, forbidden, or objectionable in them, but because they felt that random revealing of these things would bring harm to the laity. This follows the Indian example which surrounds the later Naqśbandis on South Asian soil: the pervasive notion of *adhikāra*, of spiritual entitlement, was part of the Hindu-Buddhist esoteric traditions. But the Naqśbandis' convention of initiatory secrecy backfired. It appears that their practice was quite moderate compared with those of radical lefthanded Hindu and Buddhist ritual, and really no different from such fully respectable eastern Muslim practices as *dhikr*, the constant repetition of God's names. The fact, however, that some of the things which orthodox Muslims did in a non-religious context, especially the smoking of hashish, was incorporated into the preparatory exercises of the Order, and that all this was kept a secret from the general public, gave them the name and the fame of religious radicals and heretics.

By this same process, I think, Jesus Christ and his disciples were rejected by the orthopractical Jews. His teachings were not so radically different; other preachers in his own days and considerably earlier taught more radical ideas, partly under Hellenic, partly under farther eastern influence. But his self-sponsored image as a renovator, the cliquishness of his close disciples, and his flaunting of independence worked against him. Asked by Pilate what his teachings were, he said what he had always been preaching in public, in the precincts of the School and in the Temple. Pilate, of course, couldn't care less. His counter-query "what is truth" should not be understood in the manner of simple Christian catechetes; it was a sarcastic, perfectly friendly rebuttal of Jesus's claim that he taught the Truth—an agnostic's rebuttal inspired by the philosophical relativism of educated Hellas and Rome.

Clearly, then, most of the mystical methods exemplified by persons in all the written traditions held a midway position along the orthodox-radical continuum. Their censure by the official powers, secular or ecclesiastic, was partly in response to the secrecy the mystics themselves observed.

Finally, we have the genuinely experimental, radical, usually heretical types of mystical method. The most salient example, of course, is lefthanded tantrism, which I have analyzed elsewhere in *The Tantric Tradition*. Here, what religious plebeians decry as filthy and foul is precisely what the initiate may use as nuclear to his discipline. Assigning blame either to the initiates who do certain things or to the vulgar laity who call these things wicked and sacrilegious is everyone's business in India. The apologetic dialectic of lefthanded practices is part of the *emic* parlance of one religious vision in India and in Tibet before the Chinese takeover. Lefthanded tantrics do indeed use ritualistic copulation—which is not make-believe, "symbolic" intercourse as the more liberal critics in India and Tibet thought. It is actual sexual congress used for the enstatic purpose. The core of the lefthanded tantric practice can be summarized rather briefly: while the orthodox Hindu and Buddhist doctrines stipulate that the mind and the senses have to be submerged, "killed" as the Indian vernacular puts it if union is to be achieved, the lefthanded tantrics say that the contrary is true for them: if you "kill" the mind and the senses, you kill the whole system, and nothing is achieved. They therefore harness the mind and the senses, and channel full erotic and other sensuous action toward the supreme goal, which is ecstatic to the outsider, enstatic to the insider. Sporadically, we have found such radical experimentalists in other parts of the world. There are hippie and kindred communes in North America now which use ritualistic copulation, with or, as in the old Oneida Community, without ejaculation, as part of their discipline.

The early Christian Agape, the "love feast," obviously inculcated some sort of radical mystical practice centering on a sacralized sexual act. I believe that some Christian mystics practiced copulatory methods between and around their zero-experiences, or in some cases, that copulatory processes triggered the zero-states. However, since there were hardly any known Christian mystics until this century who were not ordained monks or priests, any statements made by them or about them would eschew direct reference to such procedures. The official Christian establishment being hardline, ascetical mystagogy, mystics were part of the personnel, part of the ecclesiastic establishments. Hence, if some of them did practice a more radical type of mystical discipline, they would either keep it to themselves or so camouflage it with metaphor that the actual events could not be unambiguously presented. I think that very little about the type of mysticism practiced by individual Christian saints.can be inferred from their mystical writings. John of the Cross and the Spanish Teresa wrote a highly erotic, but metaphorical language, and I doubt that either of them underwent the radical experiment which I classify as the most antithetical to the official line. On the other hand, Christian mystics who did experiment radically might have chosen not to exceed acceptable statements, lest they be exposed, and probably prevented from working out their method. Above all, mystics—this writer not excluded—find access to the apparatus controlled by the agents of orthodoxy useful. In other words, whatever the mystic's own intuition and method, if he happens to be part of the orthodox establishment by his ordination or by some other form of membership, he will try not to alienate the orthodox agents. Though many martyrs have been mystics, most mystics are no martyrs; those who were, were so by accident. I don't think Meister Eckhart planned to spend his last years in the dungeon of his monastery. It so happens that he said the wrong things at the wrong time, but not with the depressing perseverance genuine martyrs display—people, I think, who have little but martyrdom to fall back upon, when the chips are down.

Mystical methods, then, are all good methods if they provide the goods: if they lead to the zero-experience, if they help it to re-occur, and if they bridge the gap between zero-experiences. Throughout this book, I have insisted that we treat mysticism in its own right, because it is a phenomenon that can well stand alone devoid of the artificial or historical accretions which have been attached to it so long. It becomes a pragmatic question: "good" is understood as "leading to zero-experience" and "bad" as "not leading to zero-experience." Proceeding to the chapter on the ethnography of mysticism today, we shall encounter mystics and their schools who have used instruments—drugs, sex, etc.—which all but their own flock call bad and refuse to connect with the mystic's quest.

Chapter Six

The Ethnography of Mysticism

Emile Durkheim once said that anyone who studied "religion" really studied one specific religion. Modern social sciences bear him out. What is taught in North American College Departments of Religion is either Christianity (the implicit assumption of the people who endow such chairs being that students will see the light), or else surveys of other religions under such course titles as "comparative religion," "religions of the world." No one can just teach "religion," he teaches one or the other religions, even when he thinks he teaches some sort of a universal religion, with no denominational strings attached. The simple fact remains that there is no principle underlying all religions, except some trivial ones: all religions teach to be good, to arrange life properly, to establish proper contacts with divinity or with some divinity surrogate.[1]

What about mysticism? Is there such a thing as a universal mysticism, which could be taught, understood, and absorbed without reference to any overarching religious system? Since I defined a mystic in two specific ways, incorporating all known types of mystical practice under a single scope, did that not mean that there was really but one mysticism, in contrast to "religion," of which there are many? There is indeed one mystical experience, the zero-experience. But "mysticism" means the experience *and* its interpretation, *and* the events which surround the experience and the interpretation—private events, social events, doctrinal events. Since these events are different in different places with different histories, mysticisms are different. On this level of analysis, we do indeed single out some specific phase of the world's religions, and analyze it in cross-cultural, cross-denominational perspective; e.g. the religious leader as charismatic, the rites of passage, shamans, priests, etc. Mysticism and the mystic are such single topics within the study of religion. We must see how they work in different cultural milieux.

There is such a thing as primitive mysticism. Levi-Bruhl spoke of *participation mystique*, postulating that the primitive mind does not comprehend the dichotomy between the self and nature around it—it identifies with nature, and this is part of the operation of the primitive mind. This was a totally false assumption. Subsequent investigators who actually studied "natives," not from Paris, but from the bush, learnt that there was no "primitive" language compared to any other language. But it is a fact that people in primitive societies, like people in other societies, have zero-experiences. A primitive society, by anthropological criteria, is a small, band-like society structured entirely on kinship lines, a society which does not deploy fulltime specialists for anything. Now the question of whether persons in such societies find it easier to come by, repeat, and communicate zero-experiences than people in more complex societies, cannot be answered, because we know too few mystics in too few primitive societies.

What about large-scale, literate, subsistence level agricultural societies such as those of India, China, the Middle East? We know that they generate many mystics. But we know today that western societies generate quite a few mystics too. At this moment, we cannot say at all which type of society has a higher proportion of mystics.

We reject any paper, at learned conferences, which discusses the "origin of religion," just as linguistic conventions reject presentations on the "origin of language," and physicists' conventions reject papers on a *perpetuum mobile*. The many theories of the origin of religion, propounded over the last hundred years, are delightful reading, but unacceptable, not because they cannot be proved—each of them can—but because they can not be disproved even in theory. In matters of scientific feasibility, Sir Karl Popper's dictum still stands: for a statement, or a theory, to be negotiable, it has to be verifiable and falsifiable. Whether religion rose from fear or from joy, from awe or from not being able to answer questions—we cannot know. We can, however, investigate the origins of any specific kind of religious behavior, if we have valid clues to go by, such as scriptures, priestly traditions, archaeological finds. We can also try to find the origin of any specific mysticism. But we cannot find the origin of "primitive" mysticism, since primitive societies are defined in part as having no written literature. The memory of the primitive society's lore is exactly as old as the memory of the oldest man—and that is not very old.

Zero-experiences are natural experiences. They come to some persons everywhere with no regard to their background. But the events which accompany the zero-experiences have

142

their styles. Individual and popular reactions, sermons, circum-experiential behavior—these are clusters that differ from place to place. We can speak of a Hindu mystical style, a Southern Buddhist mystical style, a Christian mystical style. In theory at least, it should then be possible to trace diffusion of mystical styles. Historians and students of comparative religion may see similarities in the mystical life which cannot be accidental where cultural contact was possible. The Central Asian and Persian sufis were thorns in the eyes of the 'ulema, and the deportment of the mystics from that area was so much closer to that tof the Indian yogis, that some connection with the Indian mystical traditions seems obtrusively present even before documents can be traced to verify the existence of such links. In our own day, of course, diffusion is no longer any problem. Indian swamis travel a good deal, and American seekers travel even more since they can afford to. Tons of popular mystical literature are printed and shipped from East to West. It is quite clearly the mark of the swami that is seen in the communes all over the American continent and in Europe.

The mystic offers a broad target for the practice of psychological speculation. My approach is anti-psychological, or rather anti-Freudian. No problem goes away when it is given a name. Fear, lust, bad mama or good mama, lecherous or impotent father—the mystic remains a mystic, he has zero-experiences, he thinks about them, talks about them—and the psychological etiology of the experience leaves him cold. Speculations about the profit or the loss which the mystical experience renders to the mystic seem to be off the mark, since the zero-experience has no caveats: a person may reject it, but if he doesn't, it is just there. If a person who has the experience dislikes it, he can of course have it analyzed out of him. I am interested in the mystic's deeds, in his delights, and in the inherent dangers. But these dangers are among the things which the mystic courts: he might well want to be what other people call insane, if sanity precludes ecstasy.

I shall investigate two geographical areas—South Asia and Euro-America. There are important mystical things happening in Japan and in the Islamic world, but I know nothing about them. The ethnography of mysticism must be a selective study or else an encyclopaedia. India and Euro-America are the areas where the action is, and is going to be, mystically speaking. The direction of the flow has been from India to the West so far, but there are signs of a reversal. The secular leaders of India want to eschew the mystical along with other progress-retarding things of India's past; but the young in the lands which have the very goods the Indian leadership wants for India are turning their eyes and their ears to India. Just as the once-despised pizza made its victorious way back into Italy from America, having been embellished by anchovies, pepperoni and other riches it did not originally possess, so yoga and mysticism, meditation and long hair, ruled out as old fashioned and superstitious by the secular leaders of modern India, may re-enter if long hair and meditation should take over the American scene.

The shaman is something like bread and butter to the anthropologist who works on religion in primitive societies. In my reviews of anthropological publications of the last decade I have found that no less than 30% of all publications on primitive religion concentrate on the shaman and his deeds. The shaman is a part-time religious or magical practitioner. Primitive societies cannot deploy fulltime specialists since everyone has to fend for his tribe's life along with his own; a separate religious job is economically unfeasible. Either by his own choice, by inheritance from some elder, by visions, by psycho-somatic conditions which western psychiatry must regard as pathological, the shaman contacts the spirit world, rides out into heaven, climbs up a spirit ladder, carries messages from the superhuman powers to his people, sometimes detects witches and other things that have gone awry, and occasionally works as a curer. He is not a priest, since he lacks moral persuasion. His job has no moral overtones; whatever fault he points out is of ritualistic omission.

Does the shaman qualify as a mystic? *Etically* speaking, I think some do. Assuming that the ontological status of the spirits and the ghosts he contacts is about the same as the ontological status of the God seen in the Desert, we must infer that the shaman generates the spirits and divinities from within himself—for where else could he get them from? He does not usually identify the spirits and the gods—but neither does the Christian mystic. He, like the latter, interprets his experience: he must speak to the spirits or they may speak through him to his village. Now in some cases, the shaman and other members of the tribe identify him with some spirit. There is no reason to doubt that many shamans have zero-experiences, which they interpret shamanistically, much as the Christian mystic must interpret his experience dualistically.

Most shamans are not mystics. They perform their jobs—mediating between the spirits of the tribe and its members, divining, curing, without having had or without seeking zero-experiences. They parallel the non-mystical saints in the Mediterranean religions. As I have shown, many saints

144

were not mystics; they led a supremely virtuous life, and so far as the canonizing agency went, they qualified. No council in Rome concerned itself with zero-experiences. Three bonafide miracles have to be wrought by the candidate for sainthood; or, if he or she has been martyred, sainthood is automatic. Having had the mystical experience was never a criterion for canonization. Similarly, the shaman must provide the stipulated goods, for unlike a priest who has the "charisma of office," as Max Weber put it, the shaman must have personal charisma; if he does not deliver the goods his society drops him as a shaman. Priests have no such problem. A man may be a bad preacher, but his priesthood cannot be removed; for the Catholic, there is no such thing as saying the mass *badly*, since whether the priest is a Thomas Aquinas or a semi-literate village yokel, the wafer is substantiated into the host as he pronounces *hoc est corpus*. But neither personal charisma nor charisma of office qualifies the shaman or the priest as a mystic. Among the Santhals in the Chotanagpur District of northeastern India, I met several shamans. At least two of them were genuine mystics. They had not been Hinduized—they certainly had not heard about the teachings of monistic Vedānta. But they had had their zero-experiences—they had *merged*. Both interpreted their experiences as professional shamans: "the *bonga* (the Santhal divinity) sat on my chest, went into my chest, and then I was the *bonga* for a day—I could not do anything—but then the *bonga* left me, and I had his powers—I could drive away the fever."

Among the Indians of the North American Plains, it is the custom for the young men to go into solitude and stay alone, with the barest amount of clothing and food, to find their guardian spirit. It may appear to them in the form of an animal, of a person, of a stone that speaks. Some field workers assure us, that Plains Indians come to believe after some years, that as youths they actually encountered their spirit, forgetting that they had not really seen the spirit. Are the spirit visions of a mystical sort frequent even today in American Indian society? It is hard to say on the basis of the reports, because anthropologists so far have not distinguished between different kinds of non-discursive human experiences. Spirit visions reported to an anthropologist are likely to be noted down as "mystical." There is no reason to doubt, however, that the proportion of mystical experiences within the spirit quest is fairly high, simply because such encounters are sought by *all* males in the tribe. The quest for any ecstatic experience, when modally pursued in a society, yields a greater number of the mystical events. Zero-experiences may accompany a more or less organized, institutionalized quest for the superhuman, or the ecstatic. Unless the member of an Indian tribe or any "primitive" identified himself as one who has sought some sort of union with the spirits, he would not qualify as a mystic. If this study has an effect on social anthropologists and people who study other cultures in the field, some might want to investigate whether tribally encouraged visionary experiences are mystical in part: whether, for example, persons in the tribe declare, in their language, that they have found union with some being and that they want to find such union again. The Plains Indians, at least as far as has been reported, do not seem to look for repeated spirit encounters; only their shamans do, this being their vocation. I would then claim that there are indeed mystics among the shamans in primitive societies.

If some shamans are mystics these primitive mystics are not any nobler than other primitives, nor is their wisdom of a different order from that of mystics belonging to literate regions. The only question that could be seriously investigated and answered is that of the shaman's tribesmen's reactions to his mystical experience. We might find that primitive people's reactions to an uninterrupted mystical experience, told by any of their tribal members or by their shamans, are much more matter-of-fact than the reactions of literate societies toward their professed mystics. Members of primitive societies I have seen do not seem to react with too much awe or amazement at anything that happens with a precedent in their setting: people have seen spirits, curers have cured snakebite, witches have been discovered and subdued, so why should there not be people who experience identity with some gods or with whatever powerful being there is?

The gap between epistemological and ontological systems is very small indeed in non-literate societies; it is small not because such people have not the intelligence to see such difference, but because no one in their surroundings misconstrued nature by bad linguistic speculation. The primitive does more or less what Wittgenstein and the earlier Ayer recommended: they do not misuse language. They use it to denote and connote things that have, to them, ontological existence. Gods and spirits and witches are quite as real, ontologically, as the deer that is hunted or the chief who is entertained. Literate societies and the nations which have generated written religions seem to have done penance for their hypertrophical theologies by dissecting the universe into *what is* —ontology—and *what might be thought of as being*—

146

epistemology. Of course, primitive man understands all these things if you tell him, or if you send him to school. Being primitive is simply the result of not going to formal schools, and not listening to theologies reinforced and complicated by a literary corpus. Meyer Fortes,[2] Evans-Pritchard[3] and other famous anthropologists have shown that primitives often have very complex theologies. On closer inspection, these are merely long, well remembered, annotated stories with intricate plots. The story teller prides himself on remembering complicated stories—the narrator in a literate society can check them in books, hence he does not have to generate theological innovations by himself. Kluckhohn reported that the Navaho singer[4] has to learn songs by heart which total, in size, the score of Wagner's *Ring*. In some societies, it costs prospective candidates for the shamanistic or the curer's office a great deal to obtain training and initiation. In others among the Chukchee in Siberia, entrance into the profession is bound up with prolonged states of acute ill-health. In still others epileptic fits—or rather, a kind of behavior which modern medicine would call "epileptic" is the condition for eligibility to the shamanistic or the curer's office.

Now mysticism is no such "office" at all. In primitive, shamanistic societies, initiation or independent entrance on the basis of visions, signs, and other phenomena is not due to one's interaction with or instruction by another person; mystics do not owe their zero-experience to any such interaction, not any more than some mystics in the western world "owe" their experience to the use of LSD[5] or psilocybin. The shamanistic office sets the scene where a shaman can be a mystic; the structure of the band-like, unspecialized society may trigger zero-experiences due to a more direct contact with the earth and nature in general, without the interposing of the game-plans of more complex societies. It is possible that the presence of a priestly order may also work as an inhibiting factor, even though there may be a high priority for meditation in such societies. In a primitive, shamanistic society, no person has to clear his experiences with anyone. He may have listeners, to whom he is just an amusing man, a storyteller, an entertainer. In an ecclesiastic society, however, his experiences would not be taken as just stories. They would be checked against rules and standards set by others—priests, clerks, and perhaps prior mystics. The shaman has no precedents to go by; he can start afresh, untrammeled by rules and conventions of precedence. His audience, the people in his tribe, may or may not take his tales of union seriously as part of his shamanistic visions, but no one would make any fuss about it. If he, as a shaman, keeps delivering the goods—contacting the spirits, reporting on things going on in the upper and nether worlds, things which concern his society, if he can find witches and advise on therapy—the means by which he came to acquire these forces are quite irrelevant to the people. They do not know heresy, they do not know about different styles of reporting and interpreting.

Among the Ojibwa Indians of Wisconsin and Minnesota, there is a dreaded "disease," the *windigo* or *wittiko*, which has provided much material for psychiatrists and anthropologists.[6] *Etically* described, it would be a sort of tribal localized cannibalism of some individuals. The *windigo* is a grotesque looking, enormous child- and adult-devouring ghost (male or female) that roams the forests. If he appears to an unwary man, he may enter and possess him. If that man does not have the proper magical protection and the spiritual resources to fend off such evil, he will become a *windigo* or, to translate the Ojibwa phrase, "he will be Windigo." People have not only confessed to being *windigo*, some have flaunted the fact. Ojibwa society reacts to such avowal in stereotypic ways, by isolating, prosecuting, but also by revering such a person. Police and court reports of the nineteenth and early twentieth centuries showed however that self-confessed *windigos* could not be prosecuted, since no person was missing anywhere. What obviously happened was that the peron imagined, day-dreamed, or dreamed that he was a *windigo*, and such statement of self-identification sufficed for the unacculturated Ojibwa to point him out as *windigo*. Now this is a strange, somewhat isolated type, yet highly relevant to us. For by the criteria I suggested, identification with a non-human agency, union with a superhuman being, plus the declaration of having experienced such union, constitutes being a mystic. The Ojibwa *windigo*, whether a shaman or an ordinary tribal member, is a mystic, a mystic who does not do any good to himself and to his society, except perhaps in the somewhat far-fetched elliptical manner suggested by Durkheim.[7] But remember that social, ethical, and other attributes, and the experiencer's operations in society, are no part of the definition of a mystic.

I now proceed to the Indian situation, which, together with the sections on contemporary Euro-American mysticism, constitutes the ethnographic focus of this study. I have, as a full-time critic of Indian culture, made more enemies in India by stating that yoga and its corollaries were the only uniquely Indian contribution to the spiritual and cultural achievements of the world, than with any other statement. The other writing societies of the world have had equally powerful literature, sculpture, architecture, theology and philosophy. But there is this one thing which India has created and systematized, and which it has given to the world. The history of the spread of Buddhism from India in all directions between 300 B.C. and 800 A.D. and, in the last fifty years the diffusion of certain modified forms of Hinduism and Buddhism to the western world demonstrate this diffusion.

Why did the various doctrines of rebirth originate in India, why were they codified there and nowhere else? The answer that the tropical climate, the constant vision of rapid growth and decay and new growth on the foundations of decay must have made Indians think that way is marvelously naif. Around the entire tropical belt, the peoples of the world have been exposed to the identical climate, identical patterns of growth and decay, and have not developed the notion of rebirth. By a wrong extension, popularizers of yoga have written that the specific climate, the abundant flora and fauna of the Indian subcontinent made the seers and the sages and their disciples contemplate nobler things, and have facilitated the creation of the yoga system, of ways of mystical union, etc. The same objection holds here—everybody around the tropical and subtropical belt has had the same ecological conditions around them for thousands of years, yet no other society developed anything comparable to the yoga system. Kabbalistic speculation is declared by some to be older, more profound, or better. This may be so, but it is not mystical, since numerical oneness with God would be a heinous heresy even for the heretically suspect Kabbalistic schools.

We simply do not know why and how yoga originated in India. Here, for once, the pious, enthusiastic statement of Indian scholars comes close to the facts, mainly because it is so vague: many thousand years ago (not 20,000, to be sure, nor 10,000, as modern Indian cultural jingoism wants it, but, say, roughly three thousand years ago), some ṛṣis (seers to whom the Veda was revealed) struck upon the idea of supererogatory meditation which would lead to supreme, irreversible poise and wisdom. Acceptance of these doctrines did not come easily: throughout the older Vedic literature, we find a preponderance of anti-meditational moods and ideas. The oldest portion of the Veda, much like most incantations of simple, illiterate societies, were exhortations, cajolings, and threats to the forces around, to keep away evil and disease, to make the rivers fow and the food grow, and to make the wombs of cows and women fertile. Very worldly wishes, but with a flair of the numinous. The gods are not only manipulable, they are really there only to be manipulated, coaxed, threatened, compelled. There are some propitiatory, pious hymns in Vedic literature, but they do not account for more than about five per cent of the total.

Around the ninth century B.C., give or take two or three centuries, it was clear that the brahmins alone held all the ritualistic prerogatives, it was they alone who could efficaciously do the coaxing, cajoling, threatening, and manipulating of the gods. Whatever other small-scale practitioners did by way of managing local deities, demons, ghosts, and witches we will never know; but the anthropologists suspect that those practitioners might not have been too different in their routines from the part-time religious specialists in most non-western societies today—shamans, diviners, curers, etc. Kings (or rather, chieftains who held or pretended to the title king *"rāja"*) had to hire priests to do the essential things. The ritual became more and more complex, and around the seventh century B.C., mastery of most royal and much ordinary domestic ritual required an impressive amount of rote learning.

It must have been about this time that some priests, and some intellectually rebellious princes, put their heads together and hit upon something new, germinally present though it might have been in the earlier traditions: a quest for something different from establishmentarian equipment, from cows, women, and wealth; different even from Indra's heaven and other heavens, where there are heady drinks and chesty women galore. This something was presumably more desirable to the intellectual, the rebel against the merit-seeking philistines, something eternal, nobler, though infinitely subtler. It was the quest for freedom from all those things, and from the desire for all those things. I think there is a parallel between those antique Asian days and our own. What the hippie, the neo-mystic, or the occultist seeks, in contrast to what the pious around him seek, is something quite different from those goods that the churches promise. Heaven is not enough, and certainly, health, wealth, and well-being are not enough: mystical insight is sought, salvation is sought, the esoteric is sought, something that makes the seeker quite different from his contemporaries. "What is it," a noble lady asked her husband, a noble seer in the *Upaniṣads*, "what is it, that one has to find, having found which nothing else remains to be sought?" Within about three hundred years, all sorts of men and women asked similar questions, approaching teachers who, presumably, had the answer, or were working at it.

150

The question is poetically variegated, but contextually identical—and so is the answer: in order to find what will transcend the usual goods, one has to turn one's gaze not outside and upwards to the gods or to the denizens of other worlds but inside oneself. It is *one's real self—you are that*; not the you that has a voice and two arms and a sex, for that is obviously not anything transcendent, not anything particularly attractive, that is the packet of things the seeker wanted to get away from. Then, within less than three centuries, a highly refined set of teachings congealed into the speculative body of pre-Buddhist India. Along with it, those rebellious seekers had devised methods for obtaining a state of mind which corroborated what they had heard and chosen as their aim: divinity and nothing less. Those gods whom not only their ancestors but all the contemporary religious establishment worshiped with much fanfare and sacerdotal exclusiveness were not really anything at all unless they were various expressions of the real self of the seeker.

Now no one knows how this notion came about. I would like to think that those masters followed a line of reasoning which I have come to take, as a modern mystic among other mystics today, and as one who is better informed about the possible options. I would like to think that those *Upaniṣadic* adepts pondered somewhat along these lines: our ancestors worshiped various gods, but since none of these gods are visible to anyone, they might all have been creations of our ancestors' fertile minds. But it was evident that the proper incantations of these gods—creations of our ancestors' minds—worked: things got done, magic succeeded. But that means that our ancestors themselves—and anyone who has the power to create the gods in his imagination—could short-circuit the route and do divine things themselves, since the divinities had been creations to begin with. Hence the most important thing is to realize one's own absolute divinity. This, the *Upaniṣadic* thinkers might have argued, is difficult because for many, many generations now, people have been extrapolating the gods, and have manipulated them from the outside, as it were. Now some people among us have had and can have an experience, far beyond that of reasoning, which corroborates this idea of basic, refined commonsense: they have *experienced* (apart from their *reasoning* which led them to realize that the gods must have been created by their ancestors) that these gods are indeed converted ecstasies—and that the universal supreme absolute was nothing but the totality of these gods, of these ecstasies within.

I do not have any literary proof for this sequence of ideas

among the rebel teachers who compiled the *Upaniṣads*—but I am making an evaluative statement: unless this was the general trend of thought, there was nothing particularly ingenious about the *Upaniṣadic* teachers, nothing particularly different in style and size from other mystics who chanced upon the zero-experience.

I impute a sufficient degree of sophistication to those teachers: at some time, long before them, their forebears extrapolated an experience which they could not bear as part of themselves, it was too large, too englobing. So they created the gods and the universal deity underlying these gods; one might call them scape-gods! Then the ritualist took over, and the extrapolated gods remained outside until some bright mystics, who made the zero-experience, put two and two together and found that there was no further need for extrapolating. The four "great dicta" (*mahāvākyāni*) regarded as the quintessence of the *Upaniṣads*, say precisely this: "All this is verily the Absolute." "Thou (*Śvetaketu* in particular, every one in general) art that (Absolute)." "I am the Absolute." and "Especially the conscious functions are the Absolute." No one said it then but I think it can be said now, about 2500 years later, with more zero-experiences, more psychology, and more comparative religion to go by: first, we created our gods and our god; then we forgot that we created them; then, by the zero-experience and by calling to our minds that we (our ancestors, that is) created them, we realize that these divine creations are we ourselves. A common sense coda clinches this knowledge: those divine beings and gods, and that supreme god—*what else could they be but us?* If there are gods outside us, powerful superhuman beings, otiose divinities, then we must not lose time attending on them. But the divinities experienced are the ones that people like us created in the first place, by placing them outside themselves into the cosmos, populating heavens, earths, and mythical seas with them. There may be gods apart from our creativeness, but that does not seem very probable to any but the believers in them. The mystics who compiled the *Upaniṣads* were not men of faith at all. They were mystics, and they had common sense. In later days, of course, all this changed; and even by the time of the Buddha, accepting the Veda as authority on a par with valid inference and direct perception seems to have been the criterion of being an *astika*, an orthodox person —in later centuries, a Hindu.

From here on, the development of *yoga* in all its complexities and intricacies was a linear process, much like the general development of other sciences. Patāñjali systematized the yoga-knowledge of his day, absorbing previous trends in his diction. The Yogasūtras [8] read like all Indian mnemonic literature: dry, arid, matter-of-fact. Nobody knows how far other schools, including the Buddhists, familiarized themselves with Patañjali's work, but it is unlikely that it remained unknown to many of the mystically motivated. The roughly two dozen extant schools of meditation all take their lead from the Yogasūtras, and the differences are of style rather than of method.

Professor Eliade suggested [9] that the entire yogic school was Indian, indigenous that is, rather than Aryan. It is a fact that we do not find much of it in the oldest parts of the Veda, the Aryan poetry. Either the Aryans settled and changed by some sort of inner growth, or they absorbed elements that had been present among the populations which they encountered in the process of migration and settlement. I will not go into the history of yogic methods. Suffice it to say that, to my knowledge, none of the disciplines of today's yogis are new in the sense of having been concocted during the past century. Some of the most recent forms—the ones better known in the West because of some Indian propaganda and much occidental gullibility—are gross oversimplifications of original methods.

A modern, religiously committed Hindu, or an occidental who has been engaged in any yoga practice, will tell you that there are four kinds of yoga—the yoga of love (bhakti), the yoga of knowledge (jñāna), the yoga of selfless action (karma), and finally, the actual, meditative "royal" yoga (rāja-yoga). Now this is a sad travesty of the facts. It is like saying that there are four kinds of medical practitioners: doctors, surgeons, chiropractors, and osteopaths, in answer to the question "how many kinds of medical practitioners are there in the world?" The "four kinds of yoga" notion goes back, entirely, and without any mitigating circumstances, to Swami Vivek-ananda's four dangerous little booklets entitled Rāja-yoga, Karma-yoga, Jñāna-yoga, and Bhakti-yoga. [10] These are incredibly naive, incredibly short excerpts from Indian literature in translations, rehashed in his talks in America and elsewhere. They were translated into virtually all western and into all Indian languages, well before the 1930's. Those who have read Vivekananda will talk Vivekananda and "four yogas" with people who they know have read Vivekananda, too. But to all other people, and to those who are marginally interested in these things, they will not reveal their source. I recall that when I was a boy of about fourteen there was a sickly looking young man in Vienna, who delivered lectures all over the place, captioned "New Investigations into the Spirit, and their Latest Results." "He is so wonderful and pious and humble, a real monk," a lady in the audience told me. Now that man gave the four yoga stuff by Vivekananda almost literally, including various expostulations in German, which Vivekananda had used in his speeches, such as "be yourself, brothers and sisters," and "everyone is great in his own place." To those who have not read Vivekananda at all, who are vaguely interested in religion, and who dislike Christian sermons, Vivekananda and his simplistic yoga-lessons sound very strange indeed, and initially fascinating. After Vivekananda, whose works penetrated Europe and America from about 1910 onward, a growing number of Indian ascetics tried their hands at similar preachments. But somehow, none of them quite seemed to make it. Swami Rāmatirtha [11] was a diffuse, more rambling early imitator of Vivekananda. The swamis of this day, who roam the earth on private invitations, all lean on Vivekananda, though they hardly ever mention him. Gandhi did not preach mysticism; but he, too, never admitted his oratorical indebtedness to Vivekananda. [12] A person is an initiate if he thinks he is an initiate, and the initiates of the past two thousand years very often did not reveal the source of their inspiration, since they wanted to bask alone in their glory, or at least in the exclusive company of the other few who had somehow derived similar inspiration from the same sources.

I am certain that Vivekananda has done more harm than good to the seekers of mystical knowledge. There is no patent on yoga-texts and on sermons based upon them. There is nothing wrong about saying that there are four yogas, four "methods," when there are really close to two dozen. After all, a teacher may cathect for his purposes what he deems fit and helpful, and disregard everything else. Yet Vivekananda's concept of *rāja-yoga*, and the way in which he taught it to very large numbers, by writing easily accessible, down-to-earth booklets, is dysfunctional. In the first place, the term "*rāja-yoga*" covers more things than *laya-yoga* or the "yoga of merging" as Vivekananda interpreted. He uses a classical epithet "royal" for this yoga, whereas the term simply refers to all yoga-types well performed. Now, in line with ancient teachers, he cautioned his readers that they must not try out these things alone, that they must find a guru; that without such personal guidance and supervision *rāja-yoga* is dangerous, it may cause insanity, etc. And yet throughout the booklet he goes right on to tell the story, using a not too good late nineteenth century translation of the Yogasūtras of Patañjali.

The book was originally intended for Americans and Europeans, and he knew quite well that gurus did not then run around freely in western countries. The booklets, like most of his other writings, were condensations or extensions of his numerous lectures, and he obviously referred to himself as the guru who might guide and goad his audiences to yogic practice. As the book stands, however, it is a dangerous tract. The reason why fewer people went haywire than one might have expected is that most people are just too incompetent, too lazy, and too full of compromise to do all the things yoga, even Vivekananda's *rāja-yoga* asks them to do. However, I know of well over a dozen cases, two of them in India, where people developed strong psychopathological symptoms which I must regard as sequels to their practice of yoga exclusively on the basis of Vivekananda's booklet.

Patañjali's yoga-canon is for people who have accepted brahmin theology. This is a fact which is systematically overlooked, not only by Vivekananda himself, but by many teachers of the Hindu Renaissance. One of their perennial mottoes was that all religions are the same, that everyone can be a yogi on the basis of his own theology, or of no theology. Theosophists, contemporaries of Vivekananda, and reformers about one hundred years before Vivekananda, all reveled in this sweet didactic harmony: theologies are different, but they are not important. To this day books entitled *Yoga for Christians, Islamic Yoga, The Agnostic Yogi, Praxis der Meditation*[13] have flooded an eager market of seekers in many lands.

Vivekananda's gospel reiterated that Hinduism is tolerant. This is quite wrong when it comes to serious business such as intra-Hindu exegesis and interpretation. Scholarly Hinduism and Buddhism, like all scholarly religions, are not tolerant. They argue, and the argument never ceases. An intelligent philosopher may show that there is a nuclear set of ideas in the Indian yoga-school systems which does not conflict with other schools, so that a degree of "tolerance" would be appropriately predictable about those systems; this has been done by Elliot Deutsch.[14] More frequently, however, the admirers of the East and their Indian tutors, the itinerant, English-speaking swamis, simply pontificate Hindu tolerance. But in the grassroot Indian religion, authority and the transmission of authority are the keynotes of the religious dialogue, if not of all religious training. There is an abysmal gap between the actual Indian *yoga* training, its performance and tradition, and what occidental converts are permitted to believe it is: an easygoing, exciting, humanistic, tolerant enterprise. It is nothing of the

155

sort. Yogic training in India is dull and severe. It is a seven-days-a-week affair, and slip-ups are punished. Nobody is hit over the head by a monk walking up and down the meditation hall as in some Zen schools in Japan. But there is austere regularity, unsmiling discipline, and not very much promise held out for eventual success. What makes it more difficult is that grassroot yoga in India has little grace-talk. Patañjali regards Īśvara, "god" if you wish, as a crutch for meditation only, as an object one may select among other possible objects. He does not pronounce upon the ontological status of divinity; in all likelihood, he did not believe in the existence of such a benign being, since he took over the world view and the theological categories of Sāṃkhya, which was the elegant philosophy of his day; and Sāṃkhya is quite overtly atheistic.

In order to be a grassroot yogi in India, there are only two possible motivations: either a man wants more mundane success (like a rich existence in his next birth, or some sort of magical conquest of wealth, power, and people, especially women), or else he wants *mukti*: he wants to be released from the cycle of birth and death, he wants to escape the drudgery of reincarnation. Now it is quite evident that, if a person wants to do yoga to achieve magical success, he could have any theology or no theology in his background, as proved by Muslims and Christians in India who avail themselves of para-yogic and magical means to achieve limited, worldly ends. But if yoga is done for spiritual purposes and not just for good health, a clear and clean mind, or for relaxation, it has to be part of a specific theological complex, which contains this assumption of rebirth as its doctrine. Now millions of India-inspired occidentals probably believe in rebirth, but *they like it.* Yoga, the supererogatory way of cracking the chain of rebirth, presupposes that the yogi *hates* rebirth, that he is thoroughly disgusted with life and living, not only with "what this life has to offer." The matter is deeply radical, and there are no two ways about it. The yogi, before he proceeds to meditate, has rejected the possibility of a more adequate existence, earthly or heavenly. The Buddha, and many of the brahmin teachers, identify life with suffering. It is not that life contains a mixture of suffering and pleasure and that suffering predominates. Life is a synonym of suffering. If a person does not accept this as an axiom, his claim to yogic genuineness is false. The logic of Hinduism and Buddhism is of a different sort from that of the Mediterranean creeds. There is no potential for progress in the Indian core-tradition. What leads to yoga is a metaphysical surfeit with any life in any body.

For the Hindu and Buddhist yogi, then, there are but two choices: either he does *some* yoga, for a specified worldly gain; or else he does it because he wants out—out of the *samsāra*, the inevitable circle of life and death, from which there is no other way out than yoga, meditation, zero-experience, enstatic consummation. Now the popular notion in India is that any yoga, any amount of supererogatory discipline, helps along toward the ultimate end, even though it is hardly ever reached in this life. The *Bhagavadgītā*, taking its own clue from the religious folklore of its days, say 400-300 B.C., and from some earlier sources, promises just this: that a man starts exactly where he left off when he died. Nothing is lost—and if a person develops yogic interests, seemingly out of the blue, without any model at home or in his immediate surroundings, then the Indian would say that he had been an unfinished yogi in his previous life. This, incidentally, has always been the way this author's early transition to the Hindu and the yoga complex was explained by Indians. There is no *tabula rasa*. When a person embarks on yoga with the ultimate goal of cessation of rebirth in mind, usually he does not think he will accomplish it in his present life. There are intermediary rewards, many of them: the *siddhis* (occult powers, ranging from seven to nineteen according to various traditions), worldly success, charismatic power. Part of the built-in dialectic is the notion that there is nothing wrong with *getting* these goods, provided the aspirant does not *want* them as he sets out on his meditative career. He must regard them as extras, pleasant and dangerous, and he must, in theory at least, reject them as they come up, or use them for "good purposes." But this never prevents India's famous legendary and historical yogis from using them—or rather, it did not prevent the people ascribing these powers to them in spite of the universal conviction that the true yogi does not want these powers. Great Tradition discourse goes along these lines: as a man takes up yoga, under the proper guidance, with the one aim of salvation from the cycle of rebirth in mind, he notices that all sorts of powers develop in him—he must reject them straight away. He may well test them, to prove to himself that he is indeed advancing on the path. If, however, he gives in to their increasing temptations, he will fall from the path; he will be a *yogabhraṣṭa*, which means quite literally "fallen from yoga," and this is a technical term known to all. Patañjali himself warned against *rasāsvāda*, "savoring the flavor," of these yogic powers. In practice, however, perfectly good yogis keep displaying their powers, *emically* speaking, telling themselves and their colleagues that they do so in order to test their own progress toward the ultimate spiritual goal.

Those people who do yoga for the admitted quest of *siddhi* can do so, and have been doing it—but their status is considerably lower in the general image. They are classed as magicians, sorcerers, or by terms which connote shamanistic status. In that case, if the term *yogi* is used at all, it is by courtesy and with the understanding that the man is not doing the real thing. A tourist attraction on the Manikarnika Ghat at Banaras in the early 1950's was a man who lifted a heavy stone with a rope tied to his penis. He was called *patthar uṭhānevālā sādhu*, lit. "the sādhu who lifts up a stone," a simple euphemism. He and similar "performers" on nail boards, contortionists, arm-raisers, etc. are all called yogi, a term almost synonymous with sādhu or holy man. He was not ever called a *sannyasi*, however, because the doctrinally sophisticated people of Banaras are well familiar with the exalted status of a *sannyasi*, a professional mystic, and an ordained member of the one of the high-powered monastic orders. The word "*sādhu*," however, covers all of these categories, at least in the popular vernacular, from the low-level performing magician or stunt-man to the most highly revered man of the spirit. I would even suggest that "*sādhu*" covers all "religious practitioners" *except* the brahmin ritualist.

All of these people know about the possibility of the zero-experience; whatever sect they belong to, dualistic, polytheistic, or non-dualist, they all know that the supreme experience can be made. Very few of them, however, claim to have had the experience, when they are asked about it by a person whom they recognized as an authority in these matters. All mystics are sadhus, but very few sadhus are mystics; all sadhus, however, know about the possibility and the importance of the zero-experience—and this situation, of course, is uniquely Indian. Whatever his educational background, a Hindu knows that he could, in theory, be a yogi, whether or not he wants to achieve the ultimate aim of emancipation stipulated by the Hindu lore. This makes the Indian different, modally speaking, from western man. Narrowed down in this manner, the obnoxious rhetoric of modern Indians "India is spiritual, the East is materialistic" would make sense.

What does the grassroot yogi in India do today? These practicing yogis in India are an unimpressive lot, when compared to the sadhus who talk about and spread yoga. It is impossible to estimate the number of people who practice yoga in the Patañjali tradition; we can only say that their social background is known. Most of them, if not all, are people belonging to the upper castes or, if they do not belong to those groups where men are initiated by the sacred thread ceremony, [15] they are people who have some compensatory ritualistic status. The image of the yogi as a beggar does not apply to them; it applies to those who professionalize yoga and who drape the uniform of poverty and asceticism, as the large majority of the sadhus do. Getting interested in yoga in India presupposes familiarity with a textual tradition, which only certain social groups provide—brahmins, people of warrior descent, the large number of merchant classes, and "high-caste" śūdras, such as we find in Kerala. Even though no one knows their numbers, I believe the proportion of practicing yogis in India to the total number of literate Hindus is about the same as that of practicing Christians to the total number of literate, nominal Christians in the western world. We have to know that religious practice in India always involves more than the minimal routine domestic rites. In certain areas, as in Tamilnad among the Smārta brahmins, the daily ritual of the male does indeed include a certain amount of yogic discipline. But elsewhere, yogic practice is supererogatory in relation to the other domestic rituals. The latter is meant to keep things going and to vouchsafe a pleasant existence in the next womb—and to replenish the forces which keep the house alive and augment its well-being. The orthodox and orthopractical brahmin feels that the domestic ritual, accompanied by certain basic yogic disciplines like *prāṇāyāma* (breath control), will give him the basic worldly goods and will keep him right on the path to better birth and, eventually, to redemption from birth—but the latter rarely becomes uppermost in his mind. If it does, then he commits himself to a more intensive yogic discipline. The transition is usually gradual. He seeks advice from a guru, not necessarily a professional (i.e. monastic) teacher, but from a person known to be experienced in meditation. Persons who jumped from merely nominal religious pursuits to yogic practice are rare in grassroot Hindu India; they are more frequent among people who have been exposed to the Hindu Renaissance, viz. to the English-language-based teachings of the modern swamis.

What does the grassroot Hindu yoga practitioner do? Some actions serve as a common denominator, while some belong to sectarian procedure and fulfill specific, segmentary stipulations.

All tradition-oriented yogic practitioners, lay and monastic, set great store by certain preparatory acts. "Ritualistic cleanliness" is first. *Etically* speaking, the practicing

159

yogi in India does not accomplish anything like the "personal hygiene" of modern western man. Many Hindus suffer from halitosis, but then this author may have been in America too long, where oral hygiene becomes an obsession.[16] *Etically* again, the kind of chemical cleanliness afforded by western soap and basic bathroom cosmetics is of course not matched by the Indian ritualistic bath, which consists of pouring cold to hot water over on's head while squatting on one's haunches, or else immersing oneself in any accumulation of water. The Hindu never undresses completely when he takes his bath—the loincloth remains there, and though the anal and the genital tracts come into contact with water and vegetarian soap, there is no intensive and extensive care. In fact, the Hindu regards the bath tub and the shower with soap as unclean—ritualistically speaking. He says that when you sit in the tub, and wash your body with soap, all the dirty water sticks to you as you get out. I have often objected that there are showers, and that even if people in the West take a bath sitting in a tub, they rinse with a shower afterwards. Yes, but the soap is unclean, it is made of animal; the suspicion lingers, even if it is pointed out that most soap is made from all sorts of herbs and perfumes. The grassroot Hindu mistrusts such claims, just as he mistrusts the occidental's conception of a "vegetarian" meal—spaghetti and bread and cake are not vegetarian, since eggpowder and other egg stuff may have been used. As to perfumes, they too don't do the job of purifying; on the contrary, they excite, they have the effect of an olfactory *uttejak* (aphrodisiac, stimulant). People on the fence, who have been westernized and who are affluent, but who follow orthodox behavior at home, take two types of baths on different occasions— the "English" bath with tub, shower, and soap, and the "bath" (*snāna*) standing in or squatting, with their loincloths on, pouring water from a mug over their heads, or by total immersion in natural water. The latter baths are the only kinds that seem to make the orthopractical feel ready for worship, and *a fortiori*, for yoga praxis which, to the high-caste person, is a sort of extended formal ritual, requiring the same preparations as regular daily ceremony. I am sure that no orthodox Hindu who has taken to yoga would, in India, take an "English" type bath in preparation for his meditation. If he is highly emancipated and if he has been exposed to the dialectic of the yogi being beyond rules, he might not take a bath at all before he begins to meditate; but if he does take one, it is the Hindu style bath which, *etically* speaking, is not a cleaning bath.

If the person is not already a vegetarian by birth—and I

would estimate that well over 90% of all people who take to yoga belong to vegetarian castes—he will probably revert to vegetarianism as he gets involved in yoga. He will probably also reduce the amount of hot spice used in his food, and he will reduce the quantity of his food intake. He will seek out *sātvik* food, i.e. pure, milk-sugar-fruit, no-spice, little-cereal food. The idea, quite current in western yoga as well as in the compromise sermons Indian swamis give in the West, that a person could do yoga and eat or drink anything whatever, is unacceptable to the grassroot yogi.

Since most people who practice yoga in India today are married, the sexual problem is important. The ancient, endemic all-Indian notion is that the retention of sperm makes a man a hero and a god; its loss makes him low and animal-like. Obviously, the married man must make a compromise, but he does so with deep and undisguised regret, once he becomes a practicing yogi. "Ladies want to weaken us," a lay yogi told me. "They want our semen—they will not say so, but they will rob us of our only power." Now just as the so-called non-vegetarian in Hindu India eats very little meat indeed, and just as the "drinker" drinks very little alcohol, since the famous *chotā peg* (about two fluid ounces) suffices to get him quite exhilarated, the orthodox married Hindu has no more sex than is absolutely necessary. The question of frequency does not come into the definition of a meat-eater, a wine-drinker, or a sex-partner.

The incipient yoga practitioner, then, eats no meat, drinks no alcohol, and abstains from sex. Society understands that. I have interviewed women in various parts of India whose husbands turned to yoga. It is impossible for anyone except an itinerant monk to elicit responses to such intimate questions. I had the feeling that the women reacted to their husbands' ever-greater withdrawal, with a sort of mental shrug. Ramakrishna Paramahansa's wife, the revered "Holy Mother" Sarada, reportedly said "who am I to stand in his way?" when he moved away from their conjugal room, never to touch her again. And presumably, if a woman takes to yoga, her husband would excuse her—except that this happens so rarely that hardly any empirical information could be gathered. Women yogis are child widows or widows.

Once the lay yogi has readied himself by such prescribed purifications, he takes to a graded course of yogic practice. He has obtained a *mantra* from his guru, [17] and if, for some reason, he has not found a guru, he will proceed using a more easily accessible *mantra*. There are *mantra* manuals in many forms; some small publishers in Northern India send them out on mail-order. Such *mantra*-collections as the *Mantramahodadhi* and the *Mantramahārṇava* list over a thousand *mantras* with the proper instructions for use, and specify the type of person who would profit by them, as well as prescribing the full course of accompanying meditative procedure. Once a person has embarked on yoga practice, the question of whether or not he has actually had a personal guru becomes unimportant. Most of the lay yoga practitioners in Northern India began meditating on the basis of manuals, which contain some sort of do-it-yourself advice. Although the official notion is that there should be a personal preceptor who gives the aspirant a *mantra* along with the initiatory instructions for meditation (*dīkṣā*), there are not enough preceptors to go around. However, if a person does obtain his *mantra* from an established monk, such a relation is regarded with considerable respect.

I suggest that a good percentage of people who begin yogic exercise by personal instructions or by utilizing manuals have had zero-experiences. Hindus are modally alert to these experiences, which are highly prestigious. Far from being embarrassed about such occurrences, as no doubt many people in the modern West are, the Hindu flaunts the experience, muses about it, visits places of pilgrimage or shrines where people who are themselves engaged in such thoughts and experiences reinforce his interests. There is, in modern India as in the old days, the ubiquitous institution of the *satsang* "assembly of the good." People with religious interests gather at a person's house, there is chanting and joint meditation, some formal worship, there are religious lectures, and the zero-experience looms as the center. There is no parallel to this in the western world. The *satsang* fulfills various functions, one of them no doubt being that of domestic entertainment. It is here that circum-zero-experiential feelings are spawned or augmented.

The practitioner has found his proper surroundings, the proper literature, and the proper discipline—which is not anything like the Christian mortification of the flesh, since the pre-yogic routine of the high-caste Hindu is quite austere to begin with.

Following the classic yogic preliminaries, systematized in the Patañjali *sūtras* and commented upon in literally hundreds of books spanning a period of twenty centuries, our typical lay Hindu yogi today proceeds as follows:

He learns to sit in the posture in which he feels most comfortable. This, of course, is related to his physical frame and his general constitution. The term is *āsana*, "sitting posture," and it is this phase of yoga and the physical *haṭha* practices, that became famous in the West long before actual yogic diffusion and infiltration. Some people, even in India, stop right there: for if a person does the yogic *āsanas* regularly, he tends to become quite satisfied with himself. But here the ways of instruction and tradition part rather radically in modern India. In classical days, there was no yoga without considerable *haṭha* practices. Since the turn of the century, however, we find a clear polarization into *dhyāna* or meditation-oriented and *haṭha-* or *āsana-* and body-oriented practitioners. Ideally, all would say, there should be an even combination of the two. But such is the compromise of the modern age, that even the grassroot yogis accept some sort of specialization. Also *haṭha* practices have acquired a mildly inferior status, since they are said to lead to *siddhi* and to support occult rather than salvational ambitions. In fact, *āsana* if done by and for itself, when accompanied by some *mantra* use and meditation, is supposed to generate occult powers. Unless a contemporary Hindu does not mind being looked upon as something of an occultist by his kinsmen and his neighbors, he will shy away from too much *haṭha* display and practice.

Once the modern Hindu householder has done his preparatory observances and has settled down to *āsana*, the visible parts of his yoga are exhausted; it is these visible "actonic chains," as Marvin Harris would call them,[18] which establish the man as a lay yogi. By about this time, his family has reserved sufficient time and space for him, to do virtually as he wants. A niche or a room in the house is tacitly given over to him, and no one will enter it from then on. It is expected that he will devote more and more time to his meditation, and if this process continues for a number of years, the man will be known to people in his locality as a yogi, a teacher. People will seek his advice. If the man's fame spreads beyond his vicinity, then he is likely to become a "saint" known over a much larger area—and this is a uniquely Indian process of professionalization. Miraculous powers will be ascribed to him, and visitors from other language areas of India will seek his instruction. From here it is not too far to the alienated forms of international neo-Hindu eclecticism which will engage us further down in this chapter. It all depends on accidental circumstances, on the eagerness of his disciples and other propagandists, and on such facticities as distance from railroad or bus stations and local climate. The person's formal education has little to do with it. In fact, there is a trend to prefer the quasi-illiterate yogi to a man of letters who has turned yogi.

163

The man will now steadily increase the duration of his breath control exercises (*prāṇāyāma*). The traditional notion is that power over one's body and one's senses can be gained by controlling that function of the body-system which is half-conscious and half-unconscious: breath. There is much variation in *prāṇāyāma* practice, and the followers of the many sub-traditions of yoga tend to keep their *prāṇāyāma* specifics to themselves and to their own disciples. The general rule, however, is that the *mantra* is "used," in relation to *prāṇāyāma*. It is used as a time-unit to regulate breathing—so and so many *thought* repetitions constitute the length of one of the four *prāṇāyāma* segments, i.e. inhaling, exhaling, keeping the air out, keeping the air in.

It is usually at this point that the practitioner feels he is getting somewhere. If he has had the zero-experience before he commenced regular yoga practice, he feels he is getting close to it. Not too frequently, *prāṇāyāma* does seem to trigger a recurrence.

The central theme of all yoga, however, is the *kuṇḍalinī* complex. Let me say that there is hardly any topic in the yoga-and-meditation universe of discourse about which so much rubbish has been spewed out, both by Indians and occidentals, over the past fifty years. It is not my intention to conduct a campaign against Swami Vivekananda's memory, but here again his dangerous, attractive little *Rāja-Yoga* volume has created a tradition of nonsense. Actual and peripheral psychiatrists and psychologists have picked it up. The most fantastic and baseless comparisons and speculations, without a shred of empirical or theoretical evidence, have been marshaled by H. Jacobs, [19] and by neo-Jungians. Jung, of course, must have read Vivekananda, but he was much too bright a scholar to take him too seriously. Not so his followers: Jungian archetypes - *kuṇḍalinī* - rebirth make up the sum of modern western mystophily.

Kuṇḍalinī means "the coiled one, fem." There is nothing mysterious about the term: *kuṇḍala* means "an earring." The *kuṇḍalinī* is the crucial function of the *imaginary* secondary body, the formalized body concept, as it were, which the yogi in the Patañjali and derived traditions uses in order to achieve the zero-experience in a systematic way. It is not some sort of a subtler body placed upon, parallel to or infusing with the fleshly body; nor is it an astral body as the theosophists and their sundry offspring claim. Patañjali and his classical commentators made it quite clear that it is *kalpanātmika*, "imaginary," it is an object our imagination has to create, and our concentrative energy has to direct itself to as a crutch for meditation, which appears almost totally impossible without some sort of formal not totally abstract object to which to attach itself. This imaginary body does indeed "look"—to the eye of the mystic's practicing imagination—like a translucent, shiny body outline, minus bones and sinews and organs. This silhouette-image contains an imaginary skeletal structure, as it were, much simpler than the actual human anatomy, of course, and indeed simpler than the traditional Indian physician's notion of the body inside. Ancient Indians never opened up dead bodies to study its organs empirically. Traditional medical science was symptomatic—and quite efficient. The horror of defilement and of ritualistic pollution was so strong in India that anatomical and physiological experimentation seemed until recently out of the question.

The *lingaśarīra*, or *sūkṣmaśarīra*, both meaning "subtle" body, are not bodies, then, but body-images. Many if not most of the later commentators in the yogic tradition were victimized by language use, in a Whorff-Sapirian fashion. [20] The adjective "*sūkṣma*" was badly chosen; if one has forgotten the original instruction denoting *sūkṣma-śarīra* as an imagined body, one must think of some actual body superimposed on the gross one, or vice versa. The term *linga-śarīra*, had it been used exclusively, and not as a terminological synonym for *sūkṣma-śarīra*, might have prevented this confusion, because *linga* in this context means "an indicator, a sign," and is closer to the intent of the original terminology, an *imagined* body.

This *linga-śarīra*, then, presents three central, parallel ducts, forming, so to speak, the spinal column of the imagined secondary body. The central duct is called "the sleeping one," *suṣumnā*. The one on the body's left side is called *īḍā*, the right one *piṅgalā*—these two connote colors as they appear to the contemplative using the *linga-śarīra* prop for their meditation.

The main impetus to latter-day nonsense, however, derives from the "centers" arranged along the *īḍa-suṣumnā-piṅgalā*. These centers are called *cakra* "circles" (cognate with Greek *kyklos*, Latin *circulum*), or in more poetic diction *padma* or lotuses. These are no Jungian "symbols"; the lotus does not "symbolize" anything; it *contains* divinities or divine powers, it is a matrix, a receptacle, but not a symbol. Symbol talk has blocked the proper understanding of any form of ritual and belief system except the one from which it originated: armchair-humanistic Judaeo-Christian-European. Jacobs, [21] and the Jungians, and the more learned hippies have taken great pains to show that these "centers" are nerve ganglia, glands, plexuses and the solar plexus, etc. They are not. The inventors of the *linga-śarīra* knew nothing about plexuses. The *cakras* are to the yogi traditionally conceived rungs on a traditionally imagined ladder; they serve as way stations, as halting points, as it were, for the yogi to check his progress. At the base of this imagined body system, in its lowest center, rests the imagined coiled up, dormant power, identified theologically with the female pole of the polarized Absolute.[22] Through the meditational process, by the use of the *mantra*, this coil is uncoiled, and it begins to move along the *īḍā-piṅgalā-suṣumnā* tract. This arousal and upward movement is an imaginary movement. There is nothing that happens in some actual shadow-body alongside or within the physical body, since there is no such shadow body. It is quite beside the point that there are nerve centers arranged along the actual physical spine; it is also quite irrelevant that there could be theoretically some sort of quasi-physical force, or some electric current which moved up that spine through whatever nerve centers there are. The *kuṇḍalinī jāgaraṇa vidhi* "kundalini arousal method" is a method of creative imagination. It creates the intuitions which may culminate in the zero-experience. Now the Hindu explanation for a zero-experience which occurs without any sort of yogic preparation, apart from the metempsychotic speculation which I mentioned earlier, is that the person who has the experience has somehow hit the *kuṇḍalinī* and made her wake up and move by chance. And here, of course, Patañjali and his commentators as well as some Buddhist tantric texts provide ample scriptural support: the ways by which this crucial arousal might happen are manifold: fasting, other types of meditation, continence, shock, love, fear, passion, divine grace (*dayā, anugraha*)—in fact the whole gamut of possible traumatic experiences. I must say that this Indian *emic* explanation does seem much more satisfying than the western occult and the western psychiatric or psychosomatic explanations which have been volunteered over the past three or four decades. The Indian explanation is liberal; it does not insist on the methods into which the greatest amount of labor and intelligence have gone. The *laya-yoga*, the "merging" yoga as transmitted from Patañjali through some 75 generations of teachers to our own day is a highly sophisticated apparatus. And yet, if other people without such training get the same experience, well and good—no jealousy, and none of the notion that important things cannot be come by without strain and pain. Vivekananda admitted that the *kuṇḍalinī* could be aroused by any of the other three yogas he knew of in addition to the Patañjali psychoexperimental complex which we are discussing here. But he and his monastic followers in the Ramakrishna Mission today make such statements as embarrassed afterthoughts, as it were. Since only a fraction of their modern followers can sit down and do the strenuous, risky, and basically asocial *kuṇḍalinī yoga*, and since liberation and the supreme intuition must traditionally be reduced to *kuṇḍalinī* language, those other, less fascinating, more work-a-day methods which do not interfrere with the business of the world, must be said to accomplish the same feat: the rising of the *kuṇḍalinī* from the lowest center, visualized as located between the rectum and the genitals, to the "thousand-petaled" lotus (*sahasrāra-padma*) in the "brain" or in the "pineal gland," as one traveling swami has said. There is no reason why zero-experiences need be explained by and reduced to *kuṇḍalinī* terminology; but such is the absorbing yogic tradition. In this terminology the zero-experience is the fusion of the *kuṇḍalinī*, apotheosized as the primordial energy, *Śakti*, with the principle of supreme cognition located in the highest sphere inside the *liṅga-śarīra*, apotheosized as her eternally waiting spouse Śiva.

There is a definite hierarchy of prestige in India. Notwithstanding the general agreement that the state of supreme consciousness, which is the stipulated ultimate aim for all *engagé* Hindus, can be attained by various means, social and non-social, the greatest praise definitely goes to the *yogi*. When this word is used alone, it always means a person who sits down and does *yoga* exercise, directly or indirectly linked to the Patañjali tradition, to *kuṇḍalinī*-arousing meditation, and to the psycho-experimental methods of ecstasy. In modern Indian usage, *yoga*, when not further qualified, stands for *laya-yoga*; the other methods, salvational ritual, intensive devotion to a personally conceived god, selfless action, and theological contemplation are always specified by some qualifying terms (*bhakti, karma, jñāna*).

Most modern Hindu aspirants, I believe, would say that the sit-down-and-do-it, experimental, *kuṇḍalinī*-type yoga is the real thing, the straight road to spiritual emancipation. *Jñāna*-procedures would take a close second. These are all intellectual, contemplative types of persistent occupation with the nuclear theological dicta which establish the numerical oneness between the individual (*jīva*) and the Absolute (*brahman*). The classical definition of this purely cognitive type of engagement as well as of its consummation is *nitya-anitya-vastu-vivekaḥ* "discrimination between eternal and ephemeral things"—the "eternal," of course, being the formless, pervasive

167

Absolute, the "Ephemeral" being everything else, including the lower theological entities, the gods and even the personally conceived supreme divinity of Hinduism. The person who does whatever he does contemplating on this distinction is a "knower" (*jñāni*) or at least a full-time seeker of "knowledge" (*jijñāsu*). Jnānis may or may not perform some sort of sit-down meditation. It seems to me that whether they do or not is accidental to the conception of a *jñāni* or a *jijñāsu*. Yet, empirically and historically speaking, both the experimental sit-down type yogis, Patāñjali, *kundalinī*-oriented, and the *jñāni-jijñāsu* type of contemplatives tend to espouse a monastic career. If he does stay on as a "householder," he does so with regret and compromise. His kin make allowances for him which would seem outrageous in any non-Indian setting; they reserve a full-time space for him, they do not bother him with worldly matters, and they treat him with the utmost deference; and as the years go by, he is looked at as a *de facto* monk who happens to be staying with them.

In theory and in fact, the *kundalinī*-applying yogi can stay at home even if the equipment, the time, the ecological paraphernalia which professional yoga, *laya-yoga* that is, requires, are hard to round up in the lay surrounding. Yet even when the modern yogi stays at home, mindful of his social duties or of his previous worldly commitments, there is an experience of monastic drift about him. In due course, as the word gets around, his house is being regarded more and more as a center of spiritual succor, and it often happens that people begin to refer to it as an *ashram*. Since the Hindu tradition greatly sensitizes its adherents to linguistic usage, the practicing person may himself refer to his house as a *matha*, an *ashrama*, or by some other term denoting the monastic complex. Also, the man would move out at the slightest provocation, if he felt that he had fulfilled his commitments. I have heard this in northern India many times: some person "became religious," he found and worshipped a guru, he became silent, contemplative, and he withdrew more and more from worldly things. Then one day "he took his towel and disappeared." The "towel" is a *cādar* or another piece of cloth which he wears and wherewith he dries himself after his bath. The image is old, and its attraction has lingered unabatedly: the term *pravraja* "sallying forth" describes the Buddha's and the other great yogis' departure from their respective homes, royal, urban, or rural as the case may be: their progress from a home into homelessness. Ideally, there is no need for such a step; the teachers of the Hindu Renaissance make it a point to tell their devotees to stay at home—*they* left *their* homes, to become monks and yogic professionals. But then, of course, someone has to stay home in order to feed and shelter the peregrinating monks.

Once a person has been identified as a saint, a holy man, nothing he does or does not do can change his title, unless he is caught *in flagrante,* and several times, engaged in disastrous things like sex or forbidden drink. But even in such a case, once his charisma is firmly established, there is a dialectic out of such dilemma: the emancipated person is not bound by social rules, and there is enough scripture to support it. Due to the leveling effects of yogic professionalization, it becomes almost impossible to say whether or not a person has had zero-experiences. People ask him just that: have you seen God, Sir? Have you realized identity with the Brahman? To all this, he will say "Yes" without a wink. I tend to give him the benefit of doubt. Since part of my definition of a mystic is that he presents himself as such, many lay practitioners in India today will qualify. There is, supplementary to or as a surrogate for the actual zero-experience, a dialectic of postulated accomplishment. The people who practice yoga are likely to know the fairly involved arguments of the dialectic of the holy. Therefore, any answer by the modern yogi to any question about his experience follows this pattern: the texts and the teachers have told us that Brahman is One—and that we are that. Whether a person actually experiences it in a zero-episode, is really beside the point, "just as milk exists, nourishes and refreshes, whether we drink it or not." The minor linguistic fallacies involved in this sort of parrying cannot bother anyone, since no one in India believes that this sort of critical querulousness is worthy of its object. Still, I think that a good percentage of the Hindus who make claims to zero-experiences have actually had one, or more. There is an ever alert, large audience for the person who dwells upon the experience. I believe that the experience simply occurs more often where there is a warm, willing, participating audience.

The yogi in the Indian tradition learns to arouse the *kuṇḍalinī* until it "pierces" its way to the upper center of the *liṅga-śarīra* where it merges with the Absolute. This is a technical process of imagination which can be learned. He interprets the zero-experience as the instant at which the *kuṇḍalinī* touches that highest point. Whether there is an invariable connection between the successful deliberate joining of the *kuṇḍalinī* to the *sahasrāra* and the reoccurrence of the zero-experience, I do not know. But this much is quite certain: the Indian yogi has a tremendous advantage over the mystics of

169

the non-yogic traditions. While the latter have to wait for "grace," or wait in despair, the Indian yogi and his disciples in India and abroad have the conviction that they own the technical know-how, the way to get there. The zero-experience is a complex, subtle, and delicate event. It defies definitions as it defies correlations with other events, guided or adventitious. But the power of identificatory belief or imagination is sufficient for the mystic who is a yogi. He has the advantage that he can try again. Mystical techniques are less widespread among non-yogic mystics. Many, like Teresa, have to wait and pray and be good.

The professional mystic in India is a very different kind of person. India is a land of ascriptions. Any person who wears a monastic garb, wears it long enough, and has an audience over a period of time, is a yogi, a professional mystic by ascription, and all the indignant remonstrances of the modern alienates, including the top-echelon leaders, seem futile vis-à-vis this perennial tradition of ascription of quality by title. "Only Siva Himself can say whether a man who wears the holy raiments is a fake or a genuine saint" is a most helpful dictum of the Tamilian Saivites; as it stands, it cannot be impugned by anyone on the grassroots level. More and more, modern India reverts to this notion by an elliptical process: the swamis are the holy men, they speak English, they do modern things, they fly in planes, they wear watches, they are punctual—and they are knowers of the *brahman*. This author is one of them—not too popular with many of his colleagues, for reasons that should be obvious to readers of this and my other works.

A professional, as opposed to a lay yogi, is a person who talks about it for a living, as it were, and most of the time. We have an analogy to certain sports. The people who compete in the Olympic Games are "amateurs"—which means that in theory, they make their living by doing something else. Whereas the "professionals" make their living exhibiting or teaching the sport. Both of them, on the top level, are about equally good. Similarly the lay and the professional yogis and mystics in India today—the married people and the monks who practice *laya* or some other yoga—share equal virtues. The difference is important on a managerial and on an interpersonal level, however. During the *kumbhamela*, the chief monastic and lay assembly of Hinduism, which takes place at intervals of six and twelve years at three holy sites in India, some fifty thousand monks of all orders and about five times as many lay people convene. When a rich man feeds participants, there is more merit in feeding the berobed monks than the pious lay

170

people. The monk's robe in India is certainly a professional dress, the ochre color is a signal and an insignium—it alone makes a man a professional yogi. There is hardly anyone interested in religious matters in India who would claim that a monk was superior as a yogi to a lay practitioner who makes the same effort; not even monks make this claim. For although the *sannyāsa* initiation, the ceremony that makes a man a monk, singles him out as a very different entity from his lay contemporaries, the difference is of a formalistic, ritualistic, and theological nature: for the monk, the zero-experience is *normative*—he is supposed to have had it. Hence, with the *post hoc ergo propter hoc* dialectic so common to religious discourse, the person who wears the robe identifies himself as one who has had the experience, and who can talk about it. "My neighbor Mr. Srinivasan may be a great yogi for all I know," a lawyer-friend of the Madras High Court told me, "but it is not written on his face. When I see a man in the garb, he beckons me to come and ask him—his robe means that!"

The professional mystics in India are almost all monastics—they have obtained ordination in orders which enjoin celibacy. For our analysis, there are two basic types of *sādhus*. The first type is the grassroot-sadhus: men of varying degrees of theological learning, from the most powerful theologians concentrated in certain regions of India, and resident in the various well established monasteries across the land, to the poor, almost illiterate mendicant sadhu who wanders from village to village, communicating modest religious material to the people. The second category is the sadhu of the Hindu Renaissance: ordained monks who speak English, and whose main audience is middle-class urban Indian. It is from this latter group alone that the internationally known swamis are recruited. Monks of the first category do not leave India—even those who could well afford to. Their audience is strictly Hindu. Whatever their personal motivations, often suspected and impugned by the Hindu population, their aim is to keep Hinduism alive. It is decidedly not the teaching of mystical practices, it is not the spread of yogic culture and meditation. Some or many of these monks of the first category may be mystics, but this is not what they regard as their homiletic subject; they speak about the good life in Hinduism, about the mythology, about the duties of people in the world; more recently they have propounded political views. In fact, there is a strong correlation between the new Hindu nationalism with its fascist elements and the oratory of some of these vocal, well informed, often erudite monks.

171

I think that the Hindu Renaissance sadhus are mostly mystics; they regard the mystical life as the object of their teaching. Whether they teach middle-class Hindus in English or in a vernacular, or whether the more successful ones among them go abroad and generate "yoga enthusiasts," the fact is that these men take mysticism seriously. They believe it can and should be taught. It is important, however, to penetrate their code. The word "mystic" or "mysticism" is hardly ever used by them, although their western disciples use it all the time. The roaming swamis know the word, of course, but it does not appear to be part of their spoken code. Instead, they use the term "realization" for the zero-experience; a "realized soul" or a "realized person" is a mystic.

For the sake of understanding this new, extremely complex situation which now obtains in India and in those parts of the western world which have sought and found spiritual tutelage from Indian sources, it is necessary to make a few criticisms which may seem overly technical to the uncommitted reader, and which give great anxiety to both the swamis and their disciples, Indian and occidental. There are not too many critics in this field. Most anthropologists and orientalists are much too absorbed in sheer description or in the deciphering of texts. The interaction between the Indian professional mystic and his eastern and western audiences, the processes of a true revitalization movement which has begun to span the globe, have not been analyzed from inside. If what the swamis teach people, at home and in the West, helps them in any manner—by relieving anxiety, diminishing mental agony, overcoming fright, fatigue, nausea, or mitigating despair—then there is merit in these teachings. I have no doubt that some such therapeutic action does indeed take place where the swamis roam. But when the swamis claim that their teachings can give people omniscience, "realization" i.e. the zero-experience, and that acceptance of their teachings will usher in world peace, then the swamis are frauds or self-deceivers. Virtually all the roaming swamis do claim these things and nothing less. Most swamis believe exactly what they say and teach—that their instruction will give zero-experience if followed, and that a large-scale acceptance of their teaching will bring world peace. The fraudulent element is the refusal to check their claims against all those standards which might either establish or destroy the validity of these claims. In other words, a phony teacher is one who refuses to be criticized, and who uses his knowledge upon those who know less than he. This is the swamis' ploy in a nutshell. The itinerant, nationally and internationally appealing swamis and yoga teachers know little or no Sanskrit, they do not know the teachings which they make their followers believe they know. With few exceptions, the yoga professionals, i.e. those who teach yoga beyond the confines of their grassroot community, teach Indian and western audiences Yoga and Vedānta which are neither Yoga nor Vedānta. They quote about a dozen passages from the *Upaniṣads* and from the *Yogasūtras*, and they insist that their teaching is the quintessence of Hinduism. Most of them really believe this. They are phonies with regard to the claims and promises they make about zero-experience, inner peace, world peace, Hindu philosophy, Yoga, Vedānta.

What are the standards whereby the teachings can and must be checked? Very simple. For Vedānta-talk, primary Vedānta literature; for Yoga-talk, primary yoga literature, together with the consensus of learned, primary-source-based opinion. The Sanskrit originals and their commentaries are the written standards; the first category of monks and Hindu scholars, the Hindu theologians who operate in Sanskrit only, not in translations, and who do *not* seek universal acceptance for the teachings involved, these are the personal standard-providers.

The professional yoga teachers do not even have to prevent their disciples (i.e. urban alienated Hindus and a fast growing flock of gullible occidentals, hippie or non-hippie, revolutionary or square, long or short-haired, sexy or puritanical, drug-taking or abstemious) from checking things with those authorities. In the first place, the followers wouldn't know where to find them. Secondly, those authorities do not speak English. Almost by definition "followers" are academically lazy people who will not learn Sanskrit. But thirdly, the standard authorities, the learned monks and *paṇḍits* in India, couldn't care less about the roaming swamis and their flock. The standard-setters are elitist, often arrogant, and outspokenly against any form of proselytization. In fact, if some eager Hindus or occidentals do penetrate to their lofty abodes in the *Maṭhas* of South India or to the learned houses of Banaras, these monastic and lay scholars try to ward them off, stall them, send them away. If they are finally cornered they do not hold out any hopes for transmission of the sacred lore to these outsiders. Some of these men of primary learning are well informed about what is going on outside. Arthur Koestler and other men of letters talked to the Śaṃkarācārya of Kāmakoṭipīṭha near Madras; he is the chief abbot of the most prestigious order of non-dualistic monks; he knew about LSD, politics, student-rebellion, free sex, and pervasive masturbation; he also knew about the roaming swamis who wear the same robe as he does, and who have many followers in India and the West. And he did not conceal his disdain for both the swamis and the followers. And yet, if claims to teaching Yoga, Vedānta, and "Hindu Philosophy" are made in India or abroad, it is only these haughty people who can tell if those claims are true. Such a confrontation, however, does not come about. Or not yet. It is the critical scholars who will crack the code sooner or later, if they can win over serious people from among the followers. People who took faith in the pamphlet-eclecticism of the swamis, the gurus, and the others who travel on invitation (the terms are synonymous on this lowbrow level of reference) may conceivably be made aware of the immense hubris—or is it sheer stupidity, or both?—underlying the claims to universal panacea made by sanctimonious little men who impress the gullible by their accent, their smell, their robe.

The process of convergence between the swami-votaries in Hindu India and the swami-votaries in Europe and America is manifest in their converging parlance. The arguments on both sides of the world are identical: what is the use of scholarship, of learning Sanskrit and theology, or the subtleties of Indian philosophy, when none of these yield "realization"? It is quite true that learning does not yield the zero-experience; but neither does *yoga*. This of course is hard to take; for what is yoga for if it does not yield "realization"? Now to this, the *ṛṣis* and the *ācāryas*, the original teachers of mystic wisdom, of Vedānta and yoga, had their answer, an answer that is certainly known to some modern seekers, but an answer that is not quoted by the roaming swamis: neither practice, nor meditation, nor any other deed takes you there. The theistic preceptors, quoting an *Upaniṣadic* passage, say that the brahman chooses those people who would realize oneness with it—and this, of course, is Grace talk. But at the back of it there is the great, relaxed, albeit somewhat cynical *nescio*, and the implication of take-it-or-leave-it. Let me talk out of school again here: among the professional monastics in India, particularly the members of the most highly elitistic orders, there is little talk about hopes for success, and novices and junior monks who dare speculate aloud about the connection between yoga praxis and zero-experiential achievement are quickly put in their place. One does yoga because that is the tradition, it is about the best thing one can do, it is so absorbing

174

that there is no time for mischief and grumbling, and there is some statistical correlation, though not a causal one, between yoga practice and zero-experience. There is an unwritten understanding between the senior, high-powered monastics in India that questions about spiritual success are neither asked nor discussed among them, and that in fact such questions give away the tyro, the beginner, the layman. As laymen and neophytes learn and mature, they cease asking questions, not because there is some extreme wisdom or insight in silence, but because they learn that there is really no predictable link between anything they or anyone else does and the occurrence or recurrence of the zero-experience.

The roaming swami does not tell his clientele about the learned elitist, aloof yogis of the *Maṭhas*, the traditional monastic centers in India, and if he does on being confronted by persons who had contact with them, he will play down their importance, using the aforesaid dialectic of "what good is bookish knowledge for 'realization'?" And of course, this dialectic gives great relief to intellectually lazy European and American seekers of eastern mystical wisdom. The great Samkarācārya, arch-yogi and arch-monastic of the 8th century, once composed a poetic tirade against a brahmin who kept boasting his grammatical knowledge of Sanskrit. Samkarācārya had this finger-waggling refrain: (when death or disease comes, or poverty, loneliness, all the miseries etc.) . . ." *nahi nahi rakṣati ud-dṛṅ-karaṇe,"*—"the morphological rule *ud-dṛṅ-karaṇe* is not going to save you"—just as the knowledge of arithmetic and geography would not save the learned man who could not swim, from drowning when the boat capsized. But Samkarācārya said nasty things about scriptural knowledge *after* he had mastered all scriptural knowledge, and mastered it so well that he went across India refuting all the masters of the scriptural knowledge who held opposing views. The upshot of all this is simply that the discursive knowledge of primary sources, the Sanskrit writ and commentary, and the tradition of theological disputation in Sanskrit (*śāstrārtha*) and its agents are standards for what is genuine and what is spurious in the teaching of yoga. True, even the quasi-yoga of Mahesh Yogi's "transcendental meditation" has given comfort to many thousands of Europeans and Americans, their number growing every minute along with the coffers of the organization; temporary relief, but some relief no doubt. So does the chiropractor and the village shaman.

I shall now present the case of a famous contemporary swami to exemplify the best of current yoga-diffusion. I have promised him a copy of this book; so let me be objective. I have known him for many years. I was a fairly well-established *sannyāsi* monk when I first met him at Uttarkashi, a monastic center in the Himalayan foothills en route to Gangotri, a somewhat inaccessible place higher up, where the Ganges enters India from the North. At that time, he was a young *sannyāsi*, very good looking, and shaved. He spoke impeccable English, and did not display the cliquish idiosyncrasies which the monks of the Ramakrishna Order constantly flaunt. He had never been with the Ramakrishna people, and that in itself was quite unusual, since English-educated and religion-motivated urban middle-class boys in Kerala, Southwestern India, tend to be attracted to that movement rather than to the more orthodox forms. When I met the young swami at Uttarkashi, he had broken away from the Swami Sivananda, the most prolific, the most grotesquely pompous and the most inordinately famous of the neo-Hindu swamis, whose latter-day "Divine Life Society" has roughly five hundred centers across the world.[23] The young swami broke away because he was bright. He joined Swami Tapovanamji Maharaj at Gangotri; Tapovanam, now deceased, was a South Indian brahmin by birth, with all the scholastic and orthopractical equipment a classical monk would need. A mine of scriptural knowledge, the non-dualistic Vedānta texts and their commentaries over a thousand years were like one big open book to him. Personally, he was a difficult man. No doubt a mystic, he did not court people. They had, in fact, a hard time to get close to him. The *sannyāsi* monks who joined his ashram—our young swami (I am speaking of 1951) among them—not only had to meditate hard and lead the austere life of the classical monks, but they also had to study scripture in Sanskrit. The young swami, an American scholar-friend whom I had taken to the Holy Mountains, and I had a long and genuinely pleasant conversation, and I was amazed at his rare lack of pretentiousness. Quite obviously, the young swami (he was about four or five years younger than I, and some three years my junior in the Order), was a mystic. He did not talk about the zero-experience, since he was at that time still very much part of the orthodox, erudite, nonchalant environment of the high-powered monks who live in that area, the most establishmentarian of all the monastic regions in India. But one can tell from the way a monk speaks, if one belongs to the tradition and if one has a minimal amount of empathy with people, when he has been through it; what one cannot tell is how often—but this is quite beside the point. (The other English

176

speaking sadhus, the roaming ones, when asked if and how often they have reached the summit, are likely to say "I have it at this very moment"; "I have achieved all there is to be achieved," etc.) We parted in amity, and I then lost sight of him.

Roughly six years later, I heard from some wealthy patrons in Delhi that Swami A (A for amazing) was about to arrive and be feted, and that he would conduct one of his famous *jñāna-yajñas* "sacrificial ceremony in the form of intuitive knowledge." The term does occur once in the canonical texts, but there it is simply an item in the list of possible sacrifices that can and ought to be made by people who have a religious target in mind. Bearded now, still handsome of course, and wearing a silken ochre robe, he arrived with eclat, secretary and all, and settled in one of the wealthiest houses in Delhi for his sojourn. From then on, I saw him sporadically, in all corners of India. The performance was identical each time, but the stage-setting around him became more and more elaborate. By 1956, he had risen to the top: to the top, that is, of the Renaissance, English-speaking, eclectic swamis, in the tradition of Vivekananda. I must say I regret this development. This monk could have been among the finest in the tradition of learning and mysticism. He chose the better life—I mean this quite rudely. He selected his audience: he never spoke in any language but English. When I ran into him at his native city in Kerala, where his doting audience were mostly Nayars like him—i.e. high-caste matrilinear *śūdras*, the dominant caste of that region of Southern India—he could have lectured in their common language, the rich and beautiful Malayalam, a Dravidian speechform with a high percentage of Sanskrit loanwords. But he didn't. The reasons for his choice are complex; but it all boils down to the problem of cathexis and identification. He identified with the Renaissance, with the eclectic, basically anti-Sanskritic, neo-Vedānta type of pamphletistic instruction and proselytization.

By 1960, he had a staff of affluent, efficient managers; there was an arrangement with the Indian Railways, which had "Swami A . . . Pilgrimage Trains" running across the length and width of the Subcontinent, between the large cities and the large shrines. He had centers and chapters in virtually all the cities of India. Today, his name is a household word wherever there are modern Hindus, and a positively numinous ring attaches to it.

A few years ago, the swami came to the United States on a visit. His secretary had written letters to many people including myself, arranging for lectures, but phrasing the inquiry in the clumsy patois of sanctity which anthropological linguists find exhilarating and non-religious people maddening. The swami "was about to grace America with his blessed appearance," he had "lectures at the most famous universities and at other centers of learning, but he could squeeze in another one," etc., etc. In Honolulu, the swami was a success; that was to be expected, since Hawaii, along with the Californian Pacific Coast, is the arch-region of neo-cultism in the western world. He scored fairly well with a general audience in New York City. Then, however, he and his management made the mistake to schedule an appearance at a large midwestern university, which is one of the three most high-powered academic centers of Indian studies in the New World. He was interviewed on internal television by a scholar who was no doubt one of the foremost authorities on Indian philosophy, accepted as such both by occidental Indologists and by Indian philosophers. Asked about some technical, but by no means too subtle points of Vedānta philosophy, the swami gave evasive answers and even second year students of Indian philosophy at that institute felt that he was hedging. When the interviewing professor suggested that Vedānta was not as simple a system as modern seekers of wisdom would have it, the swami exploded and gave a canned lecture about the superfluity of bookish learning and the arrogance of scholars who insist on it. The whole discourse is preserved on video-tape, and if anyone happens to be interested in it, he might contact this author through the publisher. I regard this as an important case of the dissimulating dialectic of the swami-yogi of this decade: a totally predictable set of cliches offered not by just some ordinary monk, but by the top professional of today. One might expect that with his power and his potentially corrective influence upon lethargic followers and the lazy, he would have assembled a slightly less stereotyped argument over the years. Not so.

On the same visit that swami addressed a large open audience at the same university. During question-period, a young Sikh student—not an Indologist, but some engineering or physical science graduate—stood up and asked a perfectly sensible question: what is the relation between yoga practice and the more down-to-earth needs of India and other undeveloped countries?—a question that bothers intelligent people in the professions in India. Instead of giving a straight answer to a straight question, however, the swami cut him short with a *Sardār*-joke.[24] At this point, all the Indian students, most not Sikhs by any means, got up and left the lecture hall in protest. When that swami tried to discredit the Sikh student, he proved my point: that the mystical life does not change people's basic habits. When the swami performed, he had two decades of famed swamihood behind him—so his habits were set, and the reply typical. Poking fun at Sikhs is one of the more inane parlor games in modern urban India. There may be no malice in it but there is a lot of stupidity, and such stereotypes should have no place in the dialogue of an illustrious professional like Swami A. If people claim that he is a mystic, that is in order; if it is stated that practicing yoga and meditation in the manner he suggests has helped many, that too is in order. But if they declare with the same degree of conviction that the man is a scholar, a sage, a saint, a perfect man, then this is a spurious claim. To be a mystic is one thing; to be perfect in the moral or any other field is quite a different thing; and these perfections are not learned by yoga techniques. You don't learn ethical behavior through yoga and meditation any more than you learn loving your neighbors by playing poker or cello. I vividly recall a performance of the swami in Calcutta. He was at the height of his glory. A *jñāna-yajña* had been arranged by a shipping magnate, an enormous *paṇḍāl*[25] had been erected which accommodated a thousand guests. The tension mounted, there was a hushed silence (very rare at religious assemblies in India) when the swami finally made his planned appearance. He walked up to the dais straight and fast. he sat down, chanted his famous loud and long OM, and gave his lecture. His lecture on Vedānta, that is. (Among grassroot scholars in India, a man is introduced as "having one lecture," or "two lectures," and if he is a great savant, he may have "three lectures.")

Anyway, the swami finished his talk in exactly one hour; as he did so, two disciples rushed up to the dais, helped him get up, and supported him as he moved slowly to the door. There was a deep silence in the audience: what a marvellously dedicated, absorbed saint! He was about thirty-eight at the time, and perfectly healthy. But of course, he knew the *gestalt* present to his audience: they had all heard that Ramakrishna Paramahamsa and Ramana Maharshi became so weak from their *sādhana*, "spiritual exercise," or so absorbed in *samādhi* that people had to prop them, feed them, raise them up from their seats, and carry them to bed. Stories of this kind, documenting the immense absorption of saints in their saintly office, abound. But how can a person get away with it, if he knows that his audience knows that he is imitating the earlier saints? Well, he knows it, but he trusts his charisma which is

179

ascriptive. Saints act in this manner, and since he is a saint, he may act, perhaps must act in this way.

Ma Anandamayi, a saintly Bengali brahmin lady over 70 has a much older reputation than Swami A. She speaks only Bengali, and some basic Hindi. But she has several fabulously appointed ashramas in India; her headquarters are at the Assi Ghat in Banaras, where I have met her a number of times. *Bhajan* and *kīrtan* [26] go on day and night wherever she goes; among her devotees, there are Food Ministers, State Ministers, Union Ministers, Governors, multi-millionaires, and at least half a dozen of the most outstanding Hindu scholars, Sanskritists and epigraphers. Outsiders complain that it is difficult, if not impossible, for an ordinary man to get near Mother Anandamayi ("blissful form"). It is beside the point whether she knows or cares. Her devotees see her walking over clouds, emerging from the sun and the moon; they identify her with Parāśakti, the supreme primordial energy, divinity incarnate, divinity herself. Many years ago, she cured people with terminal illnesses over thousands of miles, when they invoked her mentally from a distance.

I am quite sure that Mother Blissful is a genuine mystic; in fact, I have a feeling that she must have recurrent zero-experiences, since she does not seem to feel the urge to talk about it at all, unlike most other professional saints. I have observed her sitting on the dais, hundreds of people squatting around her; they all stand up and prostrate *daṇḍavat* "like unto a stick," in the orthodox fashion when she enters or leaves. She is a beautiful lady. She is not stern, she never reprimands people, she does not give them oral advice. People come to her with the toughest problems: how to retain the favor of husbands and bosses, how to see God, how to overcome nausea and disease, how to stop masturbating, how to eclipse the jealousy and hatred of others. Anandamayi gives simple, down-to-earth answers. Their profundity lies in their directness. They are not thought-out answers, but spontaneous reactions to commonsense situations. If a charismatic of the Indian kind says commonsense things to people who visit him or her in an exalted mood, then these answers take on a very special kind of numinous flavor. More amazingly, great Sanskrit scholars—people who have taught Indology at Oxford and Harvard—ask her views on highly technical philosophical and scriptural matters. Invariably, she answers "Why do you ask your little daughter these questions? I know nothing of these things." Now I am quite sure that she means this quite literally, with no affectation or hagiographic understatement.

180

Her learned audience, however, does not see it this way at all—no, they marvel at her saintly humility. For, of course, a person who has "realized" the Absolute in her mystical experience, knows everything by such intuition. This infra-verbal exchange is part of the saintly game in India, and it makes *emic* sense. The learned theologian asks the ignorant but "realized" saint; the latter answers he or she doesn't know; but in this process, *darśan* has been obtained, and this is all that counts. Were "Mother Blissful" actually to dilate upon theological themes, her audience would be about as puzzled as the little child would be if his stuffed animals did actually react to his cajoling.

Strictly speaking, the European and American clientele of the turn-of-the-century Hindu Renaissance movements is obsolete. The Ramakrishna Mission has close to a dozen centers in America and two in Europe. But the audience is stagnant and unchanging. The very young no longer go there, since they have more fascinating, more ecstatic models from India to go by—or so they think. A Ramakrishna-Vivekananda-Vedanta Center in America is typically a sizable house, bought by the resident swami over many years, on funds collected in Protestant-church-like fashion from the congregation. Each center has its bookshop, which sells the Ramakrishna Mission literature in English editions. The swami resides in one room, which he may also use for worship and meditation. I do not think that the Mission swami in America is overly keen on mystical experience, even though his shrinking congregation believes that their swami has or has had these experiences, and the neo-Vedānta *samādhi* complex is part of the sermon.

The largest room is the assembly hall for the congregation. Chairs are arranged as in any Protestant church, with a piano or a small electric organ in the back. Every Sunday morning at 11, the swami gives his sermon, which lasts 60 minutes. It is likely to be an old-time Ramakrishna Mission sermon: Ramakrishna and Vivekananda lived and preached the true Hinduism and every other religion. The stress is on *bhakti* (devotion), on the moral life (in the Protestant sense), and on the universality of the teachings of Ramakrishna and Swami Vivekananda, and their total applicability to all human situations. The mystical elements in the sermon are formalistic and tentative. One gets the impression that the swamis have begun to avoid mystical talk for fear of the encroaching vices of young radical America, sex, drugs, and wild-eyed cultism. Yet it is precisely these evasions which are bringing the eclipse of the Ramakrishna Mission in the West. The Mission did not have any real competitors in America until the end of World War II; the Zen institutions were strong, but they attracted a somewhat different audience. And the revivalistic Christian movements gave both Zen and Vedānta a wide berth.

With the advent of the beat and the consequent hippie ages things changed quite rapidly. Theodore Roszak's analysis is well taken, though not very friendly.[27] The meeting of basically different minds is coming about with increasing momentum—the political leftist radicals, the experimental psychedelicists, mystics and mysticism-seekers, and votaries of free sex. Their common denominator is negative: dislike and distrust for the establishment, secular and ecclesiastical. The generation now in power criticized its parents for their not taking the Judaeo-Christian value system seriously; but the young generation impugns the unique validity of the Judaeo-Christian values, seeing them as but one among many and more interesting options, totally unknown to their parents: Vedānta, Yoga, Zen, *Hare Krishna*, Transcendental Meditation, LSD, Rock-mysticism and unembarrassed sex.

The Ramakrishna Mission identifies completely with the generation in power. The Ramakrishna swamis inveigh against nonmarital sex, against psychedelic experiments, and against any of the more ecstatic, direct contemplative procedures. Indirectly, they dissuade their followers from learning Sanskrit: it is not necessary, all that there is has been said by Ramakrishna and Vivekananda, and the "leader" (church-American designation of the swami who runs the center) digests the needed texts for his audience, in English. No one among the Ramakrishna Mission followers I have met in America has ever doubted that their swami was qualified as an interpreter of Hindu lore. Again, we face the complex of mutual dissimulation which sustains the swami-disciple symbiosis: the swamis do not know Sanskrit, and they quite honestly believe that Sanskrit makes men "proud" and "haughty" and that the bookish learning it conveys is an obstacle rather than an aid to "god-realization". The disciples believe that the swami knows Sanskrit, but they also believe that it is unnecessary to learn anything beyond the pamphletistic literature available in the Centers. Most of them have had some sort of initiation, given by their swami, although the rule of the Ramakrishna Mission did not confer the right of giving *dīkṣā* (initiation) upon any swami except the President of the Order in his Headquarters in Belur, near Calcutta. Nevertheless, many of the swamis residing in America have somehow obtained their individual permissions to initiate. Their disciples, middle-aged Americans mostly, conduct some mild meditation, which is in no way comparable to the intense ardor displayed by the most recent Americans and Europeans who are being initiated by the hundreds every week by roaming swamis who do not belong to the Ramakrishna Mission, and by their primary occidental disciples.

Maharishi Mahesh Yogi had been well known and revered in Europe and America before the Beatles and Mia Farrow came to him. Not so in India: here, for once, the pizza-effect did not work. Mahesh Yogi's critics are not easily impressed by anything from abroad: the orthodox *sannyāsi* monks and their orthodox and orthopractical followers in learned India would have ignored Mahesh Yogi had he stayed in India and addressed himself to audiences of the kind Swami A has, just as they ignore Swami A. Mahesh Yogi, however, sought his audience in the West. He is a charming and kind man, and within limits a humorous man. And I have no reason to doubt that he is a genuine mystic. Within slightly less than a decade, he had attained world-fame; the Indian revenue-service became suspicious, but that did not harm him, as he is now firmly anchored in all parts of the western world. He flies in his helicopter, he addresses enormous assemblages in the West and, occasionally, in India. The followers of Swami A won't have anything to do with him partly because of the modern, English-speaking Hindu's antipathy toward the sensuous, an antipathy reinforced by the affluent West taking to yoga. Young, mini-skirted Hindu girls in Delhi and Bombay loved the Beatles, and therefore their Hindu parents suspect unjustly that Mahesh Yogi condones lascivity and non-austerity.

Maharishi's spoken words are as jejune as those of the other roaming swamis, but there is a difference: he gets his words printed in good type, properly proofread. "Transcendental Meditation" (a charismatic pleonasm) has caught on with some 100,000 young Europeans and Americans —college people mostly. First, one of the American initiate teachers would come to address a public audience on the campus. The listeners are told that if they want to obtain initiation, they have to undertake to make certain resolutions: they must abstain from drugs; they must attend two to three closed lectures of the senior initiate in town. Then, the initiate teacher, ordained by Mahesh Yogi, initiates the candidates separately. The initiation itself, when viewed in isolation, is pretty much what middle class laymen's initiations are in India today, but with the bare vestige of ritual accompanying the act.

"Transcendental Meditation," like any other initiatory

exercise in this general tradition so rapidly opening up to the West, does good things for people, in a therapeutic manner. Were it not for the additional claims that Mahesh Yogi and his disciples make for their brand of mini-yoga, their product would be just as good as any other yoga discipline well done. If you do "Transcendental Meditation" (or the meditation taught by Swami X, by Babaji, etc., etc.), you will find peace, poise, wisdom, and if all people did it there would be world peace, the end of alienation etc. It is quite clear to me that audiences would be much smaller if the swamis promised only as much as they can supply: relaxation, a happier mood while it lasts and, if the exercise generates deeper involvement, as it no doubt does in some cases, an opening toward zero-experiences.

The initiates into T.M. keep their mantra secret—and this, of course, is quite in line with the grassroot tradition in India: the mantra loses all its power when it is divulged. The Maharishi and his American and European operatives instruct the initiands in a highly abridged type of yoga: no posture is required, they do not even have to sit crosslegged on the floor. Only the spine must be straight (this, again, can be found in Vivekananda's pamphlets around the turn of the century). Twice a day for twenty minutes, the initiates must "listen to the inner sound of the *mantra* unfolding." This is part of the *nāda-yoga* tradition, a highly complex school in India. What Mahesh Yogi has done is obvious: he has assembled a tight-knit, abridged, segmental yoga, based eclectically on several yogic subtraditions. And it works for a while: at least for the poor, unexposed, tense, frustrated young in western countries. It is too early to say if the effects will last. What amazes and annoys the Indian expert is the ease with which initiation is given: you pay your money, you listen to a lecture or two, and then you meet the man and get your meditation, and you live happily ever after. In the Indian monastic situation, initiation is given after two years, sometimes after as many as ten years.

A youngish bearded swami holds court in a midwestern city. His disciples are young, bearded, soft-spoken, but rather full of anger, and quite intolerant. His organization in India is called the "Bliss Center," and it has divided the world into six spheres; the "New York sphere," though headquartered in Wichita, Kansas, is headed by this swami. He tours North America all the time. He addresses gatherings, mostly of students, and anyone who wishes can come to him after the lecture for initiation. In an audience of about 150, some half a dozen people, male and female students, went to the place where his disciples had arranged for him to stay (a sorority house) and obtained initiation: a *mantra* and a simple way of meditating.

This monk and in fact almost all the roaming sadhus are dead set against drugs. I have the feeling that the local authorities look at these men with some pleasure, since initiands, many of whom are recruited from the psychedelic scene, tend to renounce drugs as their price for obtaining initiation. Mahesh Yogi, of course, lost the Beatles and some other disciples, in part at least because he insisted that LSD and marijuana were bad. This is a highly incongruous, paradoxical situation: grassroot sadhus in India—not the learned monks, but the itinerants of Northern India—consume *bhāṅg* (cannabis) without any qualms, just as do laymen in many parts of the northern plains. But the swamis who go abroad don't, for they are urban boys, middle-class, college-educated men—and middle-class city people do not take *bhāṅg* at all. Not because it is supposedly unhealthy or dangerous, but because taking *bhāṅg* is tagged as rustic, superstitious, and old-fashioned.

One swami reportedly said about LSD that it was "God come to the West in the form of a drug." This oft-quoted statement is quite atypical. It was ascribed to Mahesh Yogi, but he denied it. I have the suspicion that it was concocted and put into the mouth of some swami by people who prefer to meditate with drugs rather than without.

The revolutionary outlook, the politically radical stance which most of the young espouse, becomes strangely paralyzed once they get into contact with the Indian swamis. Or rather, its dialectic is suspended for the time being. When Mahesh Yogi addressed a very large audience on the Berkeley campus of the University of Califorina, some students asked him: What, Sir, should we do about our parents who do not want to understand what we are doing? "Your parents are like God to you, *mātṛdevo bhava, pitṛdevo bhava,*" the Maharishi quoted from the *Upaniṣad.* "And what about the draft?" "Your country is like a father to you, and a father is your god—you must serve it with all your heart." There was icy silence. Once the roaming swamis philistine, uncritical, and dormantly Hindu-fascist view of things becomes known to a larger number of people, their success may well be halted.

There is Zen, and there are new creations of eastern mystery. I shall not deal with them, since they do not interest me. Let me just say that their operation in the western world should be studied and reported by a sociologist or an anthropologist who is himself a participant observer of the cult.

Just as Yoga and Vedānta have a strongly conformist aura about them in Hindu India, Zen in Japan is a much less splashy thing than it is made out to be in the West.[28] Nominally, Japan is a Buddhist country, but the Japanese are a very secular people. With the exception of the highly committed, a Japanese Buddhist may identify himself as belonging to Zen, not because he performs meditation in the Zen way, but because he is born into a Rinzai or other Zen denomination much like being born a Presbyterian. The parallel to Indian Yoga and Vedānta, and their western devotees must however not be pressed too hard. Apart from the Smārta brahmins of South India, who would refer to monistic Vedānta as the philosophy of their lineage, a Hindu is not born into a Yoga or Vedānta school, and to identify himself as a Yogi or a Vedāntin requires his doing something about it, i.e. meditation, postures, breathing and other psycho-physical control exercises. Already, it seems that the Indian type of supererogatory religious action is winning out over Zen; this may be due in a large measure to the fact that more swamis travel around America than Zen priests. While the following of Zen has remained steady in the West, Vedānta and Yoga are on the increase. Possibly the Japanese aesthetical fastidiousness creates some sort of a block: like Japanese food, Zen is a bland thing. The Indian swamis have no scruples of this sort. They paint their gods in bright colors, resembling the polychrome and oleograph prints on India's every corner.

Swami Bhaktivedanta, a lean Bengali monk, has scored fantastically with his Hare Krishna movement; "Krishna-Consciousness," as he calls it, has penetrated the roads of the large American cities, the campuses, and all urban regions. Boys and girls don the ochre robe, and move about, dancing, swaying, singing, clapping their hands quite like the Bengali rural devotees of Sri Caitanya from the late sixteenth century onward. It is much more difficult to find a troupe of "Hare Krishna" singing and dancing devotees in the streets of Calcutta than in the U.S. Indian visitors, United Nations personnel, students, and businessmen shake their heads with a blend of amazement and dismay at the sight. Except for Bengalis abroad, Hindus have hardly heard about "Hare Krishna" singing in India; only now they witness in the West what some saint, unknown to them, created a few centuries ago in rural northeastern India. "Krishna Consciousness," in the mind and in the words of Swami Bhaktivedanta and his roughly four thousand followers in North America, is a term referring to an interpreted mystical state. Since the Vaiṣṇava does not want to

186

"merge," being different from Kṛṣṇa in playful eternity, a zero-experience occurring to the Vaiṣṇava is interpreted about as negatively as a Christian orthodox mystic's experience. I asked Swami Bhaktivedanta about this—and he got quite irritated, rejecting monistic Vedānta in the same irate style in which Vaiṣṇavas have been rejecting it as a heresy for eight hundred years.

In the long run, however, I believe that the non-theistic or polytheistic ecstasy-oriented forms of westernized Vedānta may prevail among the white seekers of the light in the center. There are few black seekers in America as yet, since the blacks have more radical, and less ethereal problems to cope with at this time.

Some time late in 1970 I delivered a series of lectures at a small typical midwestern university. I spoke about the concept of mind in India. There was an informal gathering at the house of a professor, and he had announced to his classes that people whould have to sit on the floor, that there would be positively no beer nor any refreshments, and that they could meet the *swami*, viz. this author, in a less formal manner. The room was packed, and the beautiful young people were sitting on the floor, cross-legged, looking very much like a typical domestic *satsaṅg* at a Hindu's house. I spoke about yoga techniques. There was a young man behind me who took strong objection to my definition of a mystic. He was not a full-time hippie, but a student in the liberal arts division. His argument was that anyone who has a strange experience "see what I mean," that "turns him on" etc., was a mystic; and that people in the audience knew what he was saying, that he didn't have to elaborate. There were some half a dozen nods of assent, but the rest of the gathering, about fifty, got furious. A shouting match ensued; he suggested that I couldn't be shut up unless someone threw me out, so why didn't we watch T.V. and comment on the program rather than listen, and had I ever turned anyone on? The young man, told by the host professor that he was turning people off, left. Now the audience was eager, but basically disappointed; they had expected a mystical-light show. They had expected me to wave incense, sit on the floor in front of the shrine which the professor had placed in his living room, trophies from a field trip he had made to the Hindus of Guyana. They had wanted to hear me chant, to make them close their eyes, join in with OM [29] and SHANTI and groove the mystical way. Now quite clearly, and easily, I could have done all that—for this was after all what I did in India, as a professional mystic, all the time. But that was not what I had come to lecture on—and the good children took a wrong cue from the announcement. If a swami talks to people sitting on the floor, and if the people do not drink beer, there must be something meditative at hand. All this intellectual talk about books and about yoga—that is not what they really wanted to hear. On that campus as on many college campuses, there is a growing number of young people who meditate, pay for "transcendental meditation," take up the I Ching, tarot cards, and the Tibetan Book of the Dead. Many of them smoke pot and hash, and some of them still drop acid. All these things are unexceptionable in themselves, but things which should be enjoyed at different times. The central difficulty about young American neo-mysticism, campus- and commune-linked, is the uninformed, gooey eclecticism which the young espouse. "Goo" is a purely American term, I believe, for mushy, mixed food with sauce, ketchup and similar travesties. The students assembled at the professor's house were in a quandary: they wanted to agree with the cantankerous young man who wanted me out and himself in, to groove and to smoke, to chant and to smooch—all good things in their time, and even in occasional combinations. But not every meeting concerning mysticism is an orgy. Some meetings of mystics are controlled orgies as in the left-handed tantric tradition; and one may well construct or reconstruct Orphean or Bacchanalian rites, where orgies are in order. Those students wanted to agree with the young man, but on the other hand they wanted to listen to me, a rare and an authentic voice. They knew I was a Hindu monk, they knew I was a mystic—by whatever definition: I gave them mine, and that was the one I am testifying to in this book. The choice between gooey, eclectic grooving in the spirit and the pointed, non-eclectic instructions which I passed out to the assembly was one between absolute alternatives. If the eclectic alternative wins in America then mysticism will be flat, plebeian, and whatever mystical movements and ideas there now are *in nuce*, will fall in line with the older types of American religion which is basically a do-good and Sunday sermon performance. The communes have already made a start: people live together, share property or rather, reject property, and they grow and eat simple food. These are old American values and virtues. They meditate eclectically, they live eclectically—they pick up some thread from Zen according to Watts and Suzuki, they chant some "Hare Ram Hare Krishna" and of course they read the I Ching, the Book of the Dead, and Vivekanandian Vedānta; they meditate in various ways, they use some *kuṇḍalinī* mechanisms; and quite seriously, they use a secret mantra,

188

given to them by some initiator.

All this is naive eclecticism. It has to be, since the ideological underpinnings of the genuine Indian mystical tradition are of a rigorously theological sort—they presuppose acceptance of the doctrine of rebirth. This the seekers in America and Europe gladly accept. But rebirth isn't something nice or desirable at all; it is what you want to get rid of. And this desire to escape rebirth is the *only* legitimate doctrinal background for mystical contemplation. So then, if the zero-experience of the new occident will keep receiving the eclectic interpretation it now gets then there will be a new, gooey type of Sunday religion in America, supplementing the present American religion, the Protestant and Catholic remnants of a time when God promised Heaven.

The other alternative is that good taste will prevail, in some non-eclectic, tradition-based, intelligently disciplined form of yoga.

I believe, for instance, that left-handed, eroticized tantrism could and should be established in North America. This is something quite different from what the young mystical rebels are now trying to do—chanting, burning incense, making love, dropping acid, closing their eyes, and doing other congregational things; but not studying Sanskrit, and not seeking primary sources of inspiration even when they go to India and Nepal, as many, many of them have been doing over the past ten years.

It would be against both the Hindu mystical tradition and my own view to claim that mystical experience can be gained by the study of Sanskrit or Tibetan. That would be nonsense. The channels that lead to, through, and past zero-experiences have been explored in the previous chapters. I am now concerned with the genuineness of the para-mystical situation. There is no doubt in my mind that among the hippies and the other religious eclectics in the western world there are many genuine mystics, in the sense that they have zero-experiences and that they declare themselves to be mystics. The objections which I have been invoking and documenting are of the kind which I entertain about all over-interpretations of the mystical experience. Good Christian mysticism is better Christianity if it is a more camouflaged zero-experience; uncamouflaged, non-dualistic interpretation of the zero-experience, conversely, is bad Christianity. The eclectic occidental's experience is good mysticism to the degree that it does not disavow its monistic thrust. The experimentally open find it easier to enjoy the zero-experience without interpretations. This is due to the general

189

disavowal of doctrine. European and American seekers between the early decades of this century and the end of World War II were in many ways more highly inclined toward theological studies: they espoused Vedānta or Buddhism, and they read the primary texts in translations. Their new identification was with specific forms of Hinduism or Buddhism, quite unlike the present mystical generation. The latter usually are quite opposed to theological specifics. In the language of the mystical segment of the counter-culture, "turning on" and "grooving" is what counts; and if Hinduism and Buddhism are popular, it is because they are seen basically as instruments conducive to grooving. Sermonizing, the good Jewish and Christian life, why, even the words of Christ as channeled to the modern West through a crew-cut, managerially smiling clergy—these are identified as the enemy of the spirit by the young seeker of the last two decades, the hippie-decades. Furthermore, any discipline of reading, discursive and commonsense thinking, and of probing original sources is suspect, since it is seen as a method, as part of the inimical establishment. Unless it can turn them on, the young will have nothing to do with library material, and unless they can acquire a knowledge of Sanskrit and Tibetan through osmosis, by making love and by macro-diet, they will have none of it.

Until five years ago, the polarization for the young religious rebels seemed to be between Judaeo-Christian values identified as western values, and Eastern mystical values, a tangled bag of items from India, China, Tibet, the Himalayas. The Communes have blurred this polarization. From Haight-Ashbury onward, there were Jesuses alongside Śivas and Krishnas and Buddhas. The late Jack Kerouac, one of the arch-poets of mystical rebellion, wrote about Buddha, the *Dharma Bums*, Śiva, Krishna, and Jesus, with no real preference for the one over the other. I recall a drunken evening with him in Albany, New York: he retold the story of Jesus and in the next breath the story of Buddha leaving his royal palace to seek homelessness. He then warned that he would deliver the rest in Mongolian, and started rattling off some conscious, planned glossolalia, but certainly not Mongolian or any other language. Brighter than most of his admirers, he was nevertheless typical of the trend. Gary Snyder, one of the other arch-poets, spends a good deal of his time in a Zen monastery in Japan. He studies the scriptures, studies Chinese and Japanese, and does other scholarly things along with meditation. Allen Ginsberg does nothing of the sort—he is extremely intelligent and could learn Sanskrit, Chinese, Tibetan—but he won't. It is the non-learner, the sheer ecstatic, the groover who sets the style.

There are mystical movements afoot in the West which have no overt links to India; but they are few and their forces are fading. I cannot, of course, discuss orthodox Christian movements which see their members as potential mystics. There are movements which straddle an Indian-Judaeo-Christian fence: the Gurdjieff-Ouspensky-Bennett line has many emulators. There is a two-thousand-page tome published in America called the URANTIA [30] book, and the divine being Melkhizedekh, so some young devotee assured me, wrote it all by himself, and it has all the past and the future wisdom of the ages. There is a pattern to all these, shared with the Indo-eccentric movements: they all have total solutions for everything. I find total solutions depressing and boring, apart from their being silly. The India-centered movements have this one redeeming feature over the Judaeo-Christian-centered ones: they don't spell God with so Capital a G that it cows the prospective mystic into that submission which good Christians call humility and which confines zero-experimentation to either angels or heretics.

Professor Ninian Smart, the most incisive interpreter of Indian philosophy to genuine philosophical audiences in the West, has provided a model which I found helpful in coming to these conclusions. In his *Doctrine and Argument* [31] he shows that any Indian system which compromised with theism weakened its philosophical thrust to the degree in which it compromised. More theism correlates with less philosophy; more rigorous speculation correlates with less theism. I draw this analogy for mysticism: the more insistence on a personal god, the weaker the experimental and consummatory thrust of the mystic, the less ecstatic his experience, though not necessarily his report. Many mystical captions include "rapture," "heaven," "bliss," and "ecstasy" parlance. But the God who is not the mystic himself remains outside—and the rapture of juxtaposition with Him remains a man's rapture—not a god's.

I would make Smart's *Doctrine and Argument* compulsory reading for any course on mysticism. I would include R.C. Zaehner and E. Underhill [32] in that list, the latter two as negative paradigms. In a succinct article Smart [33] showed that Zaehner's distinction between "panenhenic," "monistic," and "theistic" mysticism does not stand analysis. Smart establishes an ingenious taxonomy of mystical experience which provides for various approaches and relationships, such as Zaehner's rejection of Indian mysticism, the neo-Vedāntins' acceptance of Christian mysticism, and all other actual or potential rejections or acceptances of mystics by mystics or apologists from opposed theological and cultural backgrounds. Smart lists "degrees of ramification," which run parallel to W.T. Stace's and my own "interpretation," or "degrees of interpretation." Smart concludes that, phenomenologically speaking, mysticism is the same anywhere and at any time; that the diverse reports of the mystics are due to their diverse backgrounds and their previous indoctrinations, and their "auto-interpretations"; and that their interpretations depend on ideological antecedents which have nothing to do with the mystical experience itself. Now although Smart would probably not agree to my narrow use of the term "mysticism" and "mystic," he comes to basically identical conclusions by discursively different means. This, more perhaps than any other single statement, reinforces my belief that the mystical experience is indeed one, and is "monistic" when uninterpreted, or un-"ramified" as Smart might put it.

In contrast to Smart's and Stace's analyses and to my own, Professor Hal Bridges—a historian, not a philosopher and not an anthropologist—continues the inclusive, and unduly permissive eclectic tradition set by both Judaeo-Christian writers and by the neo-Vedānta Hindus of this century. In *American Mysticisms* [34] (subtitled "from William James to Zen"), Bridges not only panegyrizes, but identifies Vedānta with the swamis-in-America stuff, lock, stock and barrel. He appends a brief note by Swami Prabhavananda of the Ramakrishna Mission in Southern California. The swami inveighs against drugs, and implies censure against any ecstatic, hedonistic reading of mysticisms. Swami Prabhavananda's translation of the *Bhagavadgītā* [35] is the cheapest and most popular; it is the worst available on the market. Bridges and Prabhavananda do not see that morality, chastity, austerity, and the whole lot of hallowed ancient things have nothing to do with the mystical experience. I doubt that the Ramakrishna Mission swamis have ever tried LSD or marijuana; but I think that even if they did, once or more often, they would not discard their rhetorical stance that the supreme cannot be "realized" through anything that is downright pleasant. Of course, the Swami does not write for Sanskritists, and Bridges probably does not know that Sanskritists would not read Prabhavananda, Nikhilananda, and the other swamis in America and Europe; but I find it annoying all the same that Prabhavananda makes coded, stereotyped statements which have no textual basis: Patañjali does *not* warn that psychedelic substances can obstruct yogic consummation any more than he warns against the use of occult power, improper food, immature attitudes, etc. It is a fact that the modern Hindus dislike the native users of *cannabis* in its various forms. But this is in line with the puritanical desensualized official culture of all "new nations": there must not be ecstasy except of the sort that can be reached only by the perfect, where the "perfect" are figures of the official hagiography which excludes the sensuous ecstatics of the mystical trade, such as the tantrics and the more radical sufi and Hindu orders, as well as the Vajrayāna Buddhist. Prabhavananda and the other swamis in America and Europe exemplify Smart's "hetero-interpretation with a high degree of ramification" or "high hetero-interpretation." The mystical insider is not impressed; sex or no sex with the zero-experience, drugs or no drugs with the zero-experience, these juxtapositions and exclusions are slanted assumptions to all those mystics who wield, in Smart's diction, "low auto-interpretation."

Chapter Seven

Analysis and Therapy

There are solid establishmentarians, more solid than Tim Leary
or Alpert-Ram Dass ever were, who make the step they made
from the establishment into the desert. The head of the best-
paying Department of Anthropology in the United States
moved to Europe where he planned to live on a bit more than
one tenth of what he earned. In Europe, I suppose, he hoped to
find the wise men who are wanting in New York City. A young
philosopher, a Wittgenstein specialist, with a doctor's degree
from the University of London, was the main speaker at a
national philosopher's convention in the States. He had many
good offers, with money and time to write books implied. But
he moved to a commune first, and then into a tree in Oregon—
quite literally—since the commune was not sufficiently austere
for him. Now we know St. Francis of Assisi did similar things,
and monks do it all the time. On the other hand, the Buddha
and I moved in the opposite direction—when he starved himself
so that he felt his belly as he touched his spine, and his spine as
he touched his belly, he found that starving oneself makes one
hollow and stupid, and conscious of the body; so he took to a
normal diet, consisting of rice and rice gruel, whereupon his
fellow-hermits turned from him, saying he had taken to
gluttony. As a monk in India, I slept on a *takhta*, a wooden
board with no sheet over it, and I ate more or less the
equivalents of rice and rice gruel. As a monk in the western
world I now eat many a good steak, listen to many good
orchestras, and drive to class in a big car with stereo-cassettes
playing Bach and Purcell. Many of my fellow monks and their
devotees now say that Agehananda has always been a glutton
and a lecher and now, living in materialistic America, it has
come out into the open. They are quite wrong. I would have
eaten steaks, listened to baroque music, etc. in India, too, had
these things been available there.

The point of these juxtapositions is that the mystical life is
a life of constant auto-therapy, and the therapies vary with the
needs of the patient. The man who has had a zero-experience

(Buddha, Leary, myself, and many more) are "patients" much like the urban people in America, and increasingly in other western lands, who have persuaded themselves that it is beneficial to be analyzed, at great cost, with a lot of time and one's total energy spent upon the process and the analyst. The mystics are patients to their fellow mystics—just as the psychoanalyst's "patient" is a self-defined patient; for he is not, of course, the certified inmate of an institution. Now just as the non-analyzed western urbanite does not understand why another person would want to be a "patient" without being sick, the non-mystic, whether the ecclesiastically religious or the non-religious, does not see why a person who is of sane mind would court experiences which place him outside the normal. The religious establishments warn the people against any direct involvement which cannot be inspected or supervised. We find that the mystic is culturally accepted only in societies which have no ecclesiastic organization or a very weak one. To this rule I find no exception: the Christian mystics who did not make the interpretational compromise of talking permissible language about the zero-experience were in trouble, as Meister Eckhart died a prisoner in the dungeon of his monastery and Giordano Bruno mounted the stake. Similarly, Al-Hallaj was impaled by the pious Muslims for announcing "I am the Law" (an al haqq) setting himself up as partner for Allah —guilty of širq, the most heinous crime for the Muslim. The Roman Church and the Muslim 'ulema were powerful, thoroughly structured organizations. Buddhism has its sangha, the monastic orders, and for sociological purposes, these are ecclesiastic organizations. But within the Buddhist monastic traditions there is a well-defined place for the mystic: he obtains his monastery's permission to settle apart from the monks, as a recluse or a hermit. These monks in Thailand and in Ceylon are greatly venerated, and they are referred to by highly honoring titles.[1] Once a monk has decided to obtain this permission and withdraws, the order has absolutely no control over him. Hinduism has no ecclesiastic organization of any sort. The various monastic traditions are autonomous and quite independent of each other, with no superordinate authority holding them together. The Hindu mystic, monk or lay, has always been free to experiment; his zero-experience not only creates charisma for him, it also generates amendments to the canonical literature.

The mystic's language is not the language of the people around him. Hindu mystics and others have spoken in erotic terms; but they also speak in self-directed clinical terms.

195

Bengali Hindus know the songs of Ramprasad, a seventeenth century mystic—"O make me mad, my Mother," addressing the cosmic mother as universal deity. Ramakrishna made it a point to quote Ramprasad; and in fact, many Indian mystics quote madness-ascribing statements of their predecessors as legitimations for their own behavior. I don't think any society has granted so much overt positive attention to the madness of the mystic language. The Sage Bharata, after whom India is called Bharat, pretended to be dumb, moving around like a madman, so that people would ignore him and leave him immersed in his ceaseless meditation. Hindu commentary of all degrees of sophistication stresses the point: the sage behaves at times like a normal man, at times like a sick man, at times like a madman— and there is no value judgment that would recommend one demeanor for the holy

R.D. Laing[2] is a mystical psychiatrist. He is controversial, in Britain more than in the experimentally maverick America. He is regarded as an anti-psychiatrist by Eysenck and other medicine- and statistics-oriented professionals. There is no way to convince them that they are wrong or short-sighted, because the very suggestion tags the person who makes it as a cohort of Laing and other mystical psychiatrists. For our purpose, one theme in Laing's work is central: that the true schizophrenic, or more widely, the patient labeled as mentally ill by any clinical terminology, can make a recovery in clinical terms, not by the various professional therapies, but by dismantling his whole person and re-creating it from scratch. We have a notable parallel to this in the successful LSD experience. A good trip may not be a strong trip; but trips that are good and strong do just this to the perceptive taker—he casts off all he is, his cognitive, affective, orectic "personality"; his *persona*, his "mask" or masks are shed one by one. If he sustains the process without capitulating to the alternative, horror and pain, he re-assembles the bits and pieces that make up the total person in the normal state to which he returns—but the bits and pieces have been washed, rinsed, and dried, as it were. The world looks different, for a blessed little while at least—not because it is different, which it isn't, but because the instruments by which he perceives it have been cleaned and oiled. In India, saints, sages, yogis, and the rishis or seers who codified the non-dualistic scriptures acted, and their followers still act, exactly like the more intelligent and the more vocal among all those occidentals whom psychiatrists, judges, policemen, and people call "paranoid-schizophrenic." Would these psychiatrists etc., if they were Hindus living in India, call the Hindu sages, yogis,

196

seers, etc. "paranoid-schiz"? Probably not, but if they did, they would make fools of themselves in the eyes of the people.

In the language of the new ethnography, then, psychiatric diagnostic terminology is *emic*; there is no *etic* terminology for madness, since there is no *etic* madness. Madness is what people in a society cannot put up with, by way of human interaction. Since the whole medical model in psychiatry is a radically wrong model[3] (v. R. Leifer), western psychologized society has taken comfort in relegating certain types of anti-social or a-social behavior to the hospital rather than to the penitentiary. Behavior which can be censured in terms of the Judaic decalogue has been given over, with very few additions and deletions, to the judge and the police. Behavior which is not mentioned as bad in the ten commandments, but which frightens, disturbs, shakes, or otherwise irritates western man in this century, has been transferred to the domain of the psychiatrist. The State now has more power than the Jewish God: for the State handles the criminal *and* the person whom people fear and hate, but whom they cannot or will not call a criminal—the mentally ill. The State imprisons thieves if it catches them, it imprisons the "mentally ill."

If a person is "schizophrenic," i.e. if psychiatrists don't like his behavior,[4] and he also suffers from ulcers (or excess of uric acid, or appendicitis, or syphilis), then he needs a physician to cure his ulcers or syphilis, and if he wants to be like all others, for reasons of his own, he needs a psychiatrist, or anyone who would do the mind-thing with him. All societies have their curers and their diagnosticians and their mind doctors. That there are people who help others to preserve, resurrect, or broaden their souls, is known to the reading public in the western world. But it is not known to the extent that proper analogies could be made. Not all talkers and wise men in primitive societies are psychiatrist-surrogates. Every society defines its physicians, and every society defines its mental helpers. Not all shamans, not all priests, and not all yogis are helpers. Some are; and among them, some types of activity, of training, of talking-to-people accomplish what the psychiatrist is supposed to do in metropolitan societies. When is a person who considers himself, or is considered by others, as mentally ill, or as in need of help other than physical, cured? In the western world and in the hagiocentric East, there are basically two incompatible answers running parallel: some curers say that a person can be cured, and in that case they will usually tell how a cured person can be recognized as cured; other curers would say that there really isn't any cure, that there are palliatives, and that helping the man survive, muddle through, get along, and function tolerably in his society or alone, is all that can be done about him. In New York City, many people are quite satisfied with the last reading. Once in analysis, always in analysis, and this becomes a way of life, with its in-groups and out-groups, its dialectic and small talk, and, of course, with its grotesque financial expenditures. Those less fortunate ones who have been certified insane and committed, want to get out, and it is they who believe that there is a cure, in theory at least. Their problems are of an order totally different from that of the analysts' steady, lucrative patients.

In India's villages, there are brahmin priests, there are low-caste priests who serve the local, non-Vedic gods, there are shamans, there are curers for snake-bite, there are Āyurvedic physicians,[5] who are generally wise men, and the occasional sadhu or monastic visitor, who comes, does his religious pep-talk, and leaves. In all villages, I have heard reports about or witnessed men and women who act in a manner which seems strange to the people around them, and which would seem clinical to occidental psychiatrists. There is abundant anthropological literature about patients, practitioners, curing, including surrogate-psychiatry.

Then there are people in all societies who regard themselves as sick, or as deviant because society refuses to view their deeds as normal; and finally there are people who believe that they are right and normal, and that, since society does not feel that way, society itself is abnormal and must be either cured or ignored. It is these people and their ways to which we now turn.

The great God Śiva is referred to as Vaidyanātha, "Lord of the Physicians." The Hindu and the Buddhist tradition calls life itself a disease, and concedes health and sanity only to those who would break out of it—suicide, of course, won't help, since rebirth is inevitable, and rebirth would bring back the very problems which a person tried to cast out in suicide. The wise man practices yoga, and seeks the zero-experience, which becomes tantamount to emancipation from the sickness of life.

Just as many curers specialize in treating the disease which once beset them, many mystics want to cure their fellow-men from the disease they were cured of—this is indeed the center of the Buddhist discipline. The Bodhisattva is one who transmits the method for emancipation; the guru in the brahmanical tradition does exactly this. The northern Buddhist tradition is most explicit: Buddhahood is karuṇa, compassion—not compassion about wars, general nausea, untoward things and physical ailments but about *dukkha* which, though it means "pain, misery," connotes *life* which *is* suffering. To the majority of the brahmin teachers, life is a mixture of pain and pleasure, though pain prevails. The Buddha, more radical, said, No, life *is* misery, it is disease, because it is attachment, addiction; shedding attachment is easier said than done; and what it boils down to is very similar, in the final analysis, to the curative devices of the sister-traditions. Doing good deeds is a delaying tactic. Rebirth as kings or as directors of the executive board, entrance into Indra's no doubt delightful heaven—all this comes to an end, leaving longing and attachment alive. But *bodhi* is the only cure since it is permanent; not only because, by Buddhist definition, everything that *is* is impermanent, but because once this state is reached, the doctrinal contrasts "permanent"—"impermanent" lapse as totally unimportant.

I shall suggest that an inversion of the common referends for "sick" may be the answer to handling the mystical situation as therapy. The identification of the mystical life, of the zero-experience and its concomitants with what is *forbidden* in any sphere of social life, religious and secular, is not only part of its attraction for seekers at all times, and especially for our own counter-culture, but the knowledge of this parameter of the illicit, in a somewhat complex but discursively clear manner, will lead us to the more methodical use of the mystical experience as therapy in future days.

Orientalists and their lay followers today have been puzzled about a specific type of statement frequently encountered in the holy writ of India. In the *Bhagavadgītā*, the Lord Kṛṣṇa says that the consummate yogi cannot do things wrong; even if he kills, he doesn't, because he does not identify with the body or the mind which kills. This has given rise to ideas both naive and dangerous. It accounts for the latent Hindu fascism which, fortunately for the world, has no power except in India. If there were no way to apply and interpret these dicta of moral inversion, the orientalist profession might better have withheld these texts from an ideologically naive public. So far, it is the spiritually minded and the weird alone in the western world who intuit the gigantic power which would be unleashed if people at large took Kṛṣṇa's advice seriously. For if they did, Hitler would be in his own. With the phony mysticism that floated around the Nazi fortresses, the top leaders might have vaguely absorbed these teachings. It is not impossible that they got hold of some translations, and, seeing themselves as Arjunas and Kṛṣṇas, acted the new Aryan heroes who made their own rules, and who believed that murdering

199

might .not be murdering after all, and that they as superior hierophants were doing what Kṛṣṇa had suggested. This sounds monstrous when said in the West, but I have heard it dozens of times enuncianted by gentle Hindu scholars who would not kill a single fly or eat a single fish.[6] I will present what I regard as the only possible, remedial way of reading Kṛṣṇa's and the other holy supermen's advice for potential supermen, cutting through the morass of a potential cosmic insanity and suggesting how the mystical rule must be understood as an instrument for individual therapy—as a cure from disease which only the mystics have so far seen as a disease. They are wrong in their ideological generalization, but right in their auto-diagnosis and their auto-therapy—and, hopefully, the light in the center will yet shine forth cleansed of the pompously glib and quite dangerous guru mania.

Mysticism in its motivation and in its pursuit constitutes what is *illicit*, anathema in any specific social and religious tradition. It is illicit even in the case of a monistic Vedānta environment, which ought to be more congenial to the mystic's efforts, since its doctrine of numerical oneness does not require any interpretation in order to be doctrinally acceptable. However, things are not that simple even in the test case of monistic Vedānta: in this tradition, it has been one thing to restate the monistic formulae first uttered long ago by the consummate mystic, the canonical seer, the *ṛṣi*, but it is quite a different thing to generate this statement, together with its total and radical eclipse of all social rules, as part of one's own experimentation.

The mystic merges, his ecstatic, often eroticized report is much more than an analogy to him; *he does it*—he actually transgresses the rules of his society, he elicits within himself the keenest pleasure, and if successful, he creates what no husband, lover, or lecher succeeds in doing: he makes orgasm permanent, uninterrupted. The intimacy with which he handles his body, his mind and other minds, and auxiliary objects around him to achieve and stabilize this state, is forbidden in *all* societies. The mystics in the Vedāntic tradition used well established, respectable codes when they talked about the experience, codes provided by the tradition, codes which implied, to their audience and to the world, that they were talking metaphor. When they spoke about the embrace of the beloved woman, they quote *śruti* and they imply a Vaihingerian "as if" in all they say and teach; when the sufi talks about hemp, wine, and embraces, his audiences read his statement as metaphorical, as a series of "as ifs."

Since intimacy makes for autonomy, total intimacy entails total autonomy, and no society so far has put up with this possibility in any individual, unless, of course, he was a god-king—and even then only for a while. Had Al Ḥallāj been an Indian Vedāntin, he would have survived—or would he? True, people were not killed in India for pronouncing religious views contrary to any commonly established religious view, and never got into a situation where the difference between direct talk and metaphor could have been a point of issue even incipiently: so grossly anti-mystical is the official 'ulema-oriented Islam that its adherents, the Muslim doctors and their powerful followers and sponsors, never even got to contemplate such distinctions. The doctors would attack Ḥallaj for being a heretic within their own tradition; the Vedānta mystic would challenge him for ever having used any other but the monistic "I am God" language. An outstanding British scholar[7] said "in the Urdu *ghazal* the radical, potentially subversive trend in mysticism is made quite explicit . . . the hero of the Urdu *ghazal*, in his mystic role . . . was crucified by the orthodox in 922 A.D. for crying out *an al ḥaqq* I am God . . . words which to the mystic express his sense of the complete merging of the individual soul in the Divine Beloved, but which to the orthodox are unspeakable blasphemies . . . ."

Before him, C.S. Lewis said "Any idealization of sexual love, in a society where marriage is purely utilitarian, must begin by being an idealization of adultery."[8] The furor that American district attorneys, policemen and most "old people," i.e. people over 30, make about LSD and pot is due, I believe, to the underlying fear of complete intimacy, which may generate complete autonomy. Billy Graham addressed thousands of youths at a rock festival late in 1969. "You can get high on Jesus, too," he told them—but the kids went around collecting signatures for a petition to legalize marijuana, and they asked Graham to pray to God for good grass. Billy Graham stands for thousands of professional ecclesiastics—they must be against intimacy, because their declarations are public, the conversions they elicit are public, and because they sense that intimacy, which is autonomous, solitary, anti-collective, is dangerous to established religion. The official culture of the western world, and for that matter of all new Asian countries as well, enjoins that the young man's body belongs to the king, or the king's surrogates. To the good American, getting plastered is perfectly in order: *"wer niemals einen Rausch gehabt, das ist kein braver Mann,"*[9] and unless he becomes an alcoholic and hence a social and a clinical problem, western man is suspect in the eyes of his neighbor if he does not drink.

Intimate drugs, intimate love, and mysticism—the most intimate of all if it were known to more establishmentarians— these are the real dangers, for they alienate a man's mind and body from the king; hence they are illicit. Mysticism was known to the priests as the supreme danger, as the irrevocable launching site for alienation from the king and his sacerdotal allies; hence they persecuted it when it appeared. The absurd sex laws which are only now being mitigated or rescinded in spite of the moralistic majority are cases in point. At the time when this is written, cunnilingus and fellatio are still culpable offenses in some twenty out of fifty American States; the term "sodomy," slyly misused and widened in lexical scope by the puritanical lawmakers of the British and American legal heritage, included every sexual contact with the exception of what Pacific tribesmen called the "missionary posture." Radical intimacy knows no bounds, and as men and women approached one another in hundreds of intensely intimate ways, thereby forgetting king and country, priest and church, total sex became total crime.

I believe that the criminal period for mysticism is yet to come, before the mystical revolution prevails. Just as western legislators have begun to remove some of those asinine laws, modifying them into innocuousness, after many centuries of dogmatic medievalism, so it will take a while, I presume, before mystical practice goes unstigmatized. The counter-culture, drugs and all, and the preachments of the harbingers of the mysterious East, swamis and Zen teachers alike, will draw the concerned attention of the more verbal people in the establishment. Then, just as it happened with such recent inventions as LSD and other "dangerous drugs," the legislator will have to have his say, and the policemen will make the arrests. What a powerful Inquisition could suppress and virtually eliminate—mysticism and the mystics—as witches, incubi and succubi, cohorts of the devil, will again be suppressed by the secular powers in the West. What had been the concern of the ecclesiastics only will become a serious concern of legislators and cops, both of whom must cater to the people at large. The *vox populi*, in our day and age, is expressed in the angry, sanctimonious, stupid, yet pathetic letters which people write to the editors of dailies across America. By and large, legislators and policemen prosecute what the people write to the papers about: drugs, free sex, disrespect for parents, teachers, and flags—these are a major subject matter. Mysticism is not known as such; it is only the hippie-end that is known and feared, not on the basis of its mystical quality, but for its link with revolution, the left, radicalism, establishment-knocking, beards, and unisex garments. In another ten years or so, the supreme autonomy which mysticism strives to confer will be known—and hell may break loose. Of course, it is unlikely that legislation will be passed directly against mystical practice. But then, it is possible: just as laws against oral-genital contacts between husband and wife have been felonies in certain States for two hundred years, mysticism may be declared as an abomination against Nature. My reading of the hatred of free sex on the part of the people at large—eastern and western alike—is that people fear autonomy in others, as they evade it themselves, hiding their autonomous potential behind many masks—wedlock, juries, sets of rules, etiquettes, politeness. Recently legislators passed a "no knock" bill—policemen, if they have reasonable suspicion that evidence could be destroyed, may break down a door without warning, lest heroin, marijuana, or LSD be flushed down the toilet. I hope this is just a nightmare: but I can see cops breaking in, without knocking, and making arrests of people sitting in the lotus posture meditating. Roman soldiers busted Christians, creating some of the best martyrs.

Autonomy, again, implies the alienation of male bodies from the State. An intellectual like the late Mr. Nehru, generally inspired by the best Fabian traditions more akin in spirit to Cambridge dons than to pandits and peasants in the Gangetic plains, waxed angrily eloquent in the Indian Parliament against some young people who had "besmirched the Flag"; with tears in his eyes, he said that he would sacrifice everything to preserve the honor of the flag. I don't think this was metaphorical speech; I believe he was serious. Somehow one would expect a more mature attitude from Nehru toward that most infantile of all silken symbols than, say, from Johnson or Nixon or Ford who had never had any humanistic or intellectual aspirations. English-speaking Indians and vocal representatives of the new nations of Asia and Africa are naively nationalistic, in spite of their bookish radicalism. I have yet to see an Indian student at an American university who really appreciates what American students do by way of acting out the counter-culture. An Indian lady doctor, an obstetrician of good repute and a U.S. resident of seven years standing, did not know the meaning of "pot" because she refuses to admit that decent people can side with the counter-culture which detests flags and which calls all the notions of patriotism and nationalism bluff. She also refuses to understand the language spoken by the counter-culture.

Once those wide, powerful circles, the silent majority and the editors of local papers, come to know about mysticism and the mystical practice as the supreme instrument of autonomy, of alienation from king, flag, country, mamma and daddy, and Rotary, they will attempt to create public opinion against it. I don't know if Jesus' saying is apposite here: that he will bring the sword, and that men will leave their parents for him. I do not know if he was talking about mystical practice—he may well have been. But if he meant to rally people around a deity whose essence they do not share, a god external to and numerically separate from his creatures, then he belongs to those who condemn autonomy as dangerous, as heresy. Hindus today, if they speak English, tend to make Christ a mystic, and beginning with Swami Vivekananda, they read his saying "I and the Father are One" as a monistic, mystical utterance, implying what the *Upaniṣadic* dicta "I am Brahman" and "Thou art That" imply. I doubt that this was Jesus' intention, for this is the only saying in the four gospels that lends itself to a mystical, monistic interpretation. I am rather inclined to read this particular statement as another attempt at reinforcing his ego-image as the Lord's prophet and messiah, comparable perhaps to Louis XIV's *L'etat c'est moi*.

We have, in the juxtaposition of mystical and non-mystical leadership, only these two types—the autonomists and the legalists. Legalists can not teach mysticism, though some of them may well practice it privately. Since legalists run the world, all who seek autonomy are *ipso facto* outside the law. Jesus probably viewed himself as an anti-legalist; and in comparison to the Judaic doctors around him, he was. Yet, if someone had dared to explain his dictum "I and the Father are One," I doubt that his answer would have been the mystical one, establishing numerical identiy between the individual and the cosmic soul. Rather, he would have issued another proof of his status as a prophet, pointing to his proximity to the Father. What was the mystical element in Jesus? Was there any at all? The esoteric readings of Christ's words are many but none of them is convincing—unless one takes the viewpoint that it is not important what the historical Jesus meant, objectively, but what he *could* have meant.

The case of Jesus is peculiarly troublesome to the mystic. Hardly a page in the gospels can be turned without finding his reassurance to himself and his audience that he fits into prophecy of the Old Text, or rather, that the messianic prophecies pointed to him. The model was "I do this today (or this is happening with, to, or about me), so that the word of the

204

prophet may be fulfilled." Jesus was still a legalist, due to his Phariseean-rabbinical training. The mystic cannot put up with a God who makes many laws. He may invoke one single universal law, containing a simple, straight injunction, like "thou shalt not kill"; but ten commandments are nine too many for a mystic. Mysticism is psycho-experimentation. One cannot experiment freely if the funding authority sets limits on one's style by imposing extraneous, irrelevant rules. Again, the mystic's God does not go into details: when I first read *Leviticus* and *Deuteronomy*, I was aghast at what seemed to me sheer blasphemy, that God should issue exact specifications about the material from which the basement of his temple was to be made, its exact length and width in inches and cubits, and literally thousands of other such ridiculous instructions. Moses, who heard it all and told it as he heard it, was of course no mystic, and he would have scorned anyone who claimed he was, had he known what a mystic was; Melkhizedech might have been one, and some other prophets, but they were few. Somehow, the Jews did not seem to mind a God who gave their artisans blueprints for ecclesiastical hardware.

The Prophet of Islam, too, encountered a highly specific God: "The Jews have 71 sects," says Allah, "the Christians have 72, but my people will have [not zero or One, as the layman might now hope to read] 73." [10] In the case of Islam, it is relatively easy to draw a line between the orthodox and the orthopractical [11] on the one side, and the mystics on the other. In no other Mediterranean religion has the official doctrine defined and condemned the mystic as in Islam. A series of historical accidents helped to polarize the issue. Mystical movements originated in areas which had been partly conquered and partly converted to Islam, areas where eastern cults had been and still were prominent ("eastern" being the ideological opposite to "mediterranean"). The 'ulema, the organ of Muslim orthodoxy, over a period of five hundred years or more, kept anathematizing utterances of the non-Arab speaking sufis, in Persia, Central Asia, and Northern India.

Until recently I thought that the fascination of Indian monism—Vedānta, certain forms of Buddhism, and mixed sectarian doctrine which made its way across the sea or the Khyber Pass into regions outside India—spread to Muslim neo-converts; and that the fact of recent conversion to Islam meant that its official, highly defined teachings had not had time to settle, or be sufficiently cemented so as to keep out extraneous influences; and that the mystically inclined in that wide culturally and linguistically heterogeneous area would derive their inspiration from India, where mysticism was part of the official religious establishment. Now I am almost certain that the Islam of the non-orthodox *sufi*, with its mystical core, was due not so much to straight Indian non-dualist, hence anti-monotheistic influences, as to the much deeper identification of the mystic as a marginal person, as one whose quest is illicit in the eyes of all "decent" people, the establishment. It so happened that Indian forms, or whatever diffused to those areas from India, provided ideological support to those who knew, resented and yet cherished their being illicit; I was led to this change of view primarily through a very visible parallel in our own day. Just as the seeking young, the hippies and the agents of the counter-culture [12] espouse India as something which is far away (hence exotic) and quite unknown in a technical sense (hence amenable to all sorts of open-ended esoteric ascriptions), so the Islamic counter-culture of Central Asia and the non-Arabic Middle East looked toward India— about whose doctrines they knew just about as much as the "Hare Krishna" people do in the Village in New York. As with the sufis of medieval Islam, so with the neo-cultists in the western world today: you select, confabulate and arrange all that is an abomination to the religious establishment, and assign it to a region from which no denial can come forth. Hindus and Buddhists who have heard about the counter-culture, about LSD and pot, about orgasm and free love-ins, have grasped that these young occidentals do things that they think sound, smell and look Indian. The Asian Buddhists and Hindus reject such connection with a horror as genuine as that of the Protestant American establishment. The establishmentarian Hindu or Buddhist will not acknowledge the actual part which orgiastic and ecstatic-experimental practice has played in the history of his tradition, if indeed he has heard about it. The modern Hindu or Buddhist eschews identification with those parts of his tradition which include ecstasy and reject the proper bourgeois religious and societal etiquette. I made a study of modern Indian reactions to the abundant erotic imagery in Hindu and Buddhist sculpture. In over a hundred modern Hindus exposed to photographs of roughly 200 erotic sculptures on the sub-continent, the invariable reaction was rejection and distaste. The more prepared and the more sophisticated simply relegated this pattern to a degenerate age: yes, those sculptures are there, but they were the result of cultural and religious contamination, with popular Buddhism in earlier and Islam in later days. But "degenerate" is an *emic* term, the *etic* translation being "What seems degenerate is abhorrent to a certain defined audience, which wants others to call it degenerate, abhorrent, etc."

Hippies and non-hippie east-directed cultists have taken up Indian music; only a handful of ethnomusicologists in the west knew anything about *tālas* and *rāgas*,[13] about the *sitār, sarod,* and *vīṇā* before the early sixties. Indians abroad preferred schmalzy Indian film music to their classical tradition. Then all of a sudden, within a year or two, the new taste bloomed, and Indian art became an increasing vogue. The Ravi Shankar and Ali Akbar Khan records sold well at high prices. "Meditation music" is more or less identified with Indian music, with a sprinkling of koto and samisen from Japan, to match things with a Zen component. I have it from a district attorney in the State of Washington that policemen were instructed to concentrate on places where the sound of *sitar* and *sarod* emerged: for that's where the psychedelic action was.

Ravi Shankar taught Indian music at the City College of New York some years ago. One night I called him to ask whether he was aware of the fact that his LPs sold so well and students flocked to his classes because his music was grist to the psychedelic mills. "I know that too well," he told me, "and I resent it. In my class, I see young people smoke hashish. I forbid them to do it. I also forbid them to enjoy openly in my class." "To enjoy" is Indian English for sexual activities of any kind. Ravi Shankar worked his class hard with Indian musicological terms and many hours of practice a day. Of an enrolled class of 120, I am told, 4 remained to the end, and these four were professional musicians. The notion that the Indian artist, who is *ipso facto* spiritual, condones sex and hemp, is totally wrong. Sex and drugs generate a strange and feared reaction in the human mind: they alienate man from king, from parents, from the proper things done and preached by the proper people at the proper place and time: they make him autonomous. And so does mysticism—but mysticism is not *known*, hence all the threats and fears and indignations I have listed so far apply to mysticism as a "not yet, but soon."

Penalties on possession of marijuana are becoming less severe. Sex legislation is being gradually softened, often unbeknownst to large audiences. When the State of New York finally mellowed on divorce legislation in the late sixties, it also changed the more despotic, prurient clauses of some ancient anti-sex legislation: oral-genital intercourse between consenting married couples is no longer an offense; and it is only a misdemeanor, no longer a felony, among unmarried consenting adults. In Texas, I understand, it is still a second degree felony. The Senate, in its deliberations on January 28, 1970, "turned back, 44 to 39, an attempt to give Health-Education-Welfare Department scientists a stronger voice in determining which drugs should be classified as dangerous under schedules which outline control procedures and penalties for use and distribution." The gist of it all was that official America has decided, at this point at any rate, to entrust the policeman rather than the scientist with matters relating to drugs, including psychedelic drugs. Senator Hughes, who had submitted the softening bill, was pointed out by Senator Hruska as in error, because Hughes wanted to "discard the Attorney General from what was intended as a law enforcement bill," a move which, according to Senator Hruska represented a "strange and alien philosophy." The American value system based on the Judaeo-Christian belief complex and the Protestant Ethic still suppresses and detests total individual autonomy. Psychedelic drugs are rejected not because they are hygienically dangerous, for then the Department of Health, Education and Welfare could be entrusted with handling the situation. But the policeman must handle it, because the results are illicit: not health is endangered, but god-king-country-establishment is alienated, its share withheld, when a man becomes autonomous and begins to use his body as he wishes, withdrawing it from the public reservoir of bodies, and seeking autonomy through mysticisms, sex, poetry, music, and drugs; let me recall that the means are irrelevant when we speak of *autonomy*; they are not, when other things are concerned.

The analogy between the psychedelic and the mystical universe of discourse must be brought home with vigor in this context. The State defines what is illicit, just as the church did when it was taken more seriously and when it had more power. The distinction between the moral, the legal, and the permissible is one for scholars and thinkers—possibly for mystics when they turn scholars and thinkers. *Making* the distinction is subversive to the occidental establishment, as it was *heretical* to the ecclesiastical doctors and their policing agents in earlier times. Senators, medically oriented psychiatrists, policemen, and judges do not make the distinction, although I have known psychiatrists, policemen, and judges who in their off-duty hours sympathize with pot smokers and, very rarely, with mystics when they are told about them. The West has had a tradition of amalgamating the heretical with the illicit, the illegal, and the immoral. Heresy, illegality, immorality, illicitness—these *must* be seen as one and

208

the same by all the inhabitants of one ideological plateau. I call this phenomenon "noxious fusion," a modally predictable tendency in one cultural group to ascribe certain unrelated themes, ideas, acts, etc. summarily where *one* of these themes is perceived. In contemporary North America, "noxious fusion" combines long hair, liberal politics, communism, drugs, anti-church, pro-Black, anti-America, pro-Vietcong, anti-war, anti-police, anarchy. When the "silent majority" American sees a clean-shaven, crew-cut male in blue jeans working on a roof, he *cannot* visualize the possibility that the man may be a homosexual, a communist, anti-war, etc. The first job of the intellectual is to unfuse the noxious fusion in which he has been brought up.

Autonomy and illicitness are being treated here on their own merit. This is the only rationally and ethically acceptable procedure. Robbins Burling, an eminent anthropological linguist, provided a good model; in reporting the linguistic structure of a language, it is totally beside the point *how* the researcher came by the material that he used in order to arrive at his statement. I am not concerned with the propriety of this specific research project, mysticism. When I state that mystical experience makes the mystic autonomous, and that its investigation must proceed on the assumption that the mystical experience can be investigated *per se*, in factual isolation, then the criteria for this study do not refer to the means, but only to the end, i.e. the mystical experience itself. It is irrelevant how a person came by his experience—through fasting, prayer, drugs, self-mortification, fornication, standing on his head, grace, listening to *Tristan and Isolde* unabridged three times in a row, etc. What counts is whether the experience satisfies criteria set up for it as autonomous. My remarks on the illicitness of the mystical life really refer to "means." In some cases, the end justifies the means; in others, it does not, and still in other cases, the question does not arise. Here I concur with my Indian preceptors, who (against the notion held by modern, sophisticated, but traditionally uninformed Hindus and Buddhists) left no doubt about their conviction that the means toward achieving divine vision, incontrovertible spiritual realization, intuition, etc., were not important. Whether you stayed at home and served family and king, whether you left them to fend for themselves, whether you fasted or glutted yourself—whatever generated the supreme experience would be taught and practiced. The fact that most methods now taught for supreme religious consummation are of the ascetic order, is a complex series of historical accidents which I cannot go into.

If we find nine ascetic, anti-sexual doctrines and one erotic sculpture, text, or instruction in a series of ten in India, this is of historical relevance only; nothing can be said about the greater correctness or suitability of the nine against the one. The problem of whether asceticism is more *moral* than fornication or peyote, and more profitable to the integrity of the state, is quite incidental to the validity of the mystical experience. The problem of illegality and moral illicitness is a problem for bad logicians, many of whom are lawmakers and policemen. *Post hoc ergo propter hoc* provides the operational basis for much law enforcement. Psychedelic drugs are *verboten* because they lead to hard drugs—an argument I have heard propounded in all seriousness by physicians, surgeons, district attorneys, and some psychiatrists. "80% of all heroin addicts have previously taken marijuana," is a motto used in all drug discussions in America. But the statement is quite as competent as "90% of all people convicted of bestiality have previously had intercourse with women." When mysticism becomes better known than it is at present, and when it becomes known that some of the means leading to mystical consummation are offensive to the moral, legal, religious, and other conventions, some pattern of public and legal action will ensue. There is, then, an endemic confusion between the *illicitness* (immorality, illegality, etc.) of some *means* to the achievement of the psychedelic experience (e.g. the ingestion of drugs), and the autonomous experience itself. What is really feared is the alienation from the norm and the autonomy some drug takers achieve. Here, the distinction between the means (drug ingestion) and the potential end (autonomy) is systematically confused, and both means and end become an abomination to the critics. Similarly once the effect of the mystical experience, i.e. alienation from the king and autonomy from social convention, becomes known to people at large, then the experience leading to this alienation will be summarily condemned.

A fascinating episode in the history of drug involvement was that of Leary and Alpert: their demise from Harvard, and their subsequent turning into the hierophants of the drug-mysticism scene. Both were well-qualified psychologists, and Leary had published a fully respectable academic book before he discovered himself through psychedelics.[14]

The one objective report about the events that led to their dismissal was written by two sober, hard-working, unbiassed sociologists.[15] One of the main objections to Leary's and Alpert's experiments with psilocybin was that they refused to program the participants on medically acceptable lines, in a

210

laboratory setting. Now Leary and Alpert insisted—not yet as prophets and cult leaders, but as scholars—that the laboratory setting was totally dysfunctional, and that it led to "bad trips" almost invariably; that a warm, loving, supportive atmosphere is essential in order to obtain the maximum benefit of the psychosomatic substance. But it was quite clear that such terms as "warm," "supportive," and particularly "loving" were outside the vocabulary of laboratory and research rules—and it was obviously Leary's and Alpert's initiatory action that catapulted them into disaster, and into the discontinuation of the Psilocybin Project. Leary and Alpert wrote "the goal of the research sessions run by the Harvard IFIF group[16] was not to produce and study frightening disturbances of consciousness, which was the goal of most psychiatric investigation of model psychoses, but to produce the ecstatic experience, to expand consciousness, to provide the subject with the most memorable, revelatory, life-changing experience of his life . . . . From the beginning of our research, our attention was directed to the *engineering of ecstasy, the preparation for, the setting for the achievement of ecstasy*" (italics added).[17]

On the opposite end, take the statement of Brendan A. Maher, chairman of the Harvard Center for Research in Personality.

"Taking a drug, sitting in a fox-hole, falling in love or falling out of an airplane all provide experiences. To the extent that we engage in any of these activities because the experience is an end in itself, then we are doing it—to speak colloquially—for 'kicks.' A university is an institution intended to provide a rather special set of experiences; experiences that lead to increased competencies, capacities for intellectual self-discipline, interest in examining all of the evidence and an understanding of the intellectual history of man. Experience *per se* is not part of a University's commissariat . . . among the members of the faculty at the Center there was a serious concern when it became apparent that not only were students being indoctrinated in the belief that communicable knowledge was the endproduct of some kind of pointless 'game,' but that the drug experience was being held out to them as a kind of redemption from the rigors of rationality." [18]

Substitute "mystical experience" for "drug," and Maher's statement could stand unchanged. Of course, the university holds no "commissariat" for conversion, but it may well hold one for the study of conversion. But conversion and its study remain respectable and acceptable, hence fundable, if they are

211

conducted extramurally and "objectively." They have no place inside the academy, its teachers must not be contaminated by it, or better, if they are, they must keep it to themselves or speak in the third person when they make a report. Allen Coult, the late founder, president, and one of the few members of the International Association for Psychedelic Anthropology, conceived of the New University, which would shift research from observation to affect-participation; getting high on acid, making love to the students, achieving mystical vision, should be the curriculum of the New University. Coult, of course, was not alone in this, though he was the most vocal proponent among the professional in the counter-culture, better read than Leary and Alpert, though probably not any less "far out" than they.

In the sixties "free" and "new" universities sprang up in every large city. The official university took a dim view of these institutions, or ignored them. Professors fired from an official university or college because of their psychedelic-prophetic activities—activities rather than views—were prominent in these counter-academies. Toronto is the only place in North America, I believe, where a university of this sort—minus pot and acid, I presume—got the official nod; some public money went into it, and there were some fine scholars on its staff. At such institutions, the courses taught are indeed unacceptable by any official academic institution as yet: yoga-meditation, breath control, ecstasies and dynamics, astrology, Zen practice, seminars in human intercourse which rightly includes the sexual sphere. The argument which keeps these courses out from the official academy is of the sort Maher projected *in rebus* Leary and Alpert, against non-descriptive, self-involving studies. I am highly sympathetic to yoga, ecstasy, orgies and all, but I do not think they can be part of the academic system. Yet they may be far more *important* for humanity today, and more interesting than the things the academician does for a living. When a lady-yogi, who conducted large classes in *haṭha-* and *rāja-yoga* in the city, requested that her yoga course be placed on the university curriculum, she was rejected—I voted against her. I will do yoga with her any time, but not in the classroom. Mysticism, yoga, lysergic acid, and the whole realm of ecstasy are beautiful and precious things, they should be practiced like making love; but they should be practiced in communities whose each and every member shares the implied world view, and for those who share and practice, the actions shared and practiced are *not* illicit, but supremely moral. But there can be no overlap into the world where people do *not* share and

212

practice. The job of the academy is to describe and to analyze from some distance, and to regard everything investigated as *object*. I am not impressed by many of my radical colleagues' arguments, Marxian and others, that the social scientist has to get involved in his subject. He should get involved as a person, if he wishes, but this involvement must not intrude upon his analysis for a simple reason: if the anthropologist and the sociologist and the psychologist and all social scientists report their findings *sub specie visionis*, inspired by their ideological, political, or religious convictions, then the result will be moral and scientific abomination. Mao and Stalin and Comrade Academician are quite wrong if they insist that there must be a people's chemistry, a proletarian physics, a revolutionary mathematics. Fortunately, there is good mathematics and physics in the U.S.S.R. and China. Trouble arose with the biological sciences, where the Soviet Union has hardly produced anything that will stand up to what the West does, *because* Soviet scientists had to toe the line, and spin an official ideological doctrine. But of course, if there is to be a people's physics and a revolutionary sociology, then Hitler, Goebbels, and Rosenberg were quite right in claiming that there is a German mythology, an Aryan physics, and a Germanic medicine.

I define the illicit as the deviant trespassing into a social segment where its content is not voluntarily accepted. Where the illicit and the deviant abide by their own rules, working out their splendor in their own circle of initiates, then the terms "deviant" and "illicit" no longer mean anything, except as terms of censure used by the outsiders against the initiates. Mysticism (even Charles Manson's, if it was genuine) was not criminal just as it wasn't green or round; the only adjectives that can qualify mystics are "genuine" and "spurious." Manson and his crew trespassed into other people's lives in a grotesque, tragical manner. If they thought that a mystical experience enjoined it on them, then their connection was as fallacious as that of other mystics who think their experience enjoins upon them the preaching of the good life.

In a well-organized interview on drugs in *Playboy* Magazine the relation between the mystical, the medical, and the legal was brought out vividly.[19] One of the participants was a policeman, a man in high national and international office, stern, stolid, and not at all bright; then there was Alan Watts, Leslie Fiedler, and Baba Ram Dass *ne* Dr. Alpert. Fiedler was the subtlest analyst of the specifically illicit part that the drug played in an infra-legal sphere. The policeman, who

213

ranted about the criminality of LSD, couldn't even begin to see why his fellow panelists harped on the connection with the religious. The mystically engaged Watts and Ram Dass evidently took it as beneath their dignity to address themselves to the policeman's harangue; but Fiedler put his finger on the matter when he said "Poets are less terrified of drugs than . . . bankers or real-estate salesmen; yet, poets know the terror of mind-expansion—the danger of walking into the world of magic, which is the danger of no-return . . . ." The drug experience could be substituted, in Fiedler's proposition, by "the mystical experience." The totally unpredictable in human experience is kin to the totally autonomous; but in the ways of the world, of society, *this* is the illicit.

The mystic should not be an ideologue as a mystic, because there is no mystical ideology. I am quite aware, however, that mystics have always believed that their experience generates a world view, an ideology, a religion. From this fact it does not follow that mystics will always believe this. I muse about the chances for a mystic who is also an intellectual by modern standards, who thinks hard and directs his capitations to diverse topics, including mysticism. But until he develops, I'll talk about actual mystics, who don't separate their experience from ideology.

Hindu pandits, Hindu swamis, and the yoga professional on the subcontinent with some very few exceptions of a very recent origin, are highly authoritarian—as is the tradition to which they adhere; they are highly puritanical; and, most embarrassing in the current light, they take the virtue of patriotism, nationalism, chauvinism, and the derived cultural jingoism for granted. I have yet to meet one India-born monk, one South Asian mystic who does not believe that a man must serve his country, that the profession of the soldier is basically a noble profession, and that parents have to be trusted.

There is no conflict here between their statements of total freedom for the "realized soul" and those strictures which our young scholars call "fascist" or which Herbert Marcuse subsumes under "surplus repression." "Total freedom" accrues to the person who has achieved the supreme status of the absolute, the swamis would say. So long as one has not reached that state, one is bound by conventions. The "realized souls," the Kṛṣṇas, the avataras, are ideologically fascistic. The *Bhagavadgītā* owes quite a bit of its popularity in India to this quality: superman, i.e. man with the zero-experience interpreted in the orthodox elitist Hindu-brahmanical fashion, may do whatever he wants, and ordinary people don't even realize his greatness. In the ideological history of India, any person who succeeded in acting the despot, while keeping up the paternalistic, patron-client atmosphere, was a candidate for avatar-hood.

If this total freedom for the totally emancipated were read in a Bacchanalian, ecstatic context, no harm would be done. I would certainly recommend such a reading: that the man who has had the zero-experience, and who interprets it as his brief to act autonomously and to interact with other people freely on a voluntary basis, should indeed go ahead and enjoy life without heeding the philistine's rebuke. But this is not how Hindu India has seen it: where culture heroes, avatars, and other hierophants did great deeds on the battlefield *and* in the field of dalliance with damsels human and divine, the latter aspect was more and more rejected as the centuries went by. Krṣṇa, simultaneous lover of 16,000 *married* milk-maids, was still blessed and praised as *jāra cora cūḍāmaṇi* "adulterer, thief, crest-jewel" in early medieval Hindi poetry; but today, the 16,000 cowherdesses, so my friend the brahmin economist at Harvard assures me, were 16,000 holy verses (*ślokas*) which Krṣṇa knew by heart!

In early Indian reports, zero-experiences created a passing or a lasting euphoria which some subjects expressed in the language of megalomania. The contents of the megalomanic episode can be either heroic and martial, or erotic—or both. I can present my own case as an example. After my second and third zero-experiences, I day-dreamed for about two days—and the daydreams had martial, musical, and erotic overtones. But at that time I did not see the connection between these seemingly unrelated themes. Several years later, however, on experimenting with LSD and some of the other new substances, I noticed that the highly euphoric phases of this model-paranoia had this threefold content in a very distinct measure: there was strong sexual interaction with the woman I took the drug with; there was a close-to-orgasmic enjoyment of Henry Purcell's *Ode on St. Cecilia's Day* and *Come Ye Sons of Art*, and here it was the trumpets that really did it, and the martial connotation was quite clear to me even while still heavily under the drug. For though I hated military things as much as anyone, I had recurrent feelings of heroic deeds done or witnessed by myself, accompanied by trumpets and trombones. Not a Christian crusader by any stretch of the imagination, I saw myself riding forth spearing infidels, not defining, of course, who exactly the infidels were, just infidels, people who stood for wrong and the evil.

215

If we view the monastic traditions of the world across dogmatic and theolgoical lines, we will be struck by the para-military character which pervades monastic institutions in all of the world's religions. (Not even excepting Buddhism: we have the highly militant Khamba monks in the Tibetan orders, distant no doubt from the top of the hierarchy, but accepted by the latter.) The early "desert fathers" [20] called themselves the vanguard of the army of God, fighting the devil in the dry desert; the later, highly ramified orders had, more often than not, military hierarchies—witness the Jesuits and other orders who have their "General" at the top.

What does this mean for the mystic? I realize, however sadly, that the ideologically detached, non-heroic, experimental mystic who separates his experience from the official world-view is somehow mysteriously and inextricably linked to all sorts of exalted social behavior and individual action, actual or imagined. All traditions support this fallacy—in fact, the mystic's conviction about a mystical-moral-heroic continuum is part of the "interpretation" of the zero-experience. There is no reason why this coded nexus should not be broken. But I think few mystics would want to break it even if they knew that it was philosophically and, in the long run, humanly more desirable and beneficial to disengage from it rather than to persist in flirting with the heroic parameters of the interpreted mystical experience. The mystic-euphoric-megalomaniac-heroic syndrome is delightful. Yet, since many mystics are men of good will, they might one day be persuaded, by rational argument and discursive study, that heroism is dysfunctional in the long run. Men of God, I would think, are preferable to soldiers of God, but then most religious traditions, at one time or the other, have called their best men of God soldiers of God. We shall have to continue arguing with theologians before we can get to the mystic, and with the poets who extol the heroic which the mystic emulates.

Chapter Eight

The Present and the Future of Mysticism

The student of religious behavior knows that a teaching, a sect, a religious organization, when revived after desuetude, is not what it was, even though it may carry the old name. Let me try to explain why groups and people who had genuine mystics amongst them did not survive, or why they were unable to sustain their claim to mystical guidance.

The theosophists were an important organization. They created and represented an important trend. I believe that Mme. Blavatsky was a fake, even though a highly charismatic fake, perhaps full of *siddhi*, occult powers, as her disciples claimed and as she implied. But Annie Besant was a great and noble woman; perhaps the finest orator in the Commonwealth in her days; a founding member and a president of the Indian National Congress; a true lover of India; and quite possibly a mystic. That she fell victim to Blavatsky was, of course, her own fault. Then there was Colonel Olcott, a good man in every way, keen on showing the West that there was beauty and unknown greatness in the East, and reminding the East of it. There was Ledbeater who, like Blavatsky, was a fake—a less dangerous one, and more pitiable. In Germany, Besant had appointed Dr. Rudolf Steiner to create and augment the theosophical call in central Europe. He separated from the mother organization and founded the Anthroposophical Society, which has its centers all over the German-speaking areas of Europe, alongside Theosophical centers. Theosophists, including the "Esoteric Society," later rechristened as the "Eastern Society," and the Anthroposophists have had their vogue. I do not know whether their membership is steady, on the decline, or gaining. But it is quite obvious that they do not compare, by way of growth, by their proselytizing and literary output, and by name and fame, to swami-centered movements, and to the Zen groups which, after establishing bridgeheads in the western world around the turn of the century, had all but monopolized the non- or anti-Christian spiritual-cum-mystical endeavors in occidental societies, until the advent of the

217

swamis after World War II.

I have not mentioned another of this century's traditions, i.e. the Gurdjieff-Ouspensky-Bennett continuum. Followers will most certainly object to this bracketing; but then this is an *etic* bracket—it does not have to make sense to the followers, if it does to the critic and the analyst. Gurdjieff was a saintly person; his teachings were quite simple and unassuming. I believe that he was a mystic who regretted having talked and having to talk about it. His followers were a motley crowd, and his interpreters moved between the bizarre and the trivial. There was nothing in his teachings that could not also be found in all other contemporary esoteric groups with an eastern-cum-Christian eclectic inspiration. But it was Gurdjieff's personality and his gentle charisma that made people rally *and* fight around him.

I gravely object to Ouspensky's writings. He did to Gurdjieff what today's English-speaking Indian teachers of Indian philosophy do to Indian philsophy. Nobody wants to be more scientific than the pseudo-scientist or the eager man who has not mastered the scientific medium. Ouspensky's quasi-mathematical interpretations of the Gurdjieffian and other spiritual lore seem to impress non-mathematicians and non-mystics alike. Ouspensky confused the cognitive with the affective; he did not see that the mystical experience—which he may or may not have had—neither required nor suffered discursive, cognitive, "scientific" explanations. Vivekananda was the man who started the "scientific" fad. Neither he nor his followers seemed to realize that they were doing a disservice to their particular brands of mysticism by trying to corroborate them with the edicts of science. Science is descriptive even where it is normative; but mysticism is neither, because states of mind are not descriptive or normative. Mysticism and the consummate religious life are not any more or less "scientific" than is agony, pleasure, orgasm, or enjoying Mozart. Descriptions of these events can, of course, be scientific to the degree that they are descriptive and analytic. But then any description of anything can be scientific. I think Vivekananda confused the meanings of "scientific" and "methodical." Yoga practice if it is to succeed must, of course, be methodical. All Indian teachers and all types of Indian tradition and training have made this abundantly clear—whether you want to make love properly, write poetry or do grammar, you must do these things systematically, and there is a method for everything that can be learned; if it is not learned, it is not really worth the effort. Good things do not come randomly—or rather, they do not persist unless there is a method to make them persist.

I have said a lot about the Ramakrishna Mission. It, too, is not a guide to the mystical future. I have indicated part of the cause for the decline of this once so hopeful Mission; but the cause of their failure is shared with the other losing movements which I am lining up in this concluding chapter.

Baha'ism is no longer new. It is certainly well organized and affluent. Alongside the so much more recent Maharishi and his Transcendental Meditation, I have seen Baha'i posters on notice boards on dozens of American campuses. In the Yellow Pages of American city telephone directories, Baha'i Assemblies are listed under "Churches, Non-denominational" or under the more appropriate "other denominations." A social scientist wrote a piece in the *Journal for the Scientific Study of Religion* a few years ago. I wrote a rejoinder in the same journal.[1] The man had marshaled statistics to show that Baha'i people in America are more involved in formal religious pursuits than Protestants. The argument is disingenuous. If a man converts to something that is quite different from the nominal faith into which he was born, it is obvious that he will be more active in the accepted faith. Perhaps the author wanted to convince himself and others that Baha'i was an old religion like Protestantism. Neither did he mention that Baha'i was a recent revivalist form of Shi'a Islam. Why all that obfuscation? The Baha'i literature, which one gets free on fine silk paper just for the asking, never mentions this; when it talks about Islam, it criticizes it—orthodox Shi'a Islam of nineteenth century Iran, that is—for having persecuted Baha'i. I believe this is the reason why Baha'i, no doubt the teaching of a mystic, does not score as a competitor with Transcendental Meditation, LSD, Zen. Any teaching which hedges about its historical roots, for whatever reason, is bound to fail in the long run—not because honesty is the best policy, which is patently not so in matters of the world, but because a mystic's teaching has to be checked against an established tradition at every point. There is no mystical teaching from scratch. Baha'ullah probably knew Persian Sufi literature, and I would think that he and his fellow-prophetess, Qurratul'Ain, also martyred like him, liked to feel themselves close to Al Ḥallāj and other Sufi mystics. To my knowledge, Baha'ullah never denied that his teaching was rooted in Islam—or rather, in the heterodox, sufi-type of mystical Islam. As it stands, Baha'ism does not generate zero-experiences; if some followers have it, they are on their own. But in order to interpret the experience, a mystic has to use the language of a tradition; unless, of course, he is the sort of mystical experimentalist who has cathected the zero-experience as all that counts, but then he doesn't talk about it in any religious manner. He talks about it in clinical, experimental, perhaps aesthetic terms.

Mr. Bennett at one time gave much of his love and most of his wealth to Subud. That teaching Indonesian-Muslim-Hindu-eclectic, with South East Asian middle-class Muslim moral standards foisted upon it, has made a strong impact on the western world, and I understand that its followers in some parts of North America are more numerous than Zen adherents in the same regions. Subud does a lot of guided interpersonal experimentation, and it has some family resemblances to Mr. Hubbard's Scientology. This seems supported by the fact that all the Subud people to whom I suggested this rejected it with unnecessary vehemence. This is like the ordinary language philosopher's wrath at being called a logical positivist—whether he likes it or not, there are family resemblances evident to any perceptive outsider. I may not like my ancestors, but I cannot help looking like them.

I think Subud has a good chance to survive and to contribute to the mystical trends of the future. I shall save the why for the end.

I must now return for a final visit to the Indian scene. Meher Baba,[2] a Parsi by birth, became a saint in the usual Indian way, by declaring himself one and by creating an audience. Then one day, in the early thirties, I believe, he took a vow of silence, at which time he announced that when he spoke again he would say the words that would save the world once and for all. When I heard about this announcement, I knew and stated repeatedly exactly what the Baba was going to say: that the world must trust him, that it must meditate, emit love, and forget hate. Years later, when Meher Baba opened his mouth on a date computed by astrologers and by the consensus of the faithful—he had friends and chapters on four continents by that time—he said these remarkable words: that the world must trust in God, meditate, spread love, and forget hate . . . .

The most grotesque of all living saints, to this author's mind, is Sai Baba, mentioned in an earlier chapter. The original Sai Baba was a Muslim *darvish*-like saint in Western India, who lived in the mid-eighteenth century. The present Sai Baba is a Telugu-speaking non-Brahman Hindu, an incarnation of the original Sai Baba. He cures terminal cancer at will at a distance of many thousands of miles, and the patient has just got to concentrate on him—visualizing Babaji (the endearing appellation for the present man), with his long hair and his flowing golden

220

robe. An ex-Civil Surgeon, F.R.C.S. is the source of this information. When thousands of people were assembled for Sai Baba's *darśan*, he distributed holy ashes (*bhasma*) to all of them from his one palm; this information did not come from a villager visiting the town where Sai Baba appeared, but from a Mr. S., Ph. D. in Economics from the London School of Economics, and advisor to the permanent Indian delegation to the United Nations. At this time, Sai Baba has some two million followers in India and abroad; his picture is seen in thousands of dwellings, palatial as well as coolie-line shanty. I believe the Sai Baba cult will spread and last, with better chances than the Ramakrishna Mission.

Swami Yogananda Paramahamsa's *Self Realization Fellowship*, with its international headquarters in a splendid structure in Los Angeles and in San Diego, California, became famous through his *Autobiography of a Yogi*. The book is running in its fifteenth English language edition, and has been translated into all European languages. It is an amazing account of miraculous deeds and things that happened to him as he met contemporary saints and mystics all over the world. He wore his hair long and was a thoroughly successful swami, both in his native Bengal and in the West. His Fellowship is holding its own at the present time, and it is probably reaching its plateau. It has a good chance to last, though it lacks the living presence of the charismatic leader.

There are two audiences with which the swamis and the other eastern mystagogues do not score. They are the professional modern philosophers, and the orientalists, people who study Asian culture professionally.

Scientists with experimental proclivities are often more naive, hence more gullible, when it comes to understanding premises. Dr. Elmer Green and future researchers on the body-and-soul systems of visiting saints apply their impressive technological know-how on impossible premises. There is one thing which the modern experimentalist and the scholastic doctors of Islam and Christianity have in common: they do not often examine the verbal premises of what they investigate. The literature on feats accompanying yoga is large in India, and thoroughly boring after a while. Swami Rama in Topeka, Kansas, may very well be able to slow down or even suspend his heart-beat for a time, to breathe imperceptibly or not at all for an hour; he may also achieve cures in people in need of cures of the psycho-somatic type. If a woman has lost faith in all doctors, sees the swami, and her child is cured the next day, then whatever the causal nexus between the swami and the child, the mother will be satisfied that the swami did it. If Dr. Green put other people, non-yogis and non-swamis under the E.E.G. and the E.C.G., computerizing the results, he might find them able to do similar feats. But even if they couldn't, even if it did require yogic discipline to accomplish these states, what follows from it? It has no bearing upon the truth of the yogic teachings, for the yogic teachings teach ecstasy, they guide and goad to the zero-experience. Doing the heart-and-breath feats does not mean having the zero-experience, nor does having the zero-experience mean being able to work these feats. From these accomplishments, no such things as world-peace, universal love and brotherhood, health, or the zero-experience follow. If the swami really believes they do, then he is either naive or a fanatic or both; if he doesn't believe it but lets people believe that he does, then he lies. The trouble with scientists who are getting interested in Indian lore is that they have been insufficiently exposed to either anthropology or to Indic studies —and, with greater damage, they do not know the beginnings of philosophical language analysis. They tend to take all that their swamis say quite literally—and they counter any challenge by the irrelevant, "disprove it" stance. Now "disproof" does not lie in the experimental or the scientific field at all; it lies in the field of prior clear thinking, premises, logic. To establish a correlation, by experiment and computation, between a man's control of heartbeat and his suspension of breath is one thing. But no relation between these things, zero-experiences, morals, world peace and questions about God and Nature can be computerized *even in theory*. This is like Gilbert Ryle's old classic: the sentence "the moon is made of green cheese on the side turned away from us" is empirically false (as was proved by the astronauts) but it was empirically falsifiable. "God is good and omnipotent" or "heartbeat control brings world peace" cannot be verified or falsified, since no statements of any sort could possibly qualify as falsifications. The error of Western experimentalists who seek to "prove" eastern wisdom is that of misplaced trust. In their minds, it takes this form: Swami X says he can control his breath and his heartbeat; he says that if a man can control his breath and his heartbeat, he sees God, has true emancipation, is a true yogi, etc. Now we test his claims— one, yes, he controls his breath; two, yes, he controls, *mirabile dictu*, his heartbeat. But now the empiricist reaches dead end: since he cannot test whether the swami sees God, is a yogi, has emancipation, etc., he takes this end of the story on faith. That the swami himself may *believe* "seeing God," etc., follows from "controlling one's breath" etc., is quite beside the point. For suppose the swami had the zero-experience, which I do not deny, then his reasoning that it followed from his controls is false reasoning based on a traditional fallacy. But why do the roughly two dozen western experimentalists who work on swamis and other oriental practitioners of the saintly profession, not ask them about the connection between "breath" or "pulse" control and the vision of God, emancipation, world-peace, etc.? There are two simple reasons for this: anthropologically untutored experimentalists tend to be so impressed by the swami's feats that they take his word for all he may say about the yogic complex—and that includes pulsation control *and* emancipation. Second, there is this white American Christian notion that a holy man should not be asked about holy things by people with a secular occupation. This is how the Protestant Ethic reinforces specialization in a subtle way—just as the chemist does not make geographical suggestions to the geographer, nor the policeman juridical proposals to the judge, the physicist, psychologist, experimentalist does not make suggestions about holy things to the holy—you don't encroach on other people's occupational domain. That is too bad, in the light of the general experience of the last three to five centuries: for it was precisely logical and other clear thinking that dethroned religious dogma. Just as Renaissance men said to priests "talk about God and the angels, but tell me how God is both all-good and omnipotent without contradicting yourself," the modern experimentalists *should* say to the swamis "you are right about breath control, pulse control, but how do these give you knowledge of God, emancipation, etc., *apart* from your believing they do?" This is much like the New Testament scene which appalls modern, sympathetic, Bible-reading Hindus. The Jews didn't believe Jesus's teachings—so he raised Jairus's daughter from the dead! What on earth, the Hindu and the philosopher ask, has the raising from the dead or any other miracle got to do with a moral teaching? How does the former prove the latter? Our modern scientists, good Christians many of them, with little philosophical and less theological acumen, fail to see that the one set of actions (miracles, marvelous controls, etc.) neither proves nor disproves any theological, moralistic, prophetic, or mystical claims. The non-theologian is basically fearful of divinity, if he is born into a theistic culture; and the non-philosopher, no matter what his technical, scientific, or other skills, does not take the trouble to seek for a cool causal concatenation when things occur which fascinate him, spilling over from a universe about which he knows nothing.

223

I wish to conclude my comments on charismatic leaders with two well-known men. Sri Aurobindo is the god-man of this age to roughly two hundred thousand very sophisticated people in India and in the West. In his well-written, somewhat pompous *Divine Life*, which I believe could be rewritten in about one-fourth of its size without loss to its content, he propounded a highly eclectic theme, a blend of yogic, Vedāntic, and incipiently Tantric ideas. The universe is quite real to him, as it is to several Vedāntic schools; hence the peak- experience is not one of extinction, or one that would cancel the world. Rather, it subsumes the world into a much higher, much more beautiful essence, the Absolute. Since Aurobindo wrote in English only, and since he was no follower and wanted to make it clear that he wasn't, he avoided Vedāntic jargon. The scene which developed around him was amazing. The Mother, who presided over the Ashram at Pondicherry after the Master moved to higher spheres, until her death in 1973, was probably a mystic; and so was he. The regimentation at the Ashram, which is as cosmopolitan a place as one could find anywhere in India, included bland food, calisthenics, complete obedience to La Mère, and lots of meditation and meditation surrogates. For a while, it seemed that the Aurobindo movement would make a big sweep into all parts of the world. Everything was very well organized indeed. The Ramakrishna Mission talks about the active and good life; the Aurobindo teachers talk about a harmonious, yogic way of living, but there is no hysterical super-claim of any sort. Some of the lower-echelon followers talk about world peace, universal love and other things which they think their way and their teachings achieve, but this is not really condoned on the top. Yet I do not believe that the Aurobindo movement, any more than the Ramakrishna Mission, will survive as a power for the mystic.

There is the famous, rather wonderful, aging J. Krishnamurti. He began as a theosophist, but he defected, an act of great insight, at the tender age of less than twenty. Mme. Besant, that great but partly benighted person, had set him up as the *avatara* of the age; he was in his early teens at that time. He was to be seated under the original *bodhi* tree, the site where the Buddha had found all there was to be found, twenty-five centuries earlier; and there, his avatarhood was to be proclaimed to the world, the nether worlds, and the upper worlds. People had come to witness the event from all over India, Australia, Europe and North America. But the night before the event, Krishnamurti vanished. He turned up in Holland less than a year later; and then he explained, quite simply, that he did not believe in his or anyone else's avatar-hood, and that he regretted to have had to do this to Mme. Besant. Since then, Krishnamurti has taught in America, Europe, and India. He has never embraced any formal monasticism, nor did he wear sartorially distinguishable robes. He has written many books, each of which makes sense. He advises people on everything they ask him. Quite recently, as he returned to Madras once more from California and Switzerland, where his largest center stands, his Hindu devotees again tried to approach him as one approaches the avatar. He got visibly annoyed. "What do you want me to talk about?" he asked. "About sex? That is an important topic now, you know." Embarrassed silence. But Krishnamurti has talked about meditation, sex, the unimportance of God, about yoga, and about everything gurus talk about. However, there is a difference: he has never initiated people. He does not tell them to meditate, or not to meditate. He does not issue moral warrants, nor religious pep-talk like the swamis. But he does talk Vedānta—a highly sophisticated, modern, non-scriptural, but authentic kind of Vedānta. He is, among the gurus of the world, a no-nonsense man—perhaps the only one. He does not reject ritualism as the city-born, middle-class swamis do, with big chips on their small shoulders. He was born a Smārta brahmin, the highest of all brahmin casts; his poor father sold him to the theosophists, to Besant and Ledbeater, along with his twin brother Laxmanamurty, who died of tuberculosis at a very early age. Is he a mystic? I believe so, but I also believe that it is really quite unimportant to him, and he does not talk about it. He is very much a precursor of the "do your own thing" style enunciated by the counter-culture in the West, minus of course the surrogate ritualistic, inversely bigoted shenanigans of the hippies, the cultists, and the wide-eyed seekers who make up the spiritual end of the youth-culture.

Prophets are given much more time than anthropologists for their words to come true, but I think that my intuitions about the future of some movements will stand. Let me explain the basis of my assessments. I think that religious, revivalist, mystical, and kindred religious movements will survive the century and will grow, to the degree that they are viable substitutes for psychotherapy and psychoanalysis. "Substitutes" means something rather special, however, since the psycho-therapeutic situation is subtler, and more open to contradictory evaluations than a straight medical situation. I would define therapy as any action or interaction that does anything *at all* to the patient. Being cured, getting better, getting worse, all these can be and are being seen as stages within the therapeutic. It is quite similar with the religious, mystical situation; movements, sects, organizations, and individual teachers will succeed, i.e. will preserve and enlarge the throng of followers, to the extent that they *do something* to their clients. In contrast, the official Protestant services, the parson's counseling, the sermon, the good life and its dialectic, *do nothing* to prospective clients from the congregation, nothing for those who seek. They do, I presume, all sorts of good things by way of arranging accustomed things into innocuous structures, for the average church-going Christian. But mystics see these people, though the majority, as the enemy. Members of the establishment have recourse, in case of crisis, to the minister. If the minister can counsel and help without being a mystic or a charismatic, then his client is not really a patient at all. Now the Ramakrishna Mission, the Aurobindo movement, and all the people and organizations that I checked off as having little or no future, are quite like the Protestant churches in the West: in the most critical and intimate realms, they do nothing to their clients, nothing by way of the diagnostic or the therapeutic. Krishnamurti, Maharishi Mahesh Yogi, and others to whom I assigned a future, *do* something to people. They may make them sick and even more miserable, they may make them ecstatic and thrill them for a day, a week, a year, perhaps longer, as with a goodly ten thousand out of a hundred thousand who have had some sort of yogic initiation in the West during the past ten years. Yoga is therapy, and mental therapy is therapy that does something to a patient—it does not have to cure, since there is no such thing as a "cure" in the psychiatric world comparable to a broken leg mended and healed. The good analyst or therapist is the person whom the patient sees as the one who had direct access to his or her inside; he may be hateful or helpful, he may improve things or worsen them—but he makes the patient feel and react, whereas bad therapists are the ones who don't change a thing.

I doubt that "Transcendental Meditation" delivers the goods that the Maharishi and his American and European middle-men promise and believe. It certainly does not confer zero-experiences, any more or any less than other psycho-experimental procedures. I must say that I have not encountered a single person who claims to have had a zero-experience and who did then seek "Transcendental" initiation to corroborate, to confirm, to stabilize it. Of the four people in the West who convinced me that they have had zero-experiences, two went to India and Ceylon and obtained orthodox initiations; the other two let it go. I lost track of one of them; the other one keeps doing what he did when he had the experience in 1960—he sells real estate. Like good analysis and good therapy, yoga does not usually change your occupation— it strengthens it. That does not mean that a person who has had the experience must necessarily keep doing what he did before he had it. But continuing or discontinuing, his choice is unconnected with the zero-experience; it has to do with his own assessment of his work. I cannot say with certainty that a zero-experience never prompts a man to reassess specific pursuits, but it is my opinion that such direct deflection from the previously established mode of action, occupation, and routine, is extremely rare.

The highly complex "drop-out" syndrome comes up at this point. Do not some rebels, male and female, attach themselves to Buddha or more recent Indian yogis? True, but in no case known to me was it a zero-experience that made the young quit, and betake themselves to Nepal or Haight-Ashbury or the East Village. In fact, a zero-experience is likely to reduce the need to move away from mamma and daddy's lair, for if it does anything directly to the average man with an average mind, it makes him more observant, more detached—it makes him see persons and events around him in a healthier, more humorous hierarchy; they fall in line, beneath the zero-experience, as less important, less pernicious, hence less serious. The people who leave their suburban homes, their colleges, or their palaces like the Buddha, do so prompted by gripes of quite a different order: dissatisfaction with society, politics, theology or simply with the general human condition radically conceived, like the Buddha—but these dissatisfactions are *not* mystical experiences. Discarding the ecology of dissatisfaction, moving out physically, may prepare the mood for a zero-experience, again as in the case of the Buddha. But is usually leads to a different organizational experience—a monastery, an ascetic grove, a Himalayan glade, a Californian mountain commune. In the new setting, a zero-experience may occur, but since people who do not change their environment also have zero-experiences, it is hard to tell whether the environmental shift and the experience are at all related.

So, then, the first factor that makes a yoga-school survive and flourish, and capture future audiences, is that the guru or gurus in question do something to their clients—or more *etically* speaking, that the clients think they are changed, that they believe the guru and follow his instructions. However they then paraphrase it, the fact remains that something happened. *Not* in the pietistic, trivial way in which the churchgoer tells himself and the world that the church, the sermon, the good Christian life did something good for him. The affect has to be part of a genuine conversion syndrome, a transference as in the case of successful analysis and therapy.

The second, equally important factor for the survival of revivalist, eclectic mystical and other neo-spiritual movements seems to be the degree to which the guru or his staff induce, persuade, or at least permit their disciples to experiment freely—and in whatever way they choose, provided that they report their gains in the terminology of the guru's teachings. Teachers who do not oppose free experimentation *on principle*, are likely to win out in this new age of the spirit, at the dawning of the age of Aquarius for whose students this book is written. It is irrelevant whether or not the guru sermonizes on the good life, on sense-control, food, chastity, loyalty, universal love and all the other virtues, so long as he does not undermine free experimentation. All the sadhus I know censure LSD, free sex, commune-life, manipulation of ecstasy, etc., as part of their instruction-packet. Yet this need not be counter-operative, *unless* they make non-experimentation with psychedelics, sex, etc., *a condition* for success. Maharishi Mahesh Yogi is a vacillating case. He seemed quite open to experimentation on the part of his disciples. Not that he would take a drug himself or achieve ecstasy through ritualized sex—being a city-boy of high caste modern India, these things are quite impossible for him as they are for the other English-speaking swamis who, since Vivekananda, were all middle-class boys. Then all of a sudden, without anyone's knowing why, he made it clear that drugs were out, and he implied that sex was out. At this point he lost the Beatles and Mia Farrow, and probably many lesser luminaries along with them. One of his senior disciples just came back from the Colorado ashram confided a new guideline to me: no drugs, no sex within the ashram compound—but no questions asked about activities outside the precincts. This is one sort of a compromise and it may be that compromises such as these will help sustain movements which would otherwise decline. The elders of the western world, and increasingly in the East, complain about permissiveness. But whatever one's value judgment the fact remains that for any movement to succeed in the future, it has to be permissive; if not overtly, then in a tacitly operational manner. From the latest evidence before me, I must say that I am rather pleasantly surprised at some of the roaming swamis' readiness to adapt. Recently I heard an otherwise unpleasant, pompous swami deliberate on yoga to a large crowd of college students. He said the usual things about yoga and inner peace, yoga and world peace, meditation against materialism, etc., but at the end, a young man whom I did not know but who must have read some of the older neo-Hindu stuff asked the swami's view about *brahmacaryam*, a term quite crucial in the Hindu Renaissance and interpreted, without significant modifications, as sexual continence by all the charismatics from Vivekananda to Gandhi. This swami, however, answered *"Brahmacaryam* means the fixing of one's mind in the Absolute, the *brahman."* Now this is not only the ancient Indian, classical, and pre-puritanical interpretation of the term; it is also its definitional meaning: *brahmani carate yasya manah* "he whose mind roams in the *brahman"*, is a *brahmacāri.* I had been emphasizing this pristine reading in India, generating considerable indignation in all quarters. I now infer that this kind of gradual relaxing of hardnosed disciplinary prescriptions and prohibitions will be conducive to yoga as therapy and to yoga as an alternative to the Judaeo-Christian way of life in this post-Christian era. Were it not for the antics of the more bizarre elements in the counter-culture, not only the hippies, but the uninformed cultists in every nook and niche in the cities of the West, some wise men of the late Bertrand Russell's stature might have become interested in these Asian options insofar as they are genuine. Many years ago, I had a short but intensive correspondence with Russell and with Sir Karl Popper. Two very different men with two very different kinds of work—but no doubt with similar good will towards a new humanism. Quite independently, of course, both of them concurred that the Indian way may indeed be an alternative, if it were cleansed from the anti-intellectual, sanctimonious dross of its promulgators, the swamis and their western clients.

Yoga per se, in its classical form, as presented by Patañjali over two thousand years ago, might well do the trick if there was a way in which to make it operational in the West, without having to be filtered through inane moralizing. Patañjali paid lip-service to the moral codes of his day, but everyone who reads Sanskrit sees immediately that it is just that—much as the logicians in the Indian tradition pay a short verbal tribute to deity, and then proceed on their own without any further mention of things divine. Patañjali suggested pure experimentation (divinity is one of the several possible crutches for meditation, and its ontological status is quite unimportant). There is a good chance that he held an atheistic world view, since his philosophical background was that of Sāṃkhya, an atheistic school within the Brahmin lore.

For yoga to become a reality and not a fad, the moralistic elements clustered around it by swami-talk have to be thrown out. Furthermore, the puritanical axioms of the modern Hindu, his fear of sex and his disregard for tenderness have to go. This element, it is important to know, is only partly moralistic. It has to do with the Indian fear of pollution, which is an intrinsic part of Indian systems of belief and interaction as well as of social ranking. P. Spratt put it neatly, in Freudian terms, when he said that the Hindu cathects his libido upon semen.[3] The fear of loss of semen and the extraordinary praise given to the man who is believed not to lose semen, *hence* to be pure, are not of a moralistic kind; they are culture-endemic, psychological if you will, and they have to do with the realm of magic and of superhuman agencies rather than with morals, although a moralistic interpretation has become standard in India since the beginning of the Indian Renaissance, culminating in Gandhi. Indian anthropology has barely come of age, and this element has been worked out as central to the understanding of things Indian, during the past two decades.

Since my *Tantric Tradition* was published, first in Britain in 1965 and then in paperback in America in 1970,[4] hundreds of enquiries have kept coming in. A new folder "Tantric Future," is growing in my filing cabinet. The left-handed, eroticized, well-suppressed tantric tradition is a resuscitable alternative to the ascetic, self-mortifying forms of yoga. The tantric theological matrix stresses the polarity of divinity as male and female, human sexual congress as a replica of the eternal divine copulation. This tradition, of course, explains very largely the abundance of erotic sculptures on shrines all over India and beyond. In recent centuries active tantric practice has become extremely rare and disguised. At this time, there are no more than three centers extant where ritualistic copulation is practiced in the tantric tradition. One of the centers was raided and broken up by the police about fifteen years ago, and any such assembly would be annihilated by the governments of the Indian States or by the Union, once it became known. So absolute is India's official and unofficial puritanism that non-marital sex is viewed on a line with theft, bribery, embezzlement, except that these things are often forgiven, whereas sex is not. "We can forgive a robber, for he is hungry," a young medical student told me, "but we cannot forgive a man who enjoys [Indian English for having sexual intercourse] for he is only selfish."

It will be objected that puritanism in this sense is not an

Indian peculiarity; that it is shared by the western establishment, and is inseparable from the moralizing that flows from the pulpit. *Playboy* and the open floodgates of pornography notwithstanding, the "good" man to the western establishment is the sexually continent man, who makes love in marriage only, and who, when he has sex outside marriage, feels duly embarrassed or guilty about it. But there is a vast difference here: in Southern Asian countries there is no dialogue between the spokesmen of puritanism and those of ecstasy and hedonistic experimentation. There may be a couple of thousand people in India who sympathize with the ecstatic and Dionysian; some are poets, some professional philosophers, and some just ordinary modern people who speak out. *The Radical Humanist*, a weekly in English, was created by M.N. Roy, the Indian Marxist. *Quest* in Bombay and *Thought* in Delhi, are modeled on *Encounter* in style and scope. Among their readers, we find the few non-puritanical Indians, people who would enter the dialectic between free hedonistic expression and traditional stricture. But they are absolutely atypical of India. In Western Europe and the Americas, the dialectic between the puritanical establishment and the sense-inspired critics is powerful and pervasive. Parsons and parents may still rant and rave against nudity and pot, against non-marital sex and its dialectic, but they are fighting a losing battle and they know it. Thousands among the critics of the establishment and of its values no longer think it necessary to compromise in any degree. It is understood in the urban West that the burden of proof has switched. Apart from isolated areas, say, the deep South, the people of the establishment know that this is so—that sex will be freer and freer, that the young will reject, defeat, and despise their elders until they come round to a wider dialectic of radical criticism—no longer of the hypocrisy of the older generations but of the very values which their hypocrisy betrays. In India, there is no such argument; parents cannot be criticized, Hinduism cannot be criticized—not radically, that is. The Indian critics criticize the hypocrisy of Hindus *vis-à-vis* their value orientation much as the past generation in the urban West criticized their parents—but the teachings of the *Bhagavadgītā*, the talks of Vivekananda, the sermons of Gandhi and the men themselves are not criticized. Few if any communist leaders, Marxist-Leninist or Maoist, have said anything against these people and these texts. The dialectic of radical criticism has simply not begun in Asia, except in some sidewalk cafes and in-group salons in Calcutta. The same goes for Srilanka: Buddhists are

231

criticized by Buddhists for their hypocrisy, but no one criticizes any part of the Buddha's teachings, the attitude about its irrevocable perfection remaining naively dogmatic.[5]

Let me project the future of therapeutic mysticism. I have said that it is bound to grow in the West, and that it is bound to decline in the areas of its origin. There is nothing astounding about this. Christianity and Buddhism were both export religions in that neither of them survived in the area of its origin, but both thrived in other lands. Why shouldn't a segment of a religious teaching, like Tantrism or Yoga, diffuse to other regions and decay where it started? There is no gainsaying the fact that both Yoga and Tantra have independent validity; that although they were formulated against the background of Hindu-Buddhist theology and speculation, their therapeutic efficacy does not any longer depend upon this background. Until a few years ago I insisted that Yoga and Tantra could not be exported. This was due to my annoyance with the haphazard, wide-eyed, anti-intellectual and undisciplined manner in which silly people in America and Europe lapped up the mysterious East without any knowledge of it, ignoring the fact that the East was no more mysterious than the West. These people refused to study primary sources (Sanskrit, Tibetan, Chinese, etc.) because they are difficult, yet claimed that they could master yoga, which had been declared much more difficult and demanding by the founders, who were scholars. But when I realized that the actual office of Yoga and Tantra was to be purely therapeutic, with no claim to world-improvement and to wisdom profound, I came to believe that the affluent West can practice yogic and tantric therapy, because the coming generations are liberal, experimental, enterprising, and not too respectful towards their ancestral traditions which regarded pleasure with disdain, put bliss into the safe hereafter, or relegated it to the domain of the sermon, that most unecstatic enterprise of the western tradition.

I am writing these final paragraphs overlooking the tea plantations in Nuwara Eliya, Srilanka. I am struck by the incredible naiveté of the political and the religious leaders in the face of the insurgency of 1971 and after. Most of the Buddhist monks either spoke for a somewhat repressive government, or they didn't speak at all; several hundred of them, nevertheless, have been arrested for terrorist activities. But the secular and the religious sermon and the stilted newspaper reports and commentaries written in nineteenth century Indo-Ceylonese English do not get near to the core-facts of the terrorist-insurgent psychology: there has been no scope for the expressive as well as the political and economic needs of the Ceylonese. Theravāda Buddhism has stifled mystical experimentation outside the narrowly defined meditational procedures recommended by the *sangha* to its members. But very few of the monks under 50 meditate. In fact, they are supposed to do other things, like teaching, talking, and generally participating in the uplift of the Ceylonese people. Several foreign Buddhist monks are about to leave Ceylon; they feel that they are not welcome *because* they came here to do Buddhism only, i.e. to meditate. I had to give several lectures, to Rotarians, Christians, and Buddhists, about the hippies and about Buddhism and other eastern teachings in the West today. I tried to explain the need for ecstasy as the base of all these movements, including such inanely jejune ones as the public gymnastics of that most highly exhibitionist of all India-derived movements, the *Hare Ram Hare Krishna* cult. Swami A.C. Bhaktivedanta, the choreographer and arch-guru of the transplanted cult, had collected the handsomest occidental boys and girls and taken them to India, where they performed for rapt audiences. The Hindus in India loved it—not because it presented an instantiation, however warped, of ecstasy, but because it shows how India has conquered the West. There is no understanding here of the mainsprings of all this esoteric quest in the West. Indians and Ceylonese still think that the West espouses Hindu or Buddhist doctrine because it is *better* than other doctrines. This, as I tried to show, is nonsense. Hinduism and Buddhism—some of their forms that is—provide the possibility of ecstatic quest in addition to or complementary to an ascetic option. Judaism and Christianity do not provide these; the Hassidim in the State of New York do not proselytize and are altogether too unattractive to catch on. Subud, Baha'i, and perhaps some other sufi-type Muslim derivatives have their following, because they condone ecstatic experimentation, even if they couch it in ascetic terms.

It is the affluent, hedonistically liberal, increasingly dedogmatized West, however, that can do it.[6] The very scene which permits all sorts of musical, artistic, aesthetical, and ethical experimentation, relinquishing canons and doctrines in favor of sheer experimentality, can readily incorporate the most esoteric doctrines, since the cognitive parts of those doctrines do not bother the radical ecstatic experimentalist. Thus emerges what, to the readers of this book, should no longer seem like a paradox: that Yoga and Tantra, the two most rigorously systematic streams of esoteric religion, should flourish in regions where morals are loose (of course, I am using the phrase

233

facetiously when establishmentarians, ecclesiastic and lay, would use it seriously literally). I think *Hair* epitomizes a lot in this line: only in countries where love ascends as the focus of a new age, not desiccated *charitas* as opposed to Eros, but Eros and charitas rolled into one, will esoteric practice thrive. The young who are bound to remain the majority and to set the relevant standards are likely to espouse Yoga and Tantra: more seriously and with more regard to primary traditions than they do now. For such grotesque oversimplifications as Hare Krishna and "Transcendental Meditation" will have to be abandoned or reformed, and informed by a serious study of primary sources. So long as the roaming swamis succeed in dissuading their wide-eyed followers from studying Sanskrit and Tibetan, and from listening to specialists who do not know English, there is little chance for such fruition. I think the reason why the young who could learn these primary things, refuse to, is not only gullibility *vis-à-vis* the berobed man with the Indian accent; also, intellectual discipline is identified with the liberal, the war-makers, and with the puritans—the "straight." With the rise of intellectually disciplined non-squares, non-puritans who would absorb and transmit the primary sources unsancti- moniously, meditating, studying, *and* copulating as they do these things, there may well come a time when a rational mysticism is generated by modern people who love to think, read, learn difficult grammars, and make love to consenting adults. A rational mysticism is not a contradiction in terms; it is a mysticism whose limits are set by reasons: a quest for the zero-experience without any concomitant claim to world- knowledge, special wisdom, or special morality. These latter three must be directly generated by reason, and by reason only.

NOTES

Chapter I

1. A.R. Louch, *Explanation and Human Action*, Berkeley & Los Angeles: Univ. of California Press, 1966.
2. Roy G. Willis, "Changes in mystical concepts and practices among the Fipo", in *Ethnology* 7, (Pittsburgh) 1968, 139-75.
3. Richard Hofstadter, *Anti-Intellectualism in American Life*, New York: Vintage Paperback No. 317, 1966.
4. Edward N. Shils, *The Intellectual between Tradition and Modernity: The Indian Situation*. The Hague: Mouton & Co., 1961.
5. R.E. Stanfield, Letter to the Editor, *New York Sunday Times Magazine Section* Oct. 12, 1969 (22-23).
6. John J. Honigman, *Personality in Culture*, New York: Harper & Row 1967, 395.
7. Mircea Eliade, *Yoga: Immortality and Freedom*, New York: Pantheon Books 1958, 37 *et passim*.
8. MIND, quarterly published by B.H. Blackwell, Oxford, is the periodical bible, so to speak of the British linguistics analyst philosophers. The term 'intersubjective' as I intend it here, was first used by a number of authors in the 50s, in that journal.
9. *The Gospel of Sri Ramakrishna*, translated by Swami Nikhilananda, first published by the Ramakrishna Math and Mission in Calcutta and Madras. This version is over 1000 pages thick. An abbreviated, manageable version was published by Swami Nikhilananda for the U.S. and Canada, and it is available by mail order from the Ramakrishna Vivekananda Center, 17 East 94th St., New York, N.Y.
10. A. Osborne, *The Collected Works of Ramana Maharshi*, Tiruvannamalai (India): Sri Ramanasrama 1963. The 'collected works' are really the collected sayings of Ramana, and they fill this slender volume.
11. The Smārta-brahmins of the Tamil, Telugu, and Malayalam speaking areas of the Dravidian South of India are no doubt the highest caste by consensus and acclaim; ideologically, they are followers of Śaṃkarā-cārya; they worship all Vedic gods on the ritualistic side, but Śiva is their tutelary deity and the monistic Advaita philosophy provides their main ideological framework.
12. The *Taittirīya Upaniṣad* of the Black Yajurveda; the most easily available, fairly good translation of this and the other chief Upaniṣads is that by Swami Nikhilananda, New York, Harper Torchbooks No. 114, (paperback) 1964, i.e. *The Upanishads—a one volume abridgement*.
13. A. Bharati "The Hindu Renaissance and its Apologetic Patterns" in *Journal of Asian Studies*, Vol. XXIX / 2, Feb. 1970.

Chapter II

1. Boris Vysheslawzeff, "Two Ways of Redemption" in Joseph Campbell (ed.) *The Mystic Vision* (Papers from the ERANOS YEARBOOKS), Princeton: University Press, 1968. Referred to as *Mystic Vision* below.

235

2. Srī Caitanya (1485-1533) was a Bengali brahmin, and the foremost devotional reformer of the late Bengali Middle Ages. His influence, although localized in Bengal and Orissa, generated a powerful millenial type movement which peaked in the 17th century all over northern India and declined thereafter. There is no doubt that Swami A.C. Bhaktivedanta "Prabhupada" (Lord's Food), the silver bullion broker of Calcutta turned saint, founder of the Hare Krishna movement in the western world, creatd a genuine duplication of the Caitanya movement in an expatriate setting, i.e. in Europe and America.

3. "Lama" Lobsang Rampa, alias Hoskins, *The Third Eye*, New York, Ballantine Publ. (latest ed.) 1972, roughly the 10th ed. One of the great literary frauds successfully perpetrated in this century. For a concise dismantlement of this and the other books produced by the man, see my editorial "Fictitious Tibet: the Origin and Persistence of Rampaism" in *Tibet Society Bulletin* No. 7, (Bloomington, Ind. 1974).

The only critically acceptable of some two dozen English translations of the *Bhagavadgītā* is the one by the late Franklin Edgerton, New York: Harper Torchbook (ppb.) No. 155, 1964.

4. *Mystic Vision.*

5. Bharati, *The Ochre Robe*, New York: Anchor-Doubleday ppb, 1970. Out of print with publishers, now available through Ross Erikson Publ., 223 Via Sevilla, Santa Barbara CA 93109.

6. The *dīkṣā-guru* is the person who formally initiates a disciple by giving him or her a *mantra* as the basis of a meditational technique. See my chapter on *dīkṣā* in *The Tantric Tradition*.

7. See Edward C. Dimock, *The Place of the Hidden Moon—Erotic Mysticism in the Vaiṣṇava Sahajīya Cult of Bengal*, Chicago: University Press 1966; Milton Singer, (ed.) *Krishna: Myths, Rituals, Attitudes*, Honolulu: East West Center Press, 1966. For a pictorial survey, see W.G. Archer's exquisite *The Loves of Krishna*, New York: Grove Press 1955.

8. *samādhi* (Sanskrit, lit. "bring into one") is the generic term for all states of consummate meditation conducing to religious goal finding. In the technical terminology of Patañjali's yoga, it is the 8th and ultimate state of contemplational perfection, and is subdivided into several categories in the Patañjali tradition of yoga techniques. In common vernacular parlance in India today, however, *samādhi* simply means intensive religious meditation; thus, any yogi or any religious person who sits crosslegged with closed eyes, or in a similar posture, is said to be doing *samādhi* (Hindi *samādhi lagā lete hain*)

9. See Ch. I., note 13.

10. The *kumbhamelā* is an all-Hindu religious assembly of monks, brahmins, and laity at several holy places in North and Central India. It takes place every twelfth year, i.e. when Jupiter enters Aquarius. The average number of participants and pilgrims has been close to half a million people during each of the past three *kumbhamelās*. The functional importance of these giant assemblies is in a way akin to the Vatican Councils for the Roman Church: it is at the *kumbhamelās* that consensus about doctrinal matters establishes informal guidelines for the monastic leaders and scholars of the land.

11. R.C. Zaehner, *Mysticism: Sacred and Profane. An Enquiry into some Praeternatural Experiences.* Oxford University Press (London & New York, ppb.) 1967. Also, *Hinduism*, Oxford Un. Pr. 1962.

12. Charles L. Stevenson, *Ethics and Language* New Haven: Yale University Press 1944. This is a seminal text in modern moral philosophy.

13. To see how cultural things—man-made constructs of any kind are built up from scratch, as it were, try Marvin Harris's *Nature of Cultural Things* (New York: Random House 1964).

14. This dictum appears in a large number of variations and modifications throughout the principal Upanisads (see Sw. Nikhilananda's *Upaniṣads* in the Harper Torchbook Series (No. 114, New York 1964).

15. Each of the Buddhist languages has a single key term denoting the supreme intuition and insight, the moment of enlightenment; the best known is the Japanese *satori*, equivalent to the Sanskrit and Pali *bodhi*.

16. *darśan(a)*, lit. 'sight' is the all-Indian term for the charismatic encounter: the guru, the god, any great man *gives darśan*, and the devotee, disciple, or the audience receives *darśan*. There is no one term parallel to this concept in any western language; it contains elements of the Christian notion of Grace, the psychological theme of sudden conversion by contact with the charismatic or with deity, and any encounter with a person or a culturally postulated divine being.

17. The *Jātakas* are a very large genre of Buddhist literature, formally the biographical account of the Buddha's many previous incarnations. There are many translations of *jatakas* and of kindred literature, both from Indian and Tibetan sources, e.g. T. Schmid *The Eighty-five Siddhas* (Stockholm 1958); George Roerich, *The Blue Annals* (2 vls) Calcutta: Royal Asiatic Society, 1949 & 1953.

18. H.H. Gerth & C. Wright Mills, (eds) *From Max Weber: Essays in Society.* New York: Oxford University Press 1958.

19. *Mystic Vision*, 241.

20. ibid., 245.

21. Aldous Huxley, *Doors of Perception and Heaven and Hell*, New York: Harper & Row 1954.

22. John Findlay, "The Logic of Mysticism" in *Religious Studies* London: Cambridge University Press, Vol. II / 2, 1967.

23. W.T. Stace, *Mysticism and Philosophy*, Philadelphia: J.B. Lippincott, 1960.

24. *ādiguru* "the pristine guru", title given to the founders of any specific religi-theological teaching.

25. *jñāni* "knower" (cognate with the Greek and Latin roots *gno-* as in gnosis, cognition, etc.); a technical term denoting the person who has achieved meditative consummation through disciplines which stress the cognitive rather than the emotional and affective aspects of religious practice.

Chapter III

1. J.L. Mehta, *The Philosophy of Martin Heidegger*, Banaras Hindu University Press, India 1968; the book appeared in an abridged paperback version, New York: Harper Torchbook No. 1605, 1971.

2. *siddhi*, the generic term for any mystical and / or occult power acquired in any manner whatsoever, by practising yogic techniques or by some extra-human gift of grace, etc. In the doctrinal literature, the achievement of supreme intuitive knowledge is called *parāsiddhi*, i.e. the supreme *siddhi*.

A person who has *siddhi* is a *siddha*.

3. *tap(a)*, *tapas*, *tapaysā*, from the root *tap-* 'to heat up' (cognate with the Latin root *tep-* as in 'tepid'), generic term for religiously motivated penance of any sort, from a daily walk in the monastery precincts to the proverbial nailboard.

4. Ruth Benedict, *Patterns of Culture*, first published in Boston in 1932, it has had some 20 reprints in various paperback editions; it still ranks as one of the three or four all-time popular anthropological classics, although very few anthropologists today share the views expressed by that great lady almost five decades ago.

5. T.L.S. Spriggs "The privacy of experience" in *Mind* LXXVIII No. 312 (Oxford) Oct. 1969.

6. A.N. Ray, "The Māṇḍukya Upaniṣad and the Kārikas of Gauḍapāda", in *Indian Historical Quarterly* XIV / 3 (Calcutta) 1938.

7. See Ch. II., note 23.

8. *digaṃbara* "clad in the four directions", i.e. nude. One of the two main sects of Jainism, referring to the fact that its monks were naked until a Muslim ruler outlawed such overly simple attire. The God Śiva himself, in Hindu lore, is often called *digaṃbara* since he is represented naked in Hindu iconographic nakedness standing for supreme indifference to worldly things.

9. *nigantha*, the generic name of the Jaina scriptures in the canonical language of the Jainas, Ardhamāgadhi.

10. *tirthaṅkara* "ford-maker", the title of the 64 founders of Jainism, the first sixty-one among them being mythical persons.

11. *anubhava* "experience'; in technical terminology, the term connotes any degree of mystical experience.

12. *japa*, the individual repetition of a *mantra* or any divine name; it is identical with the Muslim *sufi* practice of *dhikr*; rosaries in the Indian and Sufi traditions, and prayer wheels in Tibetan Buddhism are some of the accessories to *japa*.

13. *prāṇāyāma*, the techniques of breath control, part of the classical yoga system of Patāñjali, but used in virtually all meditational disciplines which originated in India.

14. See A. Bharati, MONASTICISM, in *Encyclopedia Britannica III*, Vol 12, 1974.

15. P. 155, see Ch. II, note 22.

16. *The Alan Watts Journal*, Inst. of Philosophy, Sausalito, Cal.

Chapter IV

1. By Sisirkumar Ghose (with a foreword by Aldous Huxley), London & New York: Asia Publishing House 1968.

2. publ. *Bharatiya Vidya Bhavan*, Bombay 1965.

3. ibid., p. 24.

4. *Rudrākṣa* ('red-eye') beads are made of the hard, dried berry *Eleocarpus ganitrus*. Each bead has five lines, representing the five faces of Śiva. Only monastic personnel is supposed to use these beads for *japa* (see Ch. III, note 12); laymen should use beads made of sandalwood or other substances—

for them the use of *rudrākṣa* is highly inauspicious (notwithstanding the fact that they are now being sold at Greenwich Village boutiques in New York City).

5. *The Urantia Book.* Urantia Foundation, 533 Diversey Parkway, Chicago, Ill. 60614. More about this amazing over 1000 page tome in Ch. VI.

6. *Govinda* "Cowherd" is one of the most frequent epithets of Lord Kṛṣṇa. In this pamphlet mimeographed ('cyclostyled' as it is called in India) at the Sivananda Yoga Vedanta Forest Academy in Hrishikesh, India, entitled *"Bhajan* for Englishmen", around 1952, the refrain was ". . . Govinda."

7. Surendranath Dasgupta, *History of Indian Philosophy*, 5 vls. Cambridge University Press, 1922-1955. For patient, devoted, motivated students and admirers of Indian thought, this is still the encyclopedia of Hindu, Buddhist, and Jaina philosophy.

8. See A. Bharati, "Radhakrishnan and the Other Vedanta", and Prof. S. Radhakrishnan's reply to me in *The Philosophy of Sarvepalli Radhakrishnan*, Library of Living Philosophers, ed. Paul A. Schilpp, New York: Open Court Publishers, 1952.

9. V. Raghavan, *The Indian Heritage*, Bangalore (India), Indian Institute of Culture, 1956 (preface).

10. Evelyn Underhill, *Mysticism: a Study of the Nature and Development of Man's Spiritual Consciousness*, New York: Meridian Books No. 1, 1967; Dom Cuthbert Butler, *Western Mysticism: The Teachings of Augustine, Gregory, Bernard, on Contemplation and the Contemplative Life*, New York: Harper Torchbook 312K, originally published in 1921. For no reason I could ever see, these two books have remained two classics in the study of mysticism—they are long, heavyhanded, tedious, and highly biased in favor of Christianity.

11. Ninian Smart, *Doctrine and Argument in Indian Philosophy*, London: Allen & Unwin, 1964; and Karl H. Potter, *Presuppositions of Indian Philosophies;* Englewood Cliffs, N.J.: Prenctice Hall 1963. In my opinion, these are the best and most concise introductions to Indian thought to date.

12. B.L. Atreya, *The Philosophy of the Yogavasiṣṭha*, Banaras Hindu University Press, (India) 1945.

13. *The Complete Works of Swami Vivekananda* (Vols. I-VIII). Ed. Swami Pavitrananda & Swami Yogeshwarananda, Mayavati (Almora UP); Advaita Ashrama. Also, George M. Williams, *The Quest for Meaning of Swami Vivekananda: a Study of Religious Change*, Chicago: New Horizons Press, 1974.

14. See *bibliography.*

15. See *bibliography.*

16. Indian English, particularly of the variety which I called *Swaminglish* (Bombay: *Illustrated Weekly of India*, March 17, 1974), tends to miss out on the humor such semantics imply.

17. Sri Aurobindo Pustakalaya, Pondicherry, Madras State, India.

18. See Ch. IV, note 16.

19. *ekadaśi* is the eleventh day after the full and the eleventh day after the new moon; these are days of general religious attention for Hindus. The most visible mark of these days is that a high percentage of highcaste Hindu women and some men fast, by not taking any staple food (rice, wheat), but only fruit and milk.

20. See Ch. II, note 8.

Chapter V

1. Radhakamal Mukerjee, *The Theory and Art of Mysticism*, New York & London: Asia Publishing House 1960, p. 16.

2. *cannabis sativa*, the hemp plant, yielding marijuana. Hindu takers prefer to drink it mixed with sherbet or buttermilk adding some spices—this concoction is *bhāng*, less aggressively referred to as *ṭhaṇḍāī* 'that which cools' in vernacular Hindi. Muslims prefer to smoke the weed, in which case it is called *gāñjā*.

3. *marafat*, the Urdu spelling of the Arabic technical term in sufism, *ma'rifat*, meaning gnosis, enlightenment, the state of contemplative consummation in Sufi practice and lore.

4. John Custance, *Adventure into the Unconscious*, London: Ch. Johnson Publ, 1954.

5. Thomas S. Szasz, *The Myth of Mental Illness*, New York: Harper, 1961, and later paperback editions, as Delta ppb (New York 1967).

6. Harry Stack Sullivan, *The Theory of Interpersonal Psychiatry*, New York: Norton Co., 1953. Many psychologists see this work as an alternative to Freudian therapy, on the theoretical side at least.

7. Mādhavācārya was the founder-guru of the extreme dualist school of Vedanta. The sect is headquartered in Udipi, Kannara, Southwest India. It is the least tolerant of all Vedānta schools, and makes bold of being just that. For a good statement about the complex theology of this group, see Nagaraja Sarma, *The Philosophy of Mādhava: The Reign of Realism in Indian Philosophy*, Madras: University Publication, 1960.

8. By now, *bhakti* has almost entered the large-size English dictionary as an assimilated word like avatar or yoga. It is the generic term for devotion to a personally conceived deity, and it thus contrasts with those schools that stress the abstract, impersonal, or the psycho-experimental. Thus, though tantrics worship a female or male deity in the process of mastering the incumbent techniques, they are not usually referred to as *bhaktas*. The *bhakti* schools in Hinduism divide their followers as worshippers of Viṣṇu and his incarnations including Rāma and Kṛṣṇa (Vaiṣṇavas), and of Śiva (Śaivas).

9. See F. Lessing & A. Wayman, *Mkha 'grub rje's Fundamentals of the Buddhist Tantras*. The Hague: Mouton 1968. More importantly, the many books by Herbert. V. Guenther, who is a veritable fortress of Buddhist tantric studies (as in *The Tantric View of Life*, Berkeley & London, Shambala Publ. 1972, *Tibetan Buddhism without Mystification*, Leiden: E.J. Brill 1966, and his entry on BUDDHIST MYSTICISM in the new *Encyclopedia Britannica* III Vol 3, 1974).

10. See A. Bharati, "Anthropological Approaches to the Study of Religion: Ritual and Belief Systems", in *Biennial Review of Anthropology*, B.J. Siegel ed., Stanford University Press, 1972. This is a seminal survey and analysis of the anthropological-sociological study of religious behavior between 1960 and 1970, and lists some 1000 items in its bibliography.

11. H. Evans-Wentz, *The Tibetan Book of the Dead* (*Bardo Thodöl*), in collaboration with Kazi Dandup. First published in London in 1949, this book has been redone numerous times in a paperback. It is neither a good nor a scholarly translation; Evans-Wentz did not know any Tibetan himself, and his relation to the actual Tibetan Book of the Dead is similar to Fitzgerald's relation to the actual *Rubaiyat* by Omar Khayyam—i.e.

more or less spurious. Still, quite typically, this was a volume present in all the collections of the wide-eyed seekers of the 60s, from the Village to Haight-Ashbury. At this time, Lama Chögyam Trungpa of Naropa in Boulder, and Dr. Francesca Fremantle of London are completing a first valid translation of the Book of the Dead. About the Lama, see Ch. VIII, note 6.

12. Initiation into an established meditational practice, usually by conferring a *mantra* on the initiand. See "On Mantra" and "On dīkṣā" in my *Tantric Tradition*.

13. The term 'leap-philosophy' was invented, most felicitously, by Karl H. Potter in *Presuppositions* (See Ch. IV, note 11).

14. The order of Buddhist monks. In all Buddhist countries, the term *saṅgha* or its single-term translation into the regional language, denotes the order, both as a local-regional organization and also as the much wider composite of the 'triple gem', (i.e. the Buddha, the *dharma*, and the *saṅgha*).

15. *bodhisattva*, the highest adept in Mahayana Buddhism—either by his or her spiritual achievements, or as a representation of a theophanitically conceived Buddha-form. See Har Dayal, *The Boddhisattva Doctrine in Buddhist Sanskrit Literature*, London: Trübner, Trench & Kegan Paul, 1932.

Chapter VI

1. See Ch. V. note 10.

2. Meyer-Fortes, *Oedipus and Job in West African Religion*, Cambridge: University Press, 1959.

3. E.E. Evans-Pritchard, *Theories of Primitive Religion*, Oxford: Clarendon Press 1965.

4. Clyde Kluckhohn, *Navajo Witchcraft*, Boston: Beacon Press 1962.

5. By far the best and most thoroughgoing study of this complex set of problems, persons, and essences, is Th. X. Barber's *LSD, Marijuana, Yoga, and Hypnosis*, Chicago: Aldine 1970.

6. S. Parker, "The Wittiko psychosis in the context of Ojibwa Personality and Culture", in *American Anthropologist* 62: 603-23, 1960.

7. Emile Durkheim, *The Essential Forms of Religious Life*, New York: Free Press 1965 (ppb). This book, when first published in English in 1915, became a powerful impetus to the study of religion in society, and has remained an undisputed classic up to this day.

8. Rammurti S. Mishra, *Yoga Sūtras: Textbook of Yoga Psychology*, New York: Anchor-Doubleday ppb 1973. Though the book is not an oriental-ist's dream, it is nevertheless the most readily available, and basically correct statement of classical yoga, in spite of its tedious psychologisms.

9. Mircea Eliade, *Yoga: Immortality and Freedom*, New York: Pantheon, 1958. An excellent study of the yoga complex by one of the few remaining renaissance men of this day and age.

10. Published by the Advaita Ashrama, Wellington Lane, Calcutta, and reprinted half a dozen times, these booklets have been translated into all Indian and most western languages. They are being devoured by a diffuse, uncritical mass of seekers. These brochures are incredibly simplistic.

but this may be one of the reasons for their popularity.

11. Swami Ramtirtha, M.A. *In Woods of God-Realization—The Complete Works of S.R.* Delhi: IMM Press 1910-1930.

12. Bharati, "Hindu Renaissance" See Ch. I, note 13.

13. These and scores of other booklets bearing similar titles can be found in stalls around Indian railway stations and in the bazaar areas of many metropolitan regions. Very often, some wealthy man commissions them, compiles some of them himself, and publishes them privately.

14. Eliot Deutsch, *Advaita Vedanta: a Philosophical Reconstruction.* Honolulu: East West Center Press, 1969.

15. R.B. Pandey, *Hindu Samskāras—a Socio-religious study of Hindu Sacraments.* Banaras Hindu University Publ., 1949.

16. To wit Horace Miner's fabulous "Body Ritual among the Nacirema", first published in *American Anthropologist* Vol 58, No. 3, 1956, and then republished in a number of anthologies, the best and most recent being in *Readings in Anthropology 75 / 76*, Annual Editions, the Dushkin Publishing Group Inc., Sluice Dock, Guilford CT, 1974. This collection also contains a very witty debunking of Carlos Castaneda's work, which this author regards as *infra dig.*, hence leaving it unmentioned in this book. Since I suspect that most of the readers of this book have read Castaneda, I recommend they now read Donald Barthelme's "The Teachings of Don B.: a Yankee Way of Knowledge" in this same *Readings* volume.

17. See chapter on Mantra in my *Tantric Tradition*.

18. Marvin Harris, *The Nature of Cultural Things*, New York: Random House 1964.

19. Hans Jacobs, *Western Psychotherapy and Hindu Sadhana.* London: Allen & Unwin 1961.

20. The Whorff-Sapir theory, now almost entirely rejected or coldshouldered by anthropologists and linguists, suggests that language structures and channels behavior rather than vice versa. In spite of the general misgivings about the theory, there is no doubt that it is sometimes true, and that it is almost always a good heuristic device. See *Language and Culture*, ed. H. Hoijer, American Anthropological Association Memoir No. 79, Vol. 56 / 6, Pt. 2, Washington DC 1954.

21. See note 19.

22. See *Tantric Tradition*, Ch. VIII.

23. Headquartered in California (where else), the Divine Life Society boasts some 250 centers of diverse degrees of affiliation, in the U.S. and Canada, and about 50 in western Europe. American followers in these centers display assorted kinds of Indianization and Hinduization. For free and enthusiastic information about what I regard as the most grotesque instance of American Swamification and the attempted transplant of the neo-Hindu ashram scene into the West, write to The Poconos Ashram, Sivananda Conservatory of Yoga One Science, R.D. 3, Box 400, Stroudsburg, PA 18360, or if you are in a desperate hurry to obtain salvation, call (not collect) 717 629-0481.

24. Just as in the case of the Polish jokes in America, with little knowledge of and no bearing on actual Polish achievements, the all-India joking butt is the Sardar (Sikh), and the ever recurring "Sardar jokes" are so painfully idiotic that it is embarrassing to translate them to a non-Indian audience; and of course, Sikhs don't enjoy them. The one most pervasive is the

bārah baj gayā "joke", and this is the one I believe the swami tried on the said Sikh student. The phrase means "it is 12 o'clock noon", and the theory behind it is that with the heavy turban, the Sikh at that point loses all traces of reason and intelligence he might have had. Why and how the very mention of *bārah baj gayā* persistently elicits laughter from otherwise bright people, escapes me.

25. A raised platform or dais on which 'functions' (Indian English word for any public performance) take place, from a holy man's talk to a wedding or a political speech, or a village theatrical performance. The word *paṇḍāl* has become Indian English and is used in English language publications in India and Pakistan, like 'lakh' for the number 100,000 and 'crore' for the number 10,000,000.

26. *bhajan* and *kīrtan* are roughly synonymous. They are religious responsorial litanies involving at least one leader, who may be a Brahmin priest, a monk, any saintly person, or any religiously involved lay person. For an excellent account of urban *kīrtans* see Pt. 3, The Radha Krishna *bhajans* of Madras City" in Milton Singer's important book *When a Great Tradition Modernizes*, New York: Praeger 1972.

27. In *The Making of a Counter-Culture* by Theodore Roszak, Anchor-Doubleday ppb New York 1969. In his subsequent works, somewhat astoundingly, Roszak reversed himself completely to become a virtual convert to what the first book criticized: *Where the Wasteland Ends: Politics and Transcendence in Post-industrial Society*, Anchor-Doubleday 1972, and *Pontifex: a Revolutionary Entertainment of the Mind's Eye Theater*, Anchor-Doubleday 1974.

28. Alan Watts, "Beat Zen, Square Zen, and Zen" in *Chicago Review* XII, Summer 1958, 3-11.

29. I heard a beautiful girl say under her breath that she was 'oming' every day. This morphological abomination not only shows a fast origination of a special eclectic meditation argot, but it also points to the fact that in the West, almost *anything* is counted as 'meditation', not only regular T.M. type initiation follow-ups, but things like looking at the sun, breathing in deeply, sitting on a beach and not doing things people used to do at beaches—or just gazing into the void, having a mental blank.

30. See Ch. IV, note 5.

31. See Ch. IV, note 11.

32. See Ch. IV, note 10.

33. N. Smart, "Interpretation and Mystical Experience" in *Religious Studies* Vol. I / 1, Oct. 65, 75-87. New York & London, Cambridge University press.

34. New York: Harper & Row 1970.

35. *Bhdgavadgītā—the Song of God*. Mentor Paperback (New York), several imprints since 1960. You are likely to find it on airport and Greyhound bookstalls.

Chapter VII

1. For this well documented topic, see Melford E. Spiro's seminal *Buddhism and Society*, New York: Harper & Row 1970; also, S.J. Tambiah, "The ideology of merit and the social correlates of Buddhism in a Thai village" in *Dialectic of Practical Religion*, ed. Edmund R. Leach, Cambridge

(England): University Press 1968; and Nur Yalman "Ascetic Buddhist monks of Ceylon" in *Ethnology* 3: 315-328. (Pittsburgh) 1962.

2. *R.D. Laing and Anti-Psychiatry*, eds. R. Boyers & R. Orrill, New York: Perennial Library (ppb), 1971.

3. Ronald Leifer, *In the Name of Mental Health: the Social Functions of Psychiatry*. New York: Science House, 1969.

4. The pioneer if not the discoverer of these lines of thought is Thomas S. Szasz; *The Myth of Mental Illness* (New York: Delta paperback 1967), and *Law, Liberty, and Psychiatry* New York: Macmillan 1963 were the first in a series of books written by Szasz in criticism of the official, medicine and hospital-cum-commitment oriented psychiatry.

5. On Ayurveda and Indian medicine, see Heinrich Zimmer, *Hindu Medicine*, Baltimore: Johns Hopkins Univ. Press 1948.

6. See Bharati, "Hindu Scholars, Germany, and the *Third Reich*" in *Quest* No. 44, Bombay, Jan-March 1965. This examines a situation totally unknown in the West: that extremely religious, nonviolent Hindus greatly admire Adolf Hitler. When told about the Nazi atrocities and Auschwitz, etc., these are mostly rejected as American propaganda. One very famous, gentle swami whom I spoke to about the camps, showing him a picture made after the liberation of Auschwitz, said that these corpses had been dug out from some cemetery, put together and photographed so as to spread evil notions about Hitler.

7. Ralph Russell "The pursuit of the Urdu *ghazal*", in *Journal of Asian Studies* Vol. XXIX / 2, Nov. 1969, 115 ff.

8. C.S. Lewis, *The Allegory of Love*, New York: Oxford Univ. Press (ppb) 1958

9. This is an old German counterpart adage "he who hasn't ever been plastered, can't be a good man."

10. Al Baghdādī, *Al Farq bin al farq*. trl. Selye, New York: Columbia University Press, 1930, p. 21.

11. "Orthopraxis" and "orthopractical" as juxtaposed with "orthodox," terms felicitously coined by J.A.B. van Buitenen in "On the Archaisms in the Bhāgavata Purāṇa" in M. Singer's *Krishna* book (see Ch. II, note 7)

12. See Roszak, Ch. VI, note 27.

13. Terms in Indian classical music: *tāla* is the rhythm instrumentally expressed through finger drums; *rāga* is the skeletal melody type, the melodical deep structure, as it were, generating a musical composition.

14. Timothy Leary, *Interpersonal Diagnosis of Personality*, New York: Ronald Press Co., 1957.

15. J.K. Benson & J.O. Smith, "The Harvard Drug Controversy: a case study of subject manipulation and social structure", in G. Sjober, ed., *Ethics, Politics, and Social Research*, Cambridge (Mass.): Schenkman Publ., 1967.

16. Short for "International Federation for Internal Freedom"; later, Leary renamed the organization into "League of Spiritual Development" (LSD).

17. R. Blum et al., eds. *Utopiates: The Use and Users of LSD-25*. New York: Atherton Press, 1964, p. 180.

18. B.A. Maher, "Drugs and Academic Freedom" in *Massachusetts Psychological Association Newsletter*, Oct. 1963, p. 4.

19. *Playboy*. Feb. 1970, panel discussion "The Drug Revolution".

1. James Keene, "Baha'i World Faith: redefinition of religion" in JSSR VI / 2, 1967; also my sour rebuttal of this piece in JSSR VII / 2, 1968, p. 281.

2. Meher Baba's American followers have a well appointed ashram in Myrtle Beach, S.C., and one only; numerically, they do not compare with T.M. of Divine Light (Guru Maharaj the perennial Boy); In India, his followers are probably more numerous than either Maharishi Mahesh Yogi's or The Boy's. The latter's marriage to an 8 year older American girl caused a loss of an estimated 30 percent of his Indian followers, by the old Indian tacit formula "you can't drop semen and remain a saint."

3. Philip Spratt, *Hindu Culture and Personality*, Bombay: Manaktala, 1966.

4. The American paperback edition (Anchor-Doubleday, New York 1970) is now out of print; the original British hardcover edition, in its third imprint, is still on the market with the publishers, Rider & Co., London.

5. On the occasion of the 2500th anniversary of Buddhism, celebrated in all accessible Buddhist countries, an amazing 700 page book appeared in Ceylon. Written by an author who wanted (but did not remain) incognito *Revolt in the Temple* (Sinha Publications, Colombo 1953). It is a Marxist history and peptalk about Buddhism as true Marxism. Of no scholarly merit, it apparently had a strong influence on Buddhists, lay and monastic, who felt oppressed by transition and change.

6. The Naropa and Vajradhatu Institutes in Boulder Colo., and West Barnet, Vt. ("Tail of the Tiger") were founded by an amazing Tibetan lama, Chögyam Trungpa Rinpoche. This ambitious institution, together or alongside with the Nyingma Institute under Lama Tarthang in Berkeley are no doubt the most important, serious, and genuine efforts at teaching Tibetan and eventually Tantric mysticism in America. For an evaluation of these and other Tibetan Buddhist institutions, see my editorial in *Tibet Society Bulletin* No. 8, Bloomington, Ind., Spring 1975.

BIBLIOGRAPHY

Only those books which have relevance to mysticism proper are listed here, in addition to a selection of easily accessible books not referred to in the text and the notes. In order to save space, most articles referred to in the text and the notes are not listed here again.

Archer, W.G. *The Loves of Krishna.* New York: Grove Press, 1955.

Arunachala, Sadhu. *A Sadhu's Reminiscences of Ramana Maharishi.* Tirivannamalai (India): Sri Ramanasramam Publ., 1961.

Barber, Theodore X. *LSD, Marijuana, Yoga, and Hypnosis.* Chicago: Aldine, 1970.

Beyer, St. *The Cult of Tara.* Berkeley & Los Angeles: Univ. of California Press, 1973.

Bhaktivedanta, Swami 'Prabhupada' A.C. "The Krishna Letters," correspondence between Prof. J.F. Staal of U.C. Berkeley and the Swami. In *The Daily Californian,* U.C. Berkeley, March 3, 1970.

Bharati, Agehananda. *The Ochre Robe.* Garden City: Doubleday & Co., Inc., 1970 (Ross-Erikson Publ., Santa Barbara, CA sole distributor). *The Tantric Tradition.* New York: Samuel Weiser, 1975 (ppb). *A Functional Analysis of Indian Thought and its Social Margins.* Varanasi (India): Chowkhamba Sanskrit Series Publ., 1964.

Edgerton, Franklin, trans. *Bhagavadgita.* New York: Harper Torchbook TB 115, 1964 (ppb).

Bihari, Bankey. *Sufis, Mystics, and Yogis of India.* Bombay: Bhavan's Book University, 1962.

Blum, R. a.o. eds. *Utopiates: the Use and Users of LSD-25.* New York: Atherton Press, 1964.

Bourgouignon, Erika, ed. *Religion, Altered States of Consciousness, and Social Change.* Columbus: Ohio State Univ. Press, 1973.

Boyers, R., & R. Orrill, eds. *R.D. Laing and Anti-Psychiatry.* New York: Perennial Library, 1971 (ppb).

Bridges, Hal. *American Mysticism from William James to Zen.* New York: Harper & Row, 1970.

Butler, Dom Cuthbert. *Western Mysticism.* New York: Harper Torchbook TB 312 K, first publ. 1922.

Campbell, Joseph, ed. *The Mystic Vision.* Princeton: University Press, 1968.

Custance, John. *Adventure into the Unconscious.* London: Ch. Johnson, 1954.

Dasgupta, Surendranath. *History of Indian Philosophy.* Vols. I-V. Cambridge: University Press 1922-1955.

Dayal, Har. *The Bodhisattva Doctrine in Buddhist Sanskrit Literature.* London: Kegan Paul, 1932.

Deutsch, Eliot. *Advaita Vedānta: a Philosophical Reconstruction.* Honolulu: East West Center Press, 1969.

van Buitenen, J.A.B., ed. *Source Book of Advaita Vedanta*. Honolulu: University of Hawaii Press, 1971.

Dhavamony, M. *Love of God according to Shaiva Siddhanta*. Oxford: Clarendon Press, 1971.

Domock, Edward C. *The Place of the Hidden Moon*. Chicago: University Press, 1966.

Dumoulin, H. *Oestliche Meditation und Christliche Mystik*. Munich: Karl Alber, 1966.

Durkheim, Emile. *The Essential forms of Religious Life*. New York: Free Press, 1966 (ppb).

Durr, R.A. *Poetic Vision and the Psychedelic Experience*. Syracuse: University Press, 1970.

Eliade, Mircea. *Yoga: Immortality and Freedom*. New York: Pantheon Books, 1958.

Fortes, M. *Oedipus and Job*. Cambridge: University Press, 1959.

Fremantle, A., ed. *The Protestant Mystics*. London: Weidenfels & Nicholson, n.d.

Gandalf's Garden. Monthly. London: The Citadel Press, since 1968.

Gerth, H.H. & C. Wright Mills, eds. *From Max Weber: Essays in Society*. New York: Oxford University Press, 1958.

Gose, S.K. *Mystics and Society*. New York: Asia Publishing House, 1968.

Guenther, Herbert Vighnantaka. *The Tantric View of Life*. Berkeley: Shambala, 1972.
Tibetan Buddhism without Mystification. Leiden: E.J. Brill, 1966.
sGampopa—*The Jewel Ornament of Liberation*. London: Rider & co., 1959.
The Life and Teaching of Naropa. Oxford: Clarendon Press, 1963.
The Royal Song of Saraha. Seattle, University of Washington Press, 1969.

Hopkins, J., ed. *The Hippie Papers*. Signet Books (ppb) 1968.

Huxley, Aldous. *Doors of Perception and Heaven and Hell*. New York: Harper & Row, 1954.

Isherwood, Christopher. *Ramakrishna and his Disciples*. New York: Simon & Schuster, 1965.

Jacobs, H. *Western Psychology and Hindu Sadhana*. London: Allen & Unwin, 1960.

Jyotirmayananda Sarasvati, Swami. *Praxis der MEDITATION: Theorie und Anleitung zu zehn Techniken*. Vienna: Verlag der Palme, 1970.

Leuba, J.H. *The Psychology of Religious Mysticism*. London & Boston: Routledge & Kegan Paul, 1972.

Lewis, C.S. *The Allegory of Love*. New York: Oxford Univ. Press, 1958 (ppb)

Mahesh Yogi, Maharishi. *Meditations of Maharishi Mahesh Yogi*. Bantam Book PX4282, 1969 (ppb).

Transcendental Meditation. Signet Book W5719 (ppb).
The Story of Maharishi Mahesh Yogi. ed. Martin Ebon, Signet Special T3514, 1968.
The Science of Being and Art of Living. Signet Q3512 (ppb).

de Marquette, Jacques. *Introduction to Comparative Mysticism.* Bombay: Bharatiya Vidya Bhavan, 1965.

Mishra, Rammurti S. *Yoga Sutras: Textbook of Yoga Psychology.* New York: Anchor-Doubleday, 1973 (ppb).

Nikhilananda, Swami. *The Gospel of Sri Ramakrishna.* New York: Ramakrishna Vivekananda Center, 1964 and later.
The Upanishads: a one volume abridgement. New York: Harper Torchbook TB 114, 1964.

O'Flaherty, W. Doniger. *Asceticism and Eroticism in the Mythology of Siva.* New York: Oxford University Press, 1973.

Osborne, A., ed. *The Collected Works of Ramana Maharshi.* Tirivannamalai (India): Sri Ramanasrama, 1963.

Perella, N.J. *The Kiss Sacred and Profane.* Berkeley & Los Angeles: Univ. of California Press, 1969.

Potter, Karl H. *Presuppositions of Indian Philosophy.* Englewood Cliffs, N.J.: Prentice Hall, 1963.

Prabhavananda, Swami & Christopher Isherwood. *How to know God: The Yoga Aphorisms of Patanjali.* New York: Mentor Book No. 1382 (ppb).

Radhakamal, Mukherjee. *The Theory and Art of Mysticism.* New York: Asia Publishing House, 1960.

Raju, P.T. & A. Cattell, eds. *East West Studies on Problems of the Self.* The Hague: M. Nijhoff, 1968.

Rao, M.V. Krishna. *A Brief Survey of Mystic Tradition in Religion and Art in Karnataka.* Madras: Wardha Publishing House, 1959.

Riepe, Dale. *The Philosophy of Indian and Its Impact on American Thought.* Monograph in the Series American Lectures in Philosophy, ed. M. Faber. Springfield, Ill.: Ch. C. Thomas Publ., n.d. (abt. 1970).

Roerich, George N. *The Blue Annals.* Vols. I & II, Calcutta: Royal Asiatic Society, 1949, 1953.

Roszak, Theodore. *The Making of a Counterculture.* New York: Anchor-Doubleday, 1969 (ppb).
Where the Wasteland Ends. New York: Anchor-Doubleday, 1972 (ppb)
Pontifex. New York: Anchor-Doubleday, 1974 (ppb).

Schilpp, Paul A., ed. *The Philosophy of Sarvepalli Radhakrishnan.* New York: Open Court Publ., 1956.

Schmid, T. *The Eightyfive Siddhas.* Stockholm: University Publ., 1958.

The Journal of the Scientific Study of Religion. Contains some two dozen important articles on mysticism and the mystics, since its inauguration; e.g. P. Ennis, "Ecstasy," L. Schneiderman "Mysticism" in

Vol. VI / 1, Spring 1967. JSSR is published by the Society for the
Scientific Study of Religion, Box U68A, Univ. of Connecticut, Storrs
CT 06268.

Singer, Milton, ed. *Krishna: Myths, Rituals, Attitudes.* Honolulu: East West
Center Press, 1966.

Sivananda Sarasvati, Swami. *Conquest of Mind.* Hrishikesh: Yoga Vedanta
Forest Academy, 1964.
Sivanandasrama bhajanavali. music and staff notation by Sw.
Vidyananda, Hrishikesh, 1965.
World Peace. Hrishikesh, 1957.
Samadhi Yoga. Hrishikesh, 1961.
Sure Ways of Success in Life and God Realization. Hrishikesh, 1966.
*Bliss Divine: a Book of Spiritual Essays on the Lofty Purpose of
Human Life and the Means to its Achievement.* Hrishikesh, 1958.

Smart, Ninian. *Doctrine and Argument in Indian Philosophy.* London: Allen
& Unwin, 1964.

Spiro, Melford E. *Buddhism and Society.* New York: Harper & Row, 1970.

Stace, W.T. *Mysticism and Philosophy.* London: Macmillan & Co., 1961.

Stage, W. *The Teachings of the Mystics.* New York: Mentor MJ 1181 (ppb),
1974.

Sullivan, H. Stack. *The Interpersonal Theory of Psychiatry.* New York:
Norton, 1953.

Suzuki, D.T. *Mysticism: Christian and Buddhist.* New York: Collier Books,
1962.

Tart, Charles T., ed. *Altered States of Consciousness.* esp. the chapter
"Implications of LSD and Experimental Mysticism" New York:
J. Wiley, 1969.

Underhill, Evelyn. *Mysticism: A Study in the Nature and Development of
Man's Spiritual Consciousness.* New York: Meridian Book MG1,
1967 (ppb).

The Urantia Book. Urantia Foundation, 533 Diversey Pkwy, Chicago, Ill.
60614, 1967.

Vasvani, T.L. *Prophets and Saints.* Bombay: Jaico Publ., 1957.

Vishadananda, Swami. *Spiritual Science.* 2 vols. Ottapalam / Kerala (India):
Sri Ramakrishna Ashram, n.d. (abt. 1960).

Vivekananda, Swami. *Complete Works.* Vols. I-VIII. Latest edition Calcutta:
Advaita Ashrama, 1964.

The Alan Watts Society for Comparative Philosophy, Inc. S.S. Vallejo,
P.O. Box 857, Sausalito, CA 94965. The Society keeps publishing on
all topics the late Watts was concerned with, most of them of direct
interest to readers of this book.

Wallace, Robert K. *Neurophysiology of Enlightenment: Scientific Research
on Transcendental Meditation.* New York: Maharishi International
University Press, 1974.

Williams, George M. *The Quest for Meaning of Swami Vivekananda.* Chico,
Cal.: New Horizons Press, 1974.

Windbells. Periodical published by the Zen Center, 1884 Bush Street, San Francisco CA 94109.

Yinger, Milton. *The Scientific Study of Religion.* New York: Macmillan, 1970.

Zaehner, Robert Charles. *Mysticism: Sacred and Profane.* Oxford & New York: Oxford Univ. Press, 1967 (ppb).
Hinduism. Oxford Univ. Press, 1962.

Indra, 150

Jacobs, H., 164
Jaimini, 58-59, 92
Japan, 186
Jātakas, 55
jñāna-yoga, 37, 49-50, 61, 153, 167.
    See also yoga.
John of the Cross, 139
Jung, C.G., 35-36, 57, 164

Kant, Immanuel, 116
karma, 108, 113, 116
karma-yoga, 153, 167. See also yoga.
karuna, 198
Kerouac, Jack, 190
kīrtan, 180
Kluckhohn, 147
Koestler, Arthur, 17, 81, 95, 173
Krishnamurti, J., 224-26
Krṣna, 187, 190, 199-200, 215
kumbhamela, 47, 170
kundalinī, 164, 166-69, 188
kundalinī-yoga, 167. See also yoga.

Laing, R.D., 196
laya-yoga, 166-68. See also yoga.
Leary, Timothy, 42, 49, 63, 69, 107,
    194, 210-11
Leifer, R., 197
Leviticus, 205
Lévy-Bruhl, 18, 141
Lewis, C.S., 201
Louch, A.R., 16
LSD-25 (Lysergic Acid Diethylamide),
    19, *et passim*.

Ma Anandamayi, 180
Mahābhārata, 28
Maharishi Mahesh Yogi, 34-35, 51,
    129, 175, 183-85, 219, 226, 228. *See
    also Transcendental Meditation.*
Maharshi, Ramana, 29, 46, 65, 89,
    95, 102, 109-10, 179
Maher, Brendan A., 211
Manson, Charles, 213
mantra, 77, 134, 161-63, 166, 184
mārafat, 113, 137
Marcuse, Herbert, 19, 214

Meher Baba, 73, 220
Mehta, J.L., 63
Merton, Thomas, 126
mukti, 100, 156

nāda-yoga, 184. See also yoga.
Naqsbandi, 136-37
Navaho Indians, 147
Navars, 177
Nehru, J., 203
Nichiren, 123
nirvāna, 90, 127-28
noxious fusion, phenomenon of, 209

Occam, William of, 122
Ojibwa, 148
ontology, 45, 146
Ouspensky, P.D., 218

Paramahamsa, Yogananda, 221
participation mystique, 141
Patanjali, 82-83, 85, 130, 152, 154-58,
    164, 166, 193, 229
pizza effect, 183
Popper, Karl, 70, 84, 142, 229
Playboy Magazine, 213, 231
Prabhavananda, 192
prānāyāma, 74, 159, 164
priests, 141
Protestant Ethic, 88
psilocybin, 147, 211
Purcell, Henry, 215

Radin, Paul, 62
Raghavan, V., 30
rāja-yoga, 153-55, 212. See also yoga.
Ramakrishna Paramahamsa, 29, 32,
    73, 78, 89, 97, 107, 131, 161, 167,
    176, 179, 182, 196
Ram-Dass, Baba (Richard Alpert), 42,
    194, 210-11, 213-14
Ramprasad, 196
Rāmtirtha, 154
rasāvāda, 157
realization, 172. *See* zero experience.
Rimbaud, Arthur, 59
Roszak, Theodore, 182
Roy, M.N., 120, 231
Russell, Bertrand, 229

253